Data Engineering with Alteryx

Helping data engineers apply DataOps practices with Alteryx

Paul Houghton

BIRMINGHAM—MUMBAI

Data Engineering with Alteryx

Publishing Product Manager: Heramb Bhavsar
Senior Editor: Nathanya Dias
Content Development Editor: Shreya Moharir
Technical Editor: Devanshi Ayare
Copy Editor: Safis Editing
Project Coordinator: Farheen Fathima
Proofreader: Safis Editing
Indexer: Manju Arasan
Production Designer: Aparna Bhagat
Marketing Coordinator: Nivedita Singh

First published: June 2022

Production reference: 1270522

Published by Packt Publishing Ltd.
Livery Place
35 Livery Street
Birmingham
B3 2PB, UK.

ISBN 978-1-80323-648-3

www.packt.com

For my wonderful wife Penné, for all her support and patience. And to my son Eric, for providing the energy to keep going.

Contributors

About the author

Paul Houghton is an experienced business analyst with the ability to make focused data-led decisions. He is able to utilize data from a multitude of sources, including structured company data alongside unstructured data, such as social media sites. Paul's ability to combine data from structured business sources with open and unstructured data and analyze a range of datasets enables him to make fast, accurate, and relevant business decisions.

About the reviewer

Richard Young has been a senior data scientist at OptumCare for 4 years. He has over 15 years of experience in healthcare, data modeling, and machine learning. Richard enjoys working with complex issues to solve operational and data science challenges. One of Richard's areas of specialization includes utilizing multiple data sources to discover new actionable knowledge and reduce operating costs while increasing patient care. Additionally, he is active in academia, focusing on computational neuroscience and human disease modeling and prediction. Richard currently resides in Las Vegas, NV, and is married to Alice Matthews, who is also active in academic research. He enjoys spending time in nature, camping on undeveloped sites in Nevada.

Table of Contents

3
DataOps and Its Benefits

Part 2: Functional Steps in DataOps

4
Sourcing the Data

5

Data Processing and Transformations

6

Destination Management

10

Monitoring DataOps and Managing Changes

11

Securing and Managing Access

12

Making Data Easy to Use and Discoverable with Alteryx

13

Conclusion

Index

Other Books You May Enjoy

Preface

Data analysis has become an essential skill in a variety of domains where knowing how to work with data and extract insights can generate significant value. **Alteryx** for data engineers will show you how to create a data pipeline and apply DataOps principles to the management of Alteryx data projects.

Using real-world datasets, you will learn how to use the **Alteryx Designer** to reshape, clean, and aggregate your data. Then, you will learn how to apply the DataOps principles to automate and monitor the workflows you have created, thereby ensuring the creation of the best possible datasets.

Who this book is for

If you're a data engineer, data scientist, or data analyst who wants a reliable process for developing data pipelines using Alteryx, this book is for you. You'll also find this book useful if you are trying to make the development and deployment of datasets more robust by following the DataOps principles. Familiarity with Alteryx products will be useful but is not necessary.

What this book covers

Chapter 1, *Getting Started with Alteryx*, introduces the Alteryx software suite and why you should use it as part of your data engineering processes.

Chapter 2, *Data Engineering with Alteryx*, focuses more on the specific application of Alteryx in a data engineering context. We understand the benefits of Alteryx for a data engineer and how to get started with Alteryx products.

Chapter 3, *DataOps and Its Benefits*, describes the DataOps process and why it is a good framework for data projects. It explores the principles for creating a good data product and how it can create high-performing data teams. We also explore how DataOps fits with the Alteryx products and how to leverage the principles when developing an Alteryx workflow.

Chapter 4, Sourcing the Data, explores the methods for extracting data with Alteryx. We look at the methods for connecting to local files and SQL databases in addition to the methods for extracting cloud-based data with application programming interfaces.

Chapter 5, Data Processing and Transformations, takes an example dataset from the previous chapter and describes common transformations required to process a raw dataset into an analytic resource for an organization.

Chapter 6, Destination Management, extends on the connection processes learned in *Chapter 4, Sourcing the Data,* and focuses on how to persist the dataset for future use. It examines the benefits of the saving methods and how each can be used for different applications.

Chapter 7, Extracting Value, introduces the methods for extracting insights and information from a dataset. We explore the methods for exploratory data analysis in Alteryx so that we can understand our dataset and gain organizational value from our data resources.

Chapter 8, Beginning Advanced Analytics, extends the skills learned in *Chapter 7, Extracting Value,* into the areas of spatial analytics and machine learning. We explore how to extract the geographic insights in our dataset using spatial tools. We also explore how to build a machine learning project in Alteryx using the predictive tools and the Intelligence Suite add-on.

Chapter 9, Testing Workflows and Outputs, describes how to use the message tool and the test tool to integrate testing processes and validation into our data pipeline. These checks improve the robustness of our dataset and provide early warning systems for data drift or data structure changes.

Chapter 10, Monitoring DataOps and Managing Changes, describes how to deploy continuous integration principles to an Alteryx pipeline. It allows for version and change management processes and confidence in dataset quality.

Chapter 11, Securing and Managing Access, introduces the best practices for managing an Alteryx server environment. We will learn how to manage access to workflows published to Alteryx Server and how to manage the infrastructure Alteryx Server is deployed on.

Chapter 12, Making Data Easy to Use and Discoverable with Alteryx, describes how Alteryx Connect can be used as a central data dictionary to help break the information silos in your organization and allow for the reuse of datasets across an organization.

Chapter 13, Conclusion, provides an overview of the data pipeline process we created throughout this book. It provides a final recap of all the skills you have acquired throughout the book so you can confidently apply these skills in your daily use.

To get the most out of this book

This book assumes you are familiar with general analytic and data engineering processes. You should have the most recent version of Alteryx Designer installed. The workflows have been tested on Alteryx Designer version 2022.1, but should also work on other versions. Knowledge of the Alteryx software suite will assist you with understanding the interface covered in this book; however, all examples involving Alteryx provide step-by-step instructions for following along.

Software/hardware covered in the book	Operating system requirements
Alteryx Designer	Windows
Alteryx Designer Intelligence Suite	
Alteryx Server	
Alteryx Connect	

Alteryx Server and Connect are accessed via a web browser. As a data engineer, you will need access to these platforms for automation, scaling, and collaboration.

If you are using the digital version of this book, we advise you to type the code yourself or access the code from the book's GitHub repository (a link is available in the next section). Doing so will help you avoid any potential errors related to the copying and pasting of code.

Please note that for a few images in the book, the structure of the image or the annotation is more important for your reference than the GUI text in them.

The Alteryx Designer Intelligence Suite is an add-on product that extends Alteryx Designer machine learning capabilities. If you don't have access to this add-on, the skills learned in Chapter 8, Beginning Advanced Analytics, will be limited to the predictive tools and custom code options.

Download the example workflow files

You can download the example workflow files for this book from GitHub at `https://github.com/PacktPublishing/Data-Engineering-with-Alteryx`. If there's an update to the workflows, it will be updated in the GitHub repository.

We also have other code bundles from our rich catalog of books and videos available at `https://github.com/PacktPublishing/`. Check them out!

Download the color images

We also provide a PDF file that has color images of the screenshots and diagrams used in this book. You can download it here: `https://static.packt-cdn.com/downloads/9781803236483_ColorImages.pdf`.

Conventions used

There are a number of text conventions used throughout this book.

`Code in text`: Indicates code words in the text, database table names, folder names, filenames, file extensions, pathnames, dummy URLs, user input, and Twitter handles. Here is an example: "This means we can create a `testing_workflow_validation.py` file with the `test_description` function inside it."

A block of code is set as follows:

```
from os import listdir
import os
import xml.etree.ElementTree as ET

ayx_file = ('.yxmd', '.yxmc', '.yxwz')
files = [f for f in listdir(os.getcwd()) if f.endswith(ayx_
file)]
```

Any command-line input or output is written as follows:

```
ALTER TABLE "Users" ADD PRIMARY KEY ("UserId");
```

Bold: Indicates a new term, an important word, or words that you see on screen. For instance, words in menus or dialog boxes appear in **bold**. Here is an example: "In the final workflow, we can use the **Output** tool's **Update: Insert if New** option, which will keep all our records updated."

> **Tips or Important Notes**
> Appear like this.

Get in touch

Feedback from our readers is always welcome.

General feedback: If you have questions about any aspect of this book, email us at customercare@packtpub.com and mention the book title in the subject of your message.

Errata: Although we have taken every care to ensure the accuracy of our content, mistakes do happen. If you have found a mistake in this book, we would be grateful if you would report this to us. Please visit www.packtpub.com/support/errata and fill in the form.

Piracy: If you come across any illegal copies of our works in any form on the internet, we would be grateful if you would provide us with the location address or website name. Please contact us at copyright@packt.com with a link to the material.

If you are interested in becoming an author: If there is a topic that you have expertise in and you are interested in either writing or contributing to a book, please visit authors.packtpub.com.

Share Your Thoughts

Once you've read *Data Engineering with Alteryx*, we'd love to hear your thoughts! Scan the QR code below to go straight to the Amazon review page for this book and share your feedback.

https://packt.link/r/1-803-23648-5

Your review is important to us and the tech community and will help us make sure we're delivering excellent quality content.

Part 1: Introduction

This part will describe what an Alteryx data engineer is in the context of Alteryx, while also introducing what the DataOps framework is and how it applies to Alteryx.

This part comprises the following chapters:

- *Chapter 1, Getting Started with Alteryx*
- *Chapter 2, Data Engineering with Alteryx*
- *Chapter 3, DataOps and Its Benefits*

1
Getting Started with Alteryx

In the current century, one of the core functions of all companies is to retrieve data from its source and get it into the hands of your company's analysts, decision makers, and data scientists. This data flow allows businesses to make decisions, supported by empirical evidence, quickly and with confidence. The capability also gives businesses a robust process for delivering the data flows with a significant advantage over their competition.

Creating robust data flows requires that end users find the datasets and trust the raw data source. End users need to know what transformations were applied to the dataset to build trust. They also need to know who to talk to if their needs change. **Alteryx** gives data engineers and end users a single unified place to create data pipelines and discover data resources. It also provides the context that gives end users confidence when making decisions based on any of those datasets.

This book will describe how to build and deploy data engineering pipelines with Alteryx. We will learn how to examine to apply DataOps methods to build high-quality datasets. We will also learn the techniques required for monitoring the pipelines when they are running in an automated production environment.

This chapter will introduce the Alteryx platform as a whole and the major software components within the platform. Then, we will see how those components fit together to create a data pipeline, and how Alteryx can improve your development speed and build confidence throughout your data team.

Once we understand the **Alteryx platform**, we will look into Alteryx Designer and familiarize ourselves with the interface. Next, we will set a baseline for building an Alteryx workflow and use Alteryx to create standalone data pipelines.

Next, we will investigate the server-based components of the Alteryx platform, **Alteryx Server**, and **Alteryx Connect**. We will learn how Alteryx Server can automate the pipeline execution, scale the efforts and work of your data engineering team, and serve as a central location where workflows are stored and shared. We will also learn how Alteryx Connect is used to find data sources throughout an enterprise, build user confidence with data cataloging, and build trust in the data sources by maintaining the lineage.

Finally, we will see how this book can help your data engineering work and link each part of the data engineering pipeline with the Alteryx platform applications.

In this chapter, we will cover the following topics:

- Understanding the Alteryx platform
- Using Alteryx Designer
- Leveraging Alteryx Server and Alteryx Connect
- Using this book in your data engineering work

Understanding the Alteryx platform

The **Alteryx platform** is the Alteryx software suite that combines processing, managing datasets, and analysis. While a lot of focus in the Alteryx community tends to be on the business user analyst, a data engineer's benefits are extensive. Alteryx as a whole allows for both code-free and code-friendly workflow development, giving it the flexibility to quickly transform a dataset while having the depth to make complex transformations using whatever tool or process makes the most sense.

In this section, we will learn about the following:

- What software is offered in the Alteryx platform
- How Alteryx can be used with an example business case

The software that makes the Alteryx platform

The Alteryx platform is a collection of four software products:

- **Alteryx Designer**: Designer is the desktop workflow creation tool. It is a **Graphical User Interface (GUI)** for building workflows that interact with the Alteryx Engine, which executes the workflow when run. Designer also enables automated and guided **Machine Learning (ML)** with the **Intelligence Suite** add-on. This is in addition to building your own ML data pipelines, and we will discuss both methods in *Chapter 8, Beginning Advanced Analytics.*

- **Alteryx Server**: We publish a workflow to Server when created to run the workflows on-demand or on a time-based schedule. It also holds a simple version history for referencing which version of a workflow ran a particular transformation. Finally, Server makes provision for the sharing of workflows between different users throughout a company.

- **Alteryx Connect**: The Connect catalog allows users to find and trace datasets and lineage. The population process is completed by running the *Connect Apps*, a series of Alteryx workflows with a user input for parameters that identify the different locations where the datasets reside. These apps will extract all the data catalog information and upload it to the connect database for exploration in the web browser. When the source data doesn't contain context information such as field descriptions, you can add them manually to enrich the catalog.

- **Alteryx Promote**: Promote is a data science model management tool. It provides a way to manage a model's life cycle, monitor performance and model drift, orchestrate model iterations' movements between environments, and provide an API endpoint to deploy the models to other applications.

> **Important Note**
>
> Alteryx software products have *Alteryx* as part of the name. Generally, the name *Alteryx* is dropped from the name in discussions and that will often happen throughout this book.
>
> Because the data science deployment falls into **Machine Learning Operations (MLOps)**, it isn't a core component of the **Data Operations (DataOps)** process. Thus, while you might have some interactions with the model deployment as a data engineer, we will be focusing on extracting and processing the raw datasets rather than the model management and implementation that Promote supports. As such, the Promote software will be beyond the scope of this book.

Now that we know what the Alteryx platform is and what software is available, we can look at how Alteryx will fit into a business case.

Using the Alteryx platform in a business scenario

The Alteryx platform is all about creating a process where iteration is easy. All too often, when integrating a new data source, you won't always know the answer to the following questions until late in the process:

- What is the final form of that data?
- What transformations need to take place?
- Are there additional resources that are required to enrich the data source?

Trying to develop a workflow to answer these questions with a pipeline focused on writing code, common areas of frustration appear when trying to iterate through ideas and tests. These frustrations include the following:

- Knowing when to refactor a part of the pipeline
- Identifying exactly when a particular transformation happens in the pipeline
- Debugging the process for logical errors where the error is in the data output but not caused by a coding error

The visual nature of Alteryx lets you quickly think through the pipeline, and see what transformation is happening where. When errors appear in the process, the tool will highlight the error in context.

It is also easy to trace specific records back through the process visually. This tracing renders straightforward the process of identifying when a transformation takes place that results in a logical error.

How Alteryx benefits data engineers

The Alteryx platform's key benefits to a data engineer arise in three major cases:

- **Speed of development**
- **Iterative workflow development**
- **Self-documentation** (which you can supplement with additional information)

These benefits fall under an overarching theme of making it easier to get new datasets to the end user. For example, suppose the development time, debugging, and documentation can all be made simpler. In that case, responding to requests from analysts and data scientists becomes something to take pride in rather than dreading.

Speed of development

The Alteryx platform supports the speed of development with two fundamental features:

- The visual development process
- The performance of the Alteryx Engine

The visual development process helps a data engineer by allowing them to lay out the pipeline onto the Alteryx canvas. Of course, you can create the pipeline from scratch, which is often the case if little information about the end destination is available. Still, you can build the pipeline from a data flow chart with the principal steps preplanned.

This translation process uses the transformation tools that provide the building blocks for a workflow. By aligning those tools with a logical grid across (or down) the Designer canvas, you can see each step in the pipeline. Such an arrangement allows you to focus on each step to identify when the data might diverge for a particular process and add any intermediate checks.

The other benefit is speed – the fact that the Alteryx engine performs the operations quickly. One of the reasons for this performance is that transformations take place in memory and with the minimum memory footprint required for any particular change.

For example, when a column with millions of records has a formula applied, only the **cells** (the row and column combination) that are processed are needed in memory. The result is that the transformations that Alteryx does are fast.

The location of the dataset is often the only limit to Alteryx's in-memory performance. For example, opening a large Snowflake or Microsoft SQL Server table in Alteryx can become bottlenecked by network transfers. In these cases, the InDB tools can perform calculations on the remote database to minimize the problem and reduce the volume of data transferred locally.

Iterative development workflow

The next significant benefit is the inherent iterative workflow that Alteryx development uses. When building a data pipeline, the sequencing of the transformations is vital to the dataset result.

This iterative process allows you to do the following:

- Check what the data looks like using **browse tools** and **browse anywhere** samples.
- Make modifications and establish the impact that those modifications create.
- Backtrack along the pipeline and insert new changes.

The iterative process allows the data engineer to test changes quickly without worrying about how long it will take to compile or if you haven't noticed a typo in the SQL script.

Self-documenting with additional supplementing of specific notes

Each tool in Alteryx will automatically document itself with annotations. For example, a formula tool will list the calculations taking place.

This self-documenting provides a good starting point for the documentation of the overall workflow. You can supplement these annotations by adding additional context. The further context can be renaming specific tools to reflect what they are doing (which also appears in the workflow logs). Add comment sections to the canvas or grouping processes with tool containers.

We now understand why the Alteryx platform is a powerful tool for data engineering and some of its key benefits. Next, we need to gain a deeper insight into the benefits that using Alteryx Designer can bring to your data engineering development.

Using Alteryx Designer

We have covered at a high level what the benefits of the Alteryx platform are. This section will look a bit closer at Alteryx Designer and why it is suitable for data engineering.

As mentioned previously, Designer is the desktop workflow creation tool in the Alteryx platform. You create the data pipelines and perform advanced analytics in Designer. Designer can also create preformatted reports, upload datasets to API endpoints, or load data into your database of choice.

Here, we will answer some of the questions that revolve around Designer:

- Why is Alteryx Designer suitable for data engineering
- How to start building a workflow in Designer
- How you can leverage the InDB tools for large databases
- And explain some workflow best practices

Answering the preceding questions will give you a basic understanding of why Designer is a good tool for building your data pipelines and the basis for the DataOps principles we will talk about later.

Why is Alteryx Designer suitable for data engineering?

Alteryx Designer utilizes a drag-and-drop interface for building a workflow. Each tool represents a specific transformation or process. This action and visibility of the process allow for a high development speed and emphasize an iterative workflow to get the best results. Throughout the workflow, you can check the impact of the tool's changes on the records and compare them to the tool's input records.

Building a workflow in Designer

If you open a new Designer workflow, you will see the following main interface components:

1. **Tool Pallet**
2. **Configuration Page**
3. **Workflow Canvas**
4. **Results Window**

These components are shown in the following screenshot:

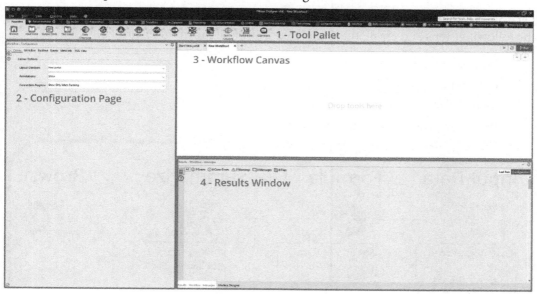

Figure 1.1 – Alteryx Designer interface

Each of these sections provides a different set of information to you while building a workflow.

The Canvas gives a visual representation of the progress of a workflow, the configuration page allows for quick reference and the changing of any settings, and the results window provides a preview of the changes made to the dataset.

This easy viewing of the entire pipeline in the canvas, the data changes at each transformation, and the speedy confirmation of settings in the workflow allow for rapid iteration and testing. As a data engineer, getting a dataset to the stakeholder accurately and quickly is the central goal of your efforts. These Designer features are focused on making that possible.

The default orientation for a workflow is left to right, but you can also customize this to work from top to bottom. Throughout this book, I will describe everything in this context, but be aware that you can change it.

> **Accessing Online Help**
>
> When working in the Designer interface, you can access the online help by pushing the *F1* button on your keyboard. Additionally, if you have a particular tool selected when you push the *F1* button, you will navigate to the help menu for that specific tool.

Let's build a simple workflow using the tools in the Favorites tool bin. We will complete the following steps and create the completed workflow shown in *Figure 1.2*:

1. Connect to a dataset.
2. Perform a calculation.
3. Summarize the results.
4. Write the results to an Alteryx yxdb file:

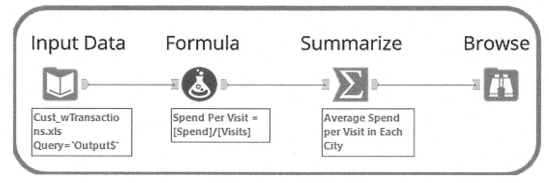

Figure 1.2 – Introduction workflow

You can look at the example workflow in the book's GitHub repository here: https://github.com/PacktPublishing/Data-Engineering-with-Alteryx/tree/main/Chapter%2001.

Using an **Input Data** tool, we can connect to the Cust_wTransactions.xls dataset. This dataset is one of the Alteryx Sample datasets, and you can find this in the Alteryx Program folder, located at C:\ProgramFiles\Alteryx\Samples\ data\SampleData\Cust_wTransactions.xls.

In *step 2* of the process, we create a field with the following steps:

I.   **Create a new field with a Formula tool**: When creating a formula, you always go through the following steps: Create a new **Output Column** (or select an existing column).

II.   **Set the data type**: Set the data type for a new column (you cannot change an existing column's data type).

III.   **Write the formula**: Alteryx has field and formula autocompletion, so that will also help for speeding up your development.

The workflow of the preceding steps can be seen in the following screenshot:

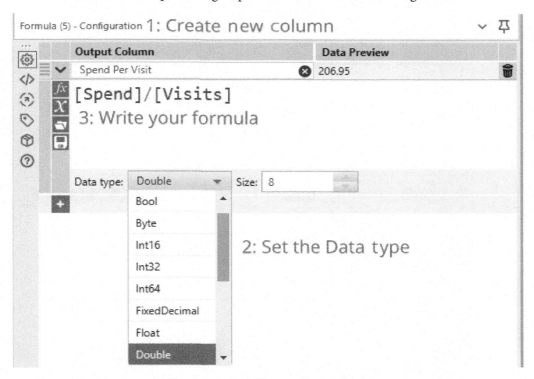

Figure 1.3 – Steps for creating a formula

The third step in the process is to summarize the results to find the average speed per customer in each city as follows:

- **Choose any grouping fields**: Select any fields that we are grouping by, such as City, and then add the action of Group By for that field.

- **Choose any aggregation fields**: Select the field that we want to aggregate, Spend Per Visit, and apply the aggregation we want to action (**Numeric** action menu | **Average** option)

The configuration for the summary described is shown in the following screenshot:

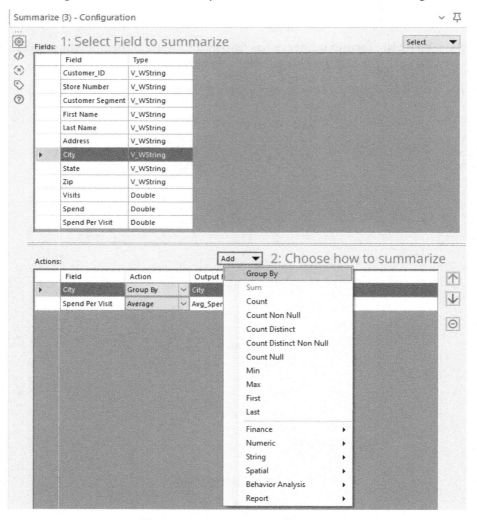

Figure 1.4 – Summarize configuration

The final step in our workflow is to view the results of the processing. We can use the **Browse** tool to view all the records in a dataset and see the full results.

The process we have looked at works well on smaller datasets or data in local files. It is less effective when working with large data sources or when the data is already in a database. In those situations, using **InDB tools** is a better toolset to use. We will get an understanding of how to use those tools in the next section.

What can the InDB tools do?

The **InDB** tools are a great way to process datasets without copying the data across the network to your local machine. In the following screenshot, we have an example workflow that uses a sample Snowflake database to process 4.1 GB of data in less than 2 minutes:

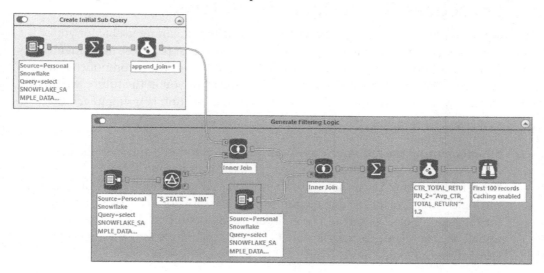

Figure 1.5 – Example workflow using InDB tools

You can look at the example workflow in the book's GitHub repository here: `https://github.com/PacktPublishing/Data-Engineering-with-Alteryx/tree/main/Chapter%2001`.

This workflow entails three steps:

1. Generate an initial query for the target data.
2. Produce a subquery off that data to generate the filtering logic.
3. Apply the filtering logic to the primary query.

When looking at the visual layout, we see the generation of the query, where the logic branches off, and how we merge the logic back onto the dataset. The automated annotations all provide information about what is happening at each step. At the same time, the tool containers group the individual logic steps together.

We will look at how to use the InDB tools in more detail in later chapters, but this workflow shows how complicated queries are run on large datasets while still providing good performance in your workflow.

Building better documentation into your workflow improves the usability of the workflow. Therefore, adding this documentation is considered the best practice to employ when developing a workflow. We will explore how we can apply the documentation in the next section.

Best practices for Designer workflows

Applying Designer best practices makes your data engineering more usable for you and other team members. Having the documentation and best practices implemented throughout a workflow embeds the knowledge of what the workflow components are doing in context. It means that additional team members, or you in the future, will be able to open a workflow and understand what each small section is trying to achieve.

The best practices fall into three areas:

1. **Supplementing the automatic annotations**: The automatic annotations that Alteryx creates for individual tools provide basic information about what has happened in a tool. The annotations do not offer an explanation or justification of the logic. Additionally, the default naming of each tool doesn't provide any context for the log outputs. We can add more information in both of these areas. We can update the tool name to describe what is happening in that tool and expand the annotation to include more detail.

2. **Using tool containers to group logic**: Adding **tool containers** to a workflow is a simple way of visually grouping processes on the canvas. You can also use specific colors for the containers to highlight different functions. For example, you can color input functions green and logic calculations in orange. These particular color examples don't matter as long as the colors are consistent across workflows and your organization.

3. **Adding comment and explorer box tools for external context**: Often, you will need to add more context to a workflow, and this context won't fit in an annotation or color grouping. You can supplement the automatic documentation with **Comment tools** for text-based notes or an **explorer box** to reference external sources. Those external sources could be web pages, local HTML files, or folder directories. For example, you can include web documentation or a README file in the workflow, thereby providing deeper context.

These three areas all focus on making a workflow decipherable at a glance and quickly understandable. They give new data engineers the information they need to understand the workflow when adopting or reviewing a project.

With a completed workflow, the next step will be making the workflow run automatically. We also need to make the datasets that the workflow creates searchable and the lineage traceable. We will use Alteryx Server and Alteryx Connect to achieve this, which we will look at next.

Leveraging Alteryx Server and Alteryx Connect

Once you have successfully created a data pipeline, the following process is to automate its use. In this section, we will use Alteryx to automate a pipeline and create discoverability and trust in the data.

The two products we will focus on are Alteryx **Server** and Alteryx **Connect**. Server is the workflow automation, scaling, and sharing platform, while Connect is for data cataloging, trust, and discoverability.

Server has three main capabilities that are of benefit to a data engineer:

- **Time-based automation of workflows**: Relying on a single person to run a workflow that is key to any system is a recipe for failure. So, having a schedule-based system for running those workflows makes it more robust and reliable.

- **Scaling of capacity for running workflows**: Running multiple workflows on Designer Desktop is not a good experience for most people. Having Server run more workflows will also free up local resources for other jobs.

- **Sharing workflows via a central location**: The Server is the central location where workflows are published to and discovered by users around the organization.

Connect is a service for data cataloging and discovery. Data assets can be labeled by what the data represents, the field contents, or the source. This catalog enables the discovery of new resources. Additionally, the **Data Nexus** allows a data field's lineage to be traced and builds trust with users to know where a field originated from and what transformations have taken place.

How can you use Alteryx Server to orchestrate a data pipeline?

Once we have created a pipeline, we may want to have the dataset extracted on a regular schedule. Having this process automated allows for more robust implementation and makes using the dataset simpler to use.

Orchestrating a data pipeline with Alteryx Server is a three-step process:

1. Create a pipeline in Alteryx Designer and publish it to Alteryx Server.
2. Set a time frame to run the workflow.
3. Monitor the running of the workflow.

This three-step process is deceptively simple and, for this introduction, only covers the most straightforward use cases. Later, in *Chapter 10*, *Monitoring DataOps and Managing Changes*, we will walk through some techniques to orchestrate more complex, multistep data pipelines. Still, those examples fundamentally come back to these three steps mentioned above.

In the following screenshot, we can see how we can define the time frame for our schedule on the Server **Schedule** page:

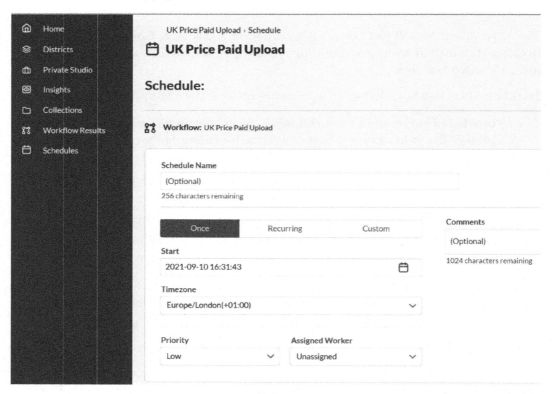

Figure 1.6 – The Alteryx Server scheduling page

On this page, we can define the frequency of a schedule, the time the schedule will occur, and provide a reference name for the schedule.

How does Connect help with discoverability?

The final piece of your data engineering puzzle is how will users find and trust the dataset you have created? While you will often generate datasets on request, you also find that users will come to you looking for datasets you have already made, and they don't know they exist.

Connect is a data cataloging and discoverability tool for you to surface the datasets in your organization and allow users to find them, request access, and understand what the fields are. It is a central place for data definitions and allows searching in terms of how content is defined.

Using this book in your data engineering work

Now that you know the basics of using Alteryx, we can investigate how Alteryx applies to data engineering. Data engineering is a broad topic and has many different definitions, depending on who is using it. So, for the context of this book, here is how I define data engineering:

Data engineering is the process of taking data from any number of disparate sources and transforming them into a usable format for an end user.

It sounds simple enough, but this definition encapsulates many variables and complexity:

- Where is the data, and how many sources are there?
- What transformations are needed?
- What is a usable state?
- How should the data be accessed?
- Who is the end user?

Chapter 2, Data Engineering with Alteryx, will expand on what this definition means. It will also explain how Alteryx products cover all the steps needed to deliver that definition.

How does the Alteryx platform come together for data engineering?

So far in this introduction, we have talked about how the parts of Alteryx can help the data engineering process independently. However, each Alteryx element also works together to build a complete, end-to-end data engineering process.

There is a common set of processes that are required when completing a data engineering project. These processes are shown in the next diagram along with what Alteryx software is usually associated with that process:

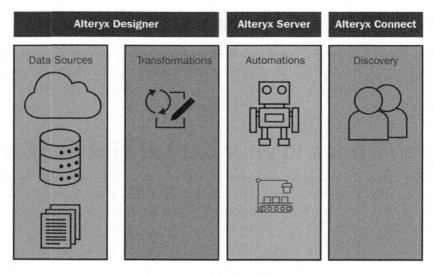

Figure 1.7 – The aspects of the data engineering process

The preceding screenshot shows Designer overlapping the data sources and transformation aspects of the processes, Server overlays the automation (which performs some of the transformations), and Connect covers the discovery section of the process.

Chapter 2, Data Engineering with Alteryx, will introduce a complete data engineering example and the DataOps principles that support data engineering in Alteryx. Finally, *Chapter 3, DataOps and Its Benefits*, will take the principles introduced and expand on why those principles will benefit data engineering and your organization.

Examples where Alteryx is used for data engineering

I want to share two example use cases where Alteryx provides an excellent platform for data engineering from my consulting work.

In the first example, my client uses Alteryx Designer to create a series of workflows to collect reference information from a third party. They automate this process on Server to extract the information from the source text files and load them into their data warehouse daily. These resources are then shared with people throughout the company and made discoverable.

The other use case is where a medium-sized business uses Alteryx to collect the core company information from scattered business APIs; finance and billing, social media and web analytics, CRM, and customer engagement. Next, the company automatically consolidates the business resources into the core reporting database. The company then discovers the centralized data sources in Connect while Alteryx populates an additional data catalog for the Business Intelligence tool.

Summary

In this chapter, we have learned the parts that make up the Alteryx platform. We have also learned how they can benefit you as a data engineer with faster development, an iterative workflow, and extendable self-documentation.

We examined an example of how to build a workflow with Designer and learned what the InDB tools can do. Finally, we introduced Server and Connect. We learned how Server can automate and scale your data engineering developments. Then we learned that Connect provides a place for user discovery of the datasets you have created.

In the next chapter, we will expand on what a data engineer is for Alteryx and how you can use Alteryx products for data engineering. Then we will introduce DataOps and why this is a guiding principle for data engineering in Alteryx.

2
Data Engineering with Alteryx

In *Chapter 1, Getting Started with Alteryx*, we began exploring the **Alteryx** platform and its use in **data engineering**. In this chapter, we will examine what the role of data engineering involves and how a person in that role would use the Alteryx platform. Throughout this book, we will assume you have a solid understanding of analytical processes but don't have any experience with Alteryx to deliver end-to-end analytic datasets. We will also learn about the DataOps framework and how an Alteryx data engineer can use it.

We will cover the following topics in this chapter:

- What is a data engineer?
- Using Alteryx products as a data engineer
- Applying DataOps as an Alteryx data engineer

What is a data engineer?

In *Chapter 1*, *Getting Started with Alteryx*, we defined data engineering as follows:

Data engineering is the process of taking data from any number of disparate sources and transforming them into a usable format for an end user.

This definition focuses on data engineering as a process and getting the data from the source to the end user. It does not consider where the data source is, who the end user is, or even the tools they use to accomplish the job. Those details are not crucial to the definition. You want to get data from the source to the user.

The definition only captures part of the complexity of the data engineering job. For example, while identifying the end user does not matter to our definition of data engineering, completing a data engineering project relies on knowing the end user.

As the data engineer, building a data pipeline requires knowing where the data is coming from, its format, and if that format has changed. Understanding these factors is the basis for delivering successful projects and trusted pipelines.

Finally, a data engineer cannot be wedded to any tool, but should use whatever device makes your work smoother and more manageable.

One tool you can use is **Alteryx**. It's a tool I find flexible and adaptable, which allows you as the data engineer, data analyst, or data scientist, to quickly iterate over a problem set, test theories, and expand the complexity into any area you need.

As a data engineer, you connect to core databases or data lakes as the source material for most of your pipelines. You will cleanse and sterilize those datasets to fit the requirements of your end user. But you won't stop with those internal datasets. You will often enrich that information with publicly available data, such as government datasets or publicly shared commercial data. You will search out commercial datasets where the cost is a direct investment in the value of your output. And you will craft metrics and features so your users will have the best chance of achieving their own goals.

As a data engineer, you are an enabler.

You can see the data engineering process in the following diagram:

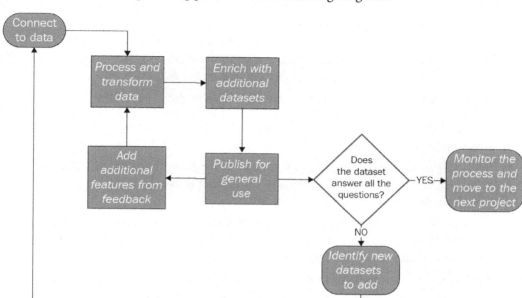

Figure 2.1 – The general data engineering process with Alteryx

So, let's finally get down to my definition of a data engineer:

A data engineer is a person who takes any available tools to collect data and then cleanse and transform the raw data to create an enriched dataset. The raw data can be from any company, commercial, or public source. The final enriched dataset is a cohesive, interpretable, and usable data source that end users trust.

With this definition of a data engineer, we need to understand how a data engineer would use Alteryx and how each Alteryx product achieves each part of the definition.

Using Alteryx products as a data engineer

With our definition of data engineering and data engineers, we ask, where does Alteryx fit in for a data engineer? In *Chapter 1, Getting Started with Alteryx*, we described a medium-sized business to demonstrate the Alteryx platform. This section will expand the above example to see how each part of the Alteryx platform works together to solve that use case and how that process follows my definition.

As a reminder, the example use case is as follows:

> *A medium-sized business uses Alteryx to collect the core company information from scattered business APIs and consolidates all these business resources into the core reporting database. The company can then find those data sources after populating the data catalogs.*

When we look at that use case, it fits with my definition of data engineering:

1. *A data engineer is a person who takes any available tools to collect data together.* In this step, you will use Designer to connect to and extract the raw data sources:

2. *Then, cleanse and transform the raw data to create an enriched dataset.* While still in Designer, you apply transformations to the dataset to combine the data sources and enrich them with additional information.

3. *Publish the final enriched data as a valuable data source.* We can publish the data source from Designer as a one-off output, but as a data engineer, you will most likely automate the process with Alteryx Server.

4. *End users can trust that data source.* With Alteryx Connect, you post the meta information about the data source and what transformations were applied to build confidence in the data source.

Working through the preceding steps, each product from the Alteryx platform fills a role in the process. **Designer** makes connecting to multiple data sources simple and performs the transformations needed. It is automated by **Server**, thus removing any key human dependency, and the pipeline can run reliably. Finally, **Connect** enables the final data output to be used by surfacing and exposing the data lineage, provides a data dictionary, and allows accessible communication of what datasets are available.

Let's look at the whole process in the following diagram and see where the Alteryx products fit in delivering each requirement:

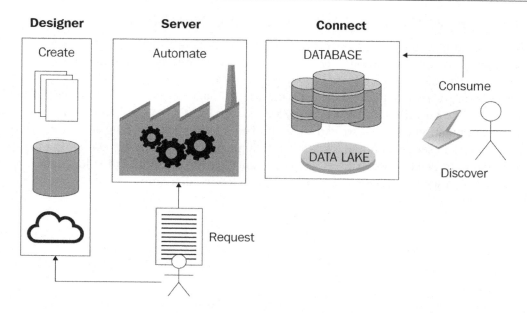

Figure 2.2 – The data pipeline for an Alteryx data engineer

From the preceding diagram, we see the overall data pipeline. Let's understand these processes next:

1. The **Create** process is where the connection to data sources happens and where the transformation and enrichment occur. Creating these processes is done by building Alteryx Designer workflows.

2. The **Automate** section encompasses where the dataset is output for users to access it and do so in an automated fashion. We discuss automation of workflows in the *Automating with Server for data engineers* section.

3. Finally, the **Connect** section is where users find and access the datasets in the data discovery platform. Finding the datasets is enabled with Alteryx Connect, allowing end users and communities to share breakdown data silos and build dataset understanding.

In the Alteryx platform, **Designer** enables the **Create** process, **Server** allows the automation process, and **Connect** enables data discovery.

Using example use cases, we can look at how to achieve each of those processes.

Creating with Designer for data engineers

The first section of the data engineering process involved creating the pipeline and completing any transformations. For our example, the dataset we are looking at is `world_data.txt`, sourced from the MySQL website (`https://downloads.mysql.com/docs/world-db.zip`) with original data sourced from Statistics Finland (`https://tilastokeskus.fi/tup/kvportaali/index_en.html`). The dataset includes population data that we can use to find a target market. Looking at the following diagram, we can see an example workflow that imports a population file containing three linked datasets. Next, those datasets are parsed and transformed into individual data tables. You can see the process as a whole in the following diagram:

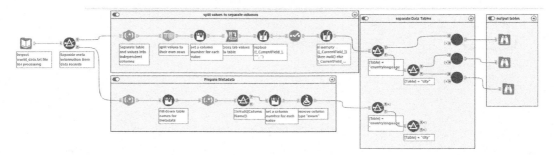

Figure 2.3 – World data table preparation

You can find the example workflows in the book's GitHub repository here: `https://github.com/PacktPublishing/Data-Engineering-with-Alteryx/tree/main/Chapter%2002`.

We can break the workflow down into five sections. They are as follows:

1. **Initial connection**: We connect to the specific file of interest with an input tool, `world_data.txt`. This file contains the global city information, population data, and language information tables. We can use this information to decide where to expand our business based on the population demographics in the cities, and the connection is shown in the following diagram:

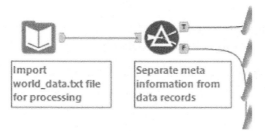

Figure 2.4 – Importing the world data file

2. **Parsing the data values**: Unfortunately, the single file holds the country information as the three related tables. Each table is a separate dataset with a different number of columns, and various data types, which we will discuss more in *Chapter 5, Data Processing and Transformations*. Additionally, the values in the columns are in the following format:

```
'table name' VALUES (value1, value2, value3,…, valueN);
```

This format requires parsing into a table format for analysis. We can use a combination of Regex for powerful text manipulation and a standard text-to-rows operation to parse the value information we need. You can learn more about Regex in Alteryx on the tool's help pages (`https://help.alteryx.com/20214/designer/regex-tool`). The process for separating the table values is shown in the following screenshot:

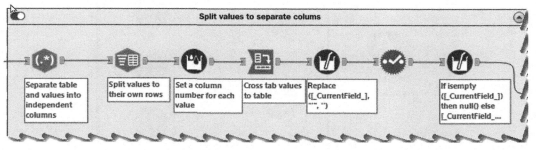

Figure 2.5 – Processing the values from the world data file

3. **Parsing the table metadata**: Next, we need to transform the table metadata. The metadata is the information that identifies what the column names are supposed to be. Using that metadata, we can confirm that the data types match the data types we set for the columns. The metadata preparation is seen in the following screenshot:

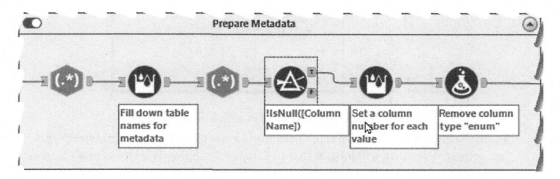

Figure 2.6 – Processing the metadata from the world data file

4. **Combining the data values and metadata**: Once we have processed the data values and metadata, we need to combine this information. We use an Alteryx standard macro to encapsulate a repeated process. To learn how to build an Alteryx macro from Alteryx Community, refer to the following link: `https://community.` `alteryx.com/t5/Alteryx-Designer-Knowledge-Base/Getting-` `Started-with-Standard-Macros/ta-p/488149`. When we make changes or updates to the process, the modifications are reflected in all locations and will minimize the errors caused by duplication. The table separation is shown in the following screenshot:

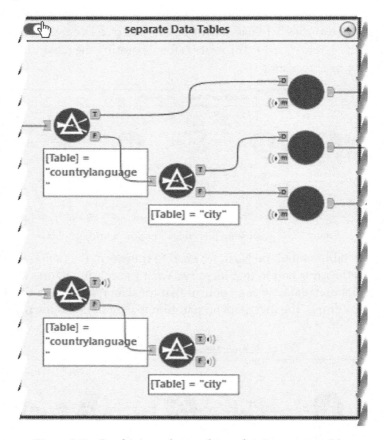

Figure 2.7 – Combining values and metadata in separate tables

In production, we would add error handling to ensure our outputs and field types are consistent, but we will look at that in *Chapter 9, Testing Workflows and Outputs*.

5. **Outputting to a storage location**: Finally, we will need to output the final datasets for use. This output location could be a local or networked folder, a relational database such as MySQL, an analytical database such as Snowflake, or a data lake for large data applications. In the workflow shown in the following screenshot, we haven't added the output tool, and the dataset is made available in a **Browse** tool for review:

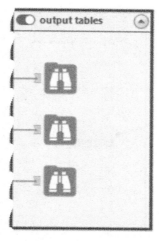

Figure 2.8 – Outputting the final world data tables

When we decide how to output the data, we will also need to determine how we want to automate this process. In the next section, we will see how we automate the process with Server.

Automating with Server for data engineers

Deciding on your output source will also inform your automation decisions. Will the output be a local file, and what uses are there for the data source? If you upload to a database (which any business should be doing for company data), how frequently does that data need to be updated and examined?

Deciding on the freshness of the data is also linked to the source. For example, is the source a static file or a regularly updated **Application Programming Interface (API)** or **File Transfer Protocol (FTP)** output? Each of these questions helps inform how often you would need to run the workflow for automation.

Now we can publish the workflow to Server (we'll look at that more in *Chapter 11, Securing and Managing Access*) and set a schedule to automate the running of the workflow. The published workflow also acts as a source-controlled version of the processing steps. Your Connect catalog will reference the changes to maintain the data lineage.

Figure 2.9 shows the process for setting a schedule on a published workflow:

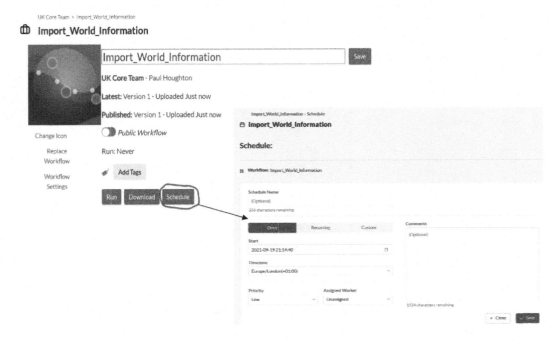

Figure 2.9 – Screen capture of the scheduling process

As you can see, there are three steps for creating the schedule:

1. First, click on the **Schedule** button.

2. Define the time and frequency of the schedule.

3. Save the schedule to start it running.

Important Note

The ability to schedule workflows on Alteryx Server requires additional permissions. If you don't have access to the **Schedule** button, you will need to speak to your Alteryx Server manager, who will change your permissions and allow the scheduling capability.

Now that we know how to schedule a workflow, we can investigate how to make the dataset discoverable. In the next section, we will see how Alteryx Connect enables the discoverability of your dataset and provides the information required for users to understand how to use the dataset.

Connecting end users with Alteryx Connect

Now that we have the workflow created and the data updating process automated, the next and final step is to get the data source to our end users. The primary end user, the person or team who requested the dataset, can quickly be informed of the data source's existence via email or Slack. However, they will still be reliant on you for finding out what the fields are, whether there is any scaling information they need to know about, or whether they want to know what transformations took place. If we can populate this information into a data dictionary, we can make the data source discovery self-service.

The following screenshot shows an example of the information that the *Connect Data Dictionary* can hold:

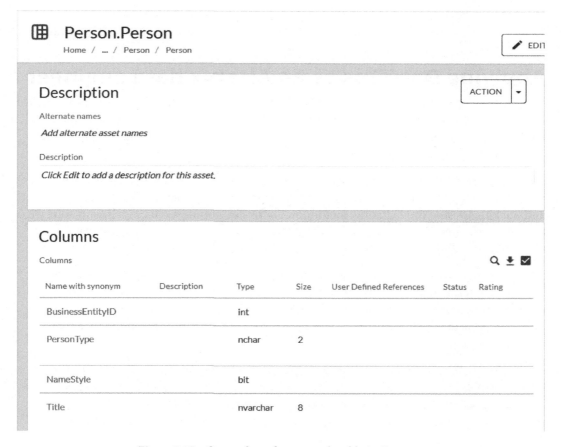

Figure 2.10 – Screenshot of an example table in Connect

The preceding screenshot shows that the example **Person** table in the **Person** database contains the extracted columns, the column types, and column sizes. These fields are all automatically populated. Additional information, such as the **Description** and **User Defined References** fields, are also extracted when available in the database. If that information is not there, it can be populated once you create the entry in Connect.

You can add alternate names for easier searching and descriptions of the table and individual fields, and request access from the data source owner. It is also possible to start a new workflow on the data source using the action button.

We will further show how Connect can make data discoverable and easy to use in *Chapter 12, Making Data Easy to Use and Discoverable with Alteryx*.

Now that we know how to enable Alteryx for your data engineering practices, we can introduce a framework to produce the best data pipelines that deliver great data products.

Applying DataOps as an Alteryx data engineer

In this chapter, we have examined how Alteryx can achieve a data engineering pipeline. We have looked at different definitions and examples of data engineering and data pipelines. However, the whole time we have been skirting around some underlying principles that underpin the process of our data engineering pipeline.

The DataOps methodology provides the structures and systems for delivering a data pipeline. It allows you to improve the cycle time and quality when producing data sources and analytics. Using the DataOps methodology for developing a data pipeline in Alteryx formalizes the iterative processes that naturally happen during development. DataOps also adds reporting and monitoring structures to ensure high data quality.

Using DataOps with Alteryx fits well as developing a workflow or pipeline in Alteryx involves an iterative process, which links to the improving cycle time. Additionally, implementing the strategies for quality improvement and management from DataOps into your Alteryx pipeline ensures the reliability of your data and the confidence that end users have in it.

DataOps extends concepts from the DevOps practices into data analytics. One of the critical principles that DataOps implements is to make the testing and deployment of new datasets as automatic as possible and integrated as soon as possible. It should also follow Agile software development practices to reduce cycle times as much as possible.

For an Alteryx data engineer, there are four main areas where we leverage the DataOps principles (which I'll explain in *Chapter 3, DataOps and Its Benefits*):

1. Data sourcing and processing
2. Storage and value extraction
3. Governance and monitoring
4. Improving access

We can build a structure into our workflows by implementing the DataOps process when developing with Alteryx. This structure makes it easier to create data pipelines and produce reliable data sources for all our end users.

Summary

In this chapter, we focused on understanding how to use Alteryx for data engineering. In the examples, we looked at how a workflow can take data from the source to the end users. We also examined how we can make those datasets more usable for both the end user who requested the data and any other user who may require that data in the future.

We also introduced DataOps and explained how the framework makes the data pipeline process automated and faster while delivering higher quality data.

In the next chapter, we will look at DataOps in more depth. We will learn how to apply DevOps with Alteryx and detail the benefits that a DevOps practice will bring to your Alteryx data engineering.

3

DataOps and Its Benefits

In *Chapter 2, Data Engineering with Alteryx*, we introduced Alteryx products, the **DataOps** framework, and how Alteryx products are accommodated within the DataOps framework. This chapter will look at the key benefits of applying DataOps and what rewards you will gain by implementing DataOps in your organization.

We will explore the principles of DataOps and investigate how they apply to Alteryx development. We will also look at the specifics of which tools in the Alteryx platform can implement the principles of DataOps.

Throughout this chapter, you will learn how Alteryx can help leverage the DataOps process and apply the principles in an Alteryx pipeline.

In this chapter, we will cover the following topics:

- The benefits the DataOps framework brings to your organization
- Understanding DataOps principles
- Applying DataOps to Alteryx
- Using Alteryx software with DataOps
- General steps for deploying DataOps in your environment

The benefits the DataOps framework brings to your organization

As a reminder, DataOps is the methodology that defines the systems and structures for building data pipelines. The most significant benefits of DataOps are as follows:

- Faster cycle times
- Faster access to actionable insights
- Improved robustness of data processes
- The ability to see the entire data flow in a workflow
- Strong security and confidence

These benefits have allowed me to deliver data pipelines to my customers and end-users faster. The speed of delivery enables end users to analyze their datasets and immediately provide the feedback needed to tune that dataset to the result they need. Additionally, the inclusion of testing, reporting, and monitoring has provided confidence in the dataset when delivering the completed project for them to maintain in the future.

For example, when building an integration pipeline for a customer, returning incremental workflow improvements faster allows feedback to be implemented in the next cycle. Next, by running a test suite that identifies our metrics during development, the end user is confident that the dataset delivers on its requirements. Additionally, we can use the test suite in production to ensure that the dataset continues to deliver on the requirements as expected.

These benefits are delivered through automation and reduced duplication. How we can achieve these benefits is explained in the next section.

Faster cycle times

With DataOps, we can achieve faster cycle times by applying a consistent process in developing the data pipelines. Furthermore, implementing this consistency means that a lot of the setup portion of a project is standardized, and we can minimize the duplication of processes across projects.

The faster cycle time also helps both end users and data engineers to enjoy the process more as they see tangible results sooner, and all parties can progress to the next step in their analysis.

Faster access to actionable insights

We can achieve actionable insights by standardizing repetitive parts of the process, for example, having a standardized and documented process for connecting external sources to internal databases. Additionally, any data tasks, such as everyday cleansing and control table updates, can be made into a reusable macro to simplify that part of the process.

Improved robustness of data processes

Implementing robust monitoring processes, such as applying **Statistical Process Controls (SPCs)**, enables end users to be confident in the results of the data pipeline. The SPCs are an automated system for identifying when the variations in your dataset fall outside acceptable limits. These standardized processes allow teams to detect when errors might emerge and catch the outliers in the datasets so that they can be processed appropriately.

Provides an overview of the entire data flow

The core workflows in Alteryx give an overview of the process at the transformation level. For example, watching the data flow through a workflow, checking the transformations at each point, and monitoring the process controls provide an overview of the entire process.

When you add that to Connect's data lineage features, you can see the entire data flow from source through transformation, stopping at any intermediate staging files prior to final ingestion and consumption. This complete view of the data flow means we can assess the impact of any process changes. Again, this helps deliver the DataOps principles by improving data pipeline transparency and interaction between teams and developers.

Strong security and conformance

Finally, having a centralized platform for the analytics process allows for better management of the entire data estate. Having a view of who is interacting with data assets, which users should have access to those assets, and a centralized process for managing those processes allows for tight control of security and governance of the data pipeline.

With these benefits explained, we can learn what the DataOps principles are. We can also link the application of the DataOps principles to the benefits they will bring when we implement them in an organization.

Understanding DataOps principles

The DataOps principles are the set of guidelines that help deliver datasets and pipelines more efficiently. According to the DataOps manifesto (`https://dataopsmanifesto.org/en/`), 18 different principles are recommended. Those principles fall into three main pillars that form the basis of DataOps:

- **People**
- **Delivery**
- **Confidence**

We can see the pillars and a summary of the principles in *Figure 3.1*, and we will look at each principle in detail later in this chapter:

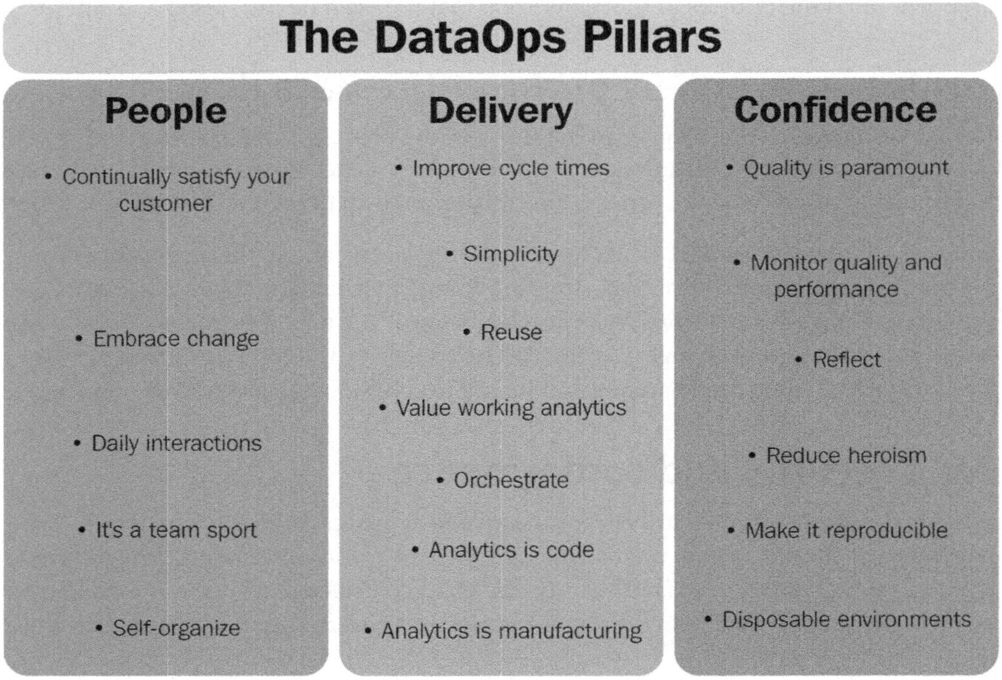

The DataOps Pillars

People	Delivery	Confidence
• Continually satisfy your customer	• Improve cycle times	• Quality is paramount
	• Simplicity	• Monitor quality and performance
• Embrace change	• Reuse	• Reflect
• Daily interactions	• Value working analytics	• Reduce heroism
• It's a team sport	• Orchestrate	• Make it reproducible
• Self-organize	• Analytics is code	• Disposable environments
	• Analytics is manufacturing	

Figure 3.1 – The pillars and principles of the DataOps framework

But for now, we will investigate the themes of each pillar:

- The **People pillar** focuses on the culture that DataOps is trying to instill. It looks at both the data teams delivering the datasets and the end users who will consume the dataset. The principles in this pilar also encourage a close, iterative link between the end user and the data engineer, borrowing ideas from the Agile Development Framework.

- The **Delivery pillar** focuses on how to deliver a finished data product to the end user. It encompasses the production of resources, how the process is automated, and how, once delivered, a dataset can be continuously improved and developed.

- The **Confidence pillar** focuses on building each step of the data pipeline to ensure confidence in the process and that the final output is accurate; knowing that if there is a request to repeat the processing of a pipeline, the result would be the same; and knowing that when a decision is made based on the data provided, that decision and the insight it drives is the best and the most accurate it can be.

Let's look at each of the pillars and the principles that fit into those pillars.

The People pillar

As mentioned, the People pillar is all about the culture that DataOps wants to drive. It focuses on putting the end user or customer at the center of every decision made when delivering a data pipeline.

We can apply the following principles to achieve this culture:

- **Continually satisfy your customer**: Throughout the development process, communicate your progress with your customer and update the pipelines you are creating based on their feedback.

- **Embrace change**: Always be prepared to update and adapt your workflow and systems to implement the best practices as they evolve.

- **Daily interactions**: Communicate with your team and customers frequently to ensure expectations are always aligned.

- **It's a team sport**: Build a team with diverse roles, skills, and backgrounds and then, any individual assumptions about a particular topic can be tested and accessed collectively.

- **Self-organize**: Having a collection of skills in the team allows individuals to organize themselves into the best groups for any specific project that arises.

The DataOps principles that constitute the People pillar, described above, focus on creating a communicative culture. With a team of data engineers, data analysts, and data scientists, you can collectively solve any request made to you by the organization.

The Delivery pillar

Getting data reliably to the end user can be as challenging to deliver. Being able to serve data requests quickly and efficiently to the end user is made possible by the Delivery pillar. By following the Delivery pillar, you can make decisions quickly:

- **Improve cycle times**: It would be best to design processes to deliver a working data pipeline to the end user as soon as possible rather than create and deliver a monolithic approach.

- **Simplicity**: When you make each step in the data pipeline as simple as possible, this aids in troubleshooting the workflow. If you separate parts of the process into independent actions, it can help to isolate potential delivery issues.

- **Reuse**: Whenever possible, you should create reusable, easily implemented data processes. You can then reimplement those processes in new workflows.

- **Value working analytics**: Delivering a working dataset allows analytics to start, and the dataset can be refined once a functional pipeline is available.

- **Orchestrate**: This means having unified processes for managing the entire data pipeline, from pipeline creation, to automation, to monitoring.

- **Analytics is code**: By treating the analytic tools as code, they can be managed and reverted to a known working state and released in a systematic process.

- **Analytics is manufacturing**: You can continuously improve the process through many minor, incremental updates and modifications.

You are better able to serve and judge a data request by following these six principles. By implementing the **improve cycle times**, **simplicity**, and **reuse** principles, you can quickly create new datasets and minimize excess work. When a process is rebuilt or overcomplicated, it is harder to deliver a good data product. Improving cycle times means that a more extensive project is delivered in smaller chunks to ensure smooth completion.

The value working analytics principle focuses not on creating a pipeline or what tools you use to achieve the dataset, but on the actual data product delivered.

Finally, the last three principles are the functional parts of the data pipeline delivery. When you can orchestrate a process from ingestion to insight, you control all the different environments involved. You can manage the tool versions and server environment configuration. The Analytics is code principle highlights the fact that the process used to deliver a data product can be examined and checked. The Analytics is manufacturing principle highlights the fact that the pipeline you create is an analytic insights product, which means you can continuously improve the process.

The Confidence pillar

The Confidence pillar is about creating the conditions to support the confidence of your end users in your data pipeline. For example, suppose end users have doubts regarding the datasets due to inconsistent processing or unexplained errors. In that case, the issues erode the value of your pipeline, and those users will not engage with your datasets. The following principles help build the systems needed to ensure that your end users are confident that the data you are providing is accurate and valuable to them:

- **Quality is paramount**: Making sure the datasets and pipelines you deliver provide accurate values is central to producing a valuable dataset.

- **Monitor quality and performance**: Designing systems to monitor the datasets you create and the performance of the data pipelines should be included as part of the development cycle and not an addition to an otherwise completed project

- **Reflect**: You should take the time to go back over established data pipelines and apply any new skills you have learned or learn about new features added to your software stack.

- **Reduce heroism**: Finding ways to transfer pipeline-specific knowledge will reduce dependency on specific people and allow team members to switch between projects when needed.

- **Make it reproducible**: Ensuring that a pipeline can be rerun at any time so that you can recreate the dataset if needed.

- **Disposable environments**: You should be able to quickly and easily create development and deployment environments. This ease of creation means any testing process has minimal impact on secondary systems and developers can implement changes confidently, as what they are doing can be controlled.

These six principles combine to provide the systems and controls to support your data pipeline deployments. In addition, they provide the mechanisms for managing the data and pipelines while also emphasizing that processes should be continuously improved when put into production.

If end users don't have confidence in a dataset or developers aren't confident in the environments they are trying to develop, it can result in stagnating datasets and poor pipeline performance. However, you can manage and minimize those risks if you implement these pillars.

Applying DataOps to Alteryx

Now that we know the principles and the pillars of DataOps, how does DataOps work with Alteryx? Like any tool you can use with DataOps, some principles integrate into the Alteryx platform very easily. In contrast, other principles need to be considered carefully for the best results.

Supporting the People pillar with Alteryx

Building a culture with Alteryx to support the People pillar enables the flexibility to approach any problem. You can continually deliver the minimum viable product to the customer and adapt to customers' demands with fast development speeds. Alteryx Development follows an iterative process that matches the DataOps principles. Additionally, lean manufacturing, which also forms the basis of DataOps principles, encourages the continuous improvement that Alteryx development supports.

Another benefit of the Alteryx platform for the People pillar is the code-friendly capabilities of the software. While Alteryx is primarily a code-free, GUI-based tool, features such as the Python tool, the R tool, and the Run command tool allow external processes to be integrated into a workflow easily. This flexibility enables you to leverage a range of tools within the same platform.

Leveraging the team sport and self-organizing principles with Alteryx is about applying the mentality that delivers the best results for an Alteryx developer. This mentality is to work iteratively and take advantage of the community resources available. Additionally, with multiple team members working together, each person can look at the problem and identify any issues and questions that might impede a project's progress.

Using Alteryx to deliver data pipelines

The principles in the Delivery pillar are focused on getting data to end users as quickly and efficiently as possible. Alteryx can help by leveraging its code-free base practically and delivering quickly through fast iterations and simple, easy-to-understand workflows. Additionally, you can easily reuse processes by packaging them into macros.

How you deliver a project in Alteryx has a strong correlation with the DataOps principles. For example, development is cycled quickly through each iteration, the visual workflow can be easily understood and followed, and you can package any repeated sections or processes for reuse.

The principle of valuing working analytics, where you deliver a complete project in smaller working chunks, is leveraged at each stage in workflow development. For example, when building an Alteryx workflow, the datasets are checked frequently with the browse anywhere feature, examined in-depth with browse tools, and can be sense checked using summary functions, charts, and test checks. In addition, a working pipeline is needed to deliver a dataset to your end user and that pipeline enables you to verify the process used.

We fill the final three principles in the Alteryx platform as part of the underlying make-up of the software. Alteryx manages process orchestration either inside the ecosystem or by leveraging outside tools to deliver the end-to-end pipeline. Each Alteryx workflow contains the details of the specific software version that ran the data pipeline. Because the specifics are held in the Alteryx file's XML recording the pipeline, treating an Alteryx workflow as you would any other code with standard software version control can be executed.

One challenge with treating an Alteryx workflow as code is that because it is a visual interface, the small visible changes that an Alteryx data engineer might make can cause the difference in tracking in version control software challenging to interpret. This challenge stems from deciding whether this change in the XML is essential to the workflow or just visual.

Building confidence with Alteryx

Ensuring the quality and performance of Alteryx pipelines is not created automatically within the Alteryx platform. Recording the workflow runtime information happens automatically, saving the run details in the Alteryx Server database, but it must be deliberately extracted and analyzed. You can employ sub-workflows or sub-processes in the data pipeline to check the quality of the records.

Alteryx can leverage the principle of reducing heroism through the readability of the workflows. This readability means that other data engineers can take over a pipeline relatively quickly. Even when unplanned, this easy workflow handover is supported by the self-documenting nature of an Alteryx workflow. When documentation best practices are adhered to, the handover process is even more straightforward. Even so, you can navigate unplanned handovers with automated documentation.

Alteryx leverages the reproducible development and disposable environment principles because Alteryx does not change the underlying data without explicitly forcing a write process. Because all workflows are non-destructive, developers can test and iterate ideas and try novel processes without affecting the underlying data infrastructure. Additionally, when creating a new environment for an Alteryx developer, the base install contains the functionality required to run any workflow.

The limitation of this in the Alteryx environment is that it doesn't include any custom reusable macros. However, suppose a consistent process is implemented to save and access these reusable processes, such as saving to a consistent network location or cloud storage provider. In that case, you can easily add those macros to any new development environment.

Deploying DataOps with Alteryx starts with understanding the mindset and places where you are using Alteryx. Where we can achieve this has been discussed, but we also need to see how to use each Alteryx program in DataOps projects.

Using Alteryx software with DataOps

The Alteryx platform components of Designer, Server, and Connect deliver the parts needed to support the DataOps framework pillars and fulfill the principles that make up those pillars. Each of the different software components fits across the People, Delivery, and Confidence pillars, serving the various functions needed to deliver in a DataOps framework.

In *Figure 3.2,* we have the same pillars from earlier, but with an overlay of where each Alteryx product interacts with the different pillars:

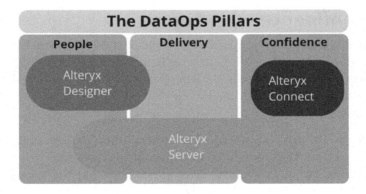

Figure 3.2 – DataOps pillars overlayed with the Alteryx products

In the diagram, we can see the three DataOps principles and how Designer supports the People and Delivery pillars, Connect enables the Confidence pillar, while Server supports the principles across all pillars.

Alteryx Designer

Building a DataOps pipeline will always start with development in Alteryx Designer. First, the quick iteration that I have been speaking about allows for continuous satisfaction and allows the data engineer to embrace any changes during the project. Next, Designer enables the team sport and self-organization principles. Each person in the team can interact using the same visual design process while bringing their expertise with any specific language or tool and leveraging that in Alteryx.

For the Delivery pillar, you can find the repeated processes that appear in a data pipeline and extract them into a reusable macro. We can make these macros available to other team members so that they don't have to recreate work. It also increases the simplicity of the process as the visual clutter associated with the standardized approach can be simplified to a single tool.

Finally, you can build confidence in the datasets with Designer by designing performance and monitoring solutions. Next, ensuring the quality of datasets is enabled by creating insight dashboards that monitor data processing.

Alteryx Server

The next component for supporting DataOps is Server. This allows the automation of pipelines created in Designer. This central processing of workflows also manages the process for simple version control and the sharing of workflows and parameterized applications throughout the organization.

Once you save the workflows to Server, any insights you develop in relation to quality control can be automatically populated and monitored in the Server Gallery web interface. Automating running workflows in Server removes the *heroism* or *key man risk* that might otherwise be present for an Alteryx data pipeline.

Finally, centralizing workflows to a single server gallery allows silos to be broken across organizations and cross-company teams to be established. Additionally, those cross-company teams can self-organize using collections for sharing and management when Server administrators set the permissions to allow it.

Alteryx Connect

The final orchestrating capability is incorporated into the Alteryx platform by using Connect to share all resources across the organization from Alteryx or elsewhere. In addition, the Connect platform allows for the discovery of reusable workflow components, existing datasets and reports, and any other content assets that might answer the end user's questions without needing a new project.

Showing the lineage of the datasets strengthens users' confidence. When users see the transformations and where other colleagues use the datasets, they gain community validation for a dataset. In addition, the Connect software can reveal the quality monitoring workflows, insights, and dashboards that are already available.

The People pillar is supported by putting users who need access to an asset in contact with its owners. It can build a community knowledge base around those existing assets for users and facilitate communication to answer different questions.

We have talked about the concepts of how Alteryx works with DataOps and what each Alteryx program delivers within DataOps. We can now investigate the steps to deploy a DataOps project with Alteryx.

General steps for deploying DataOps in your environment

Now that we know what the DataOps principles are and what parts of Alteryx build the DataOps pipeline, how would you implement DataOps into your company? The best way to demonstrate this would be to introduce an example we will use for our example process throughout the rest of this book.

The data pipeline example we will be following is this:

As a company, we want to enrich our marketing efforts by integrating regularly updated public datasets. We need to identify the source of these datasets (and make sure we have the legal authority to use them) and transform them to match our company areas. Then, we have to make them available to both the data science team for machine learning and to our operational teams across the organization.

This problem statement works well in identifying the process we need to implement, shown in *Figure 3.3*:

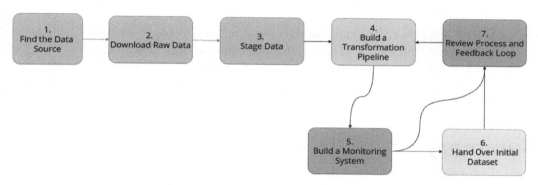

Figure 3.3 – An example process for starting a DataOps project

With the method shown in the preceding diagram, we can explore what each step represents:

1. **Find the Data Source**: When identifying the public data source, we need to ensure that we have a commercial license to use it. This license is necessary to safeguard the fact that any value we extract for the business is legal. We should also investigate the creation of the raw data and ensure that we address any ethical concerns.

2. **Download Raw Data**: Once we have identified the dataset we want, we need to begin the extraction process. We should have an automated process for extracting the data so that any data updates are collected.

3. **Stage Data**: With the raw data in hand, we need to save this to a company-controlled location for future transformations. This raw dataset should also never be modified so future analysis can start from the unaltered raw data.

4. **Build a Transformation Pipeline**: With the raw data in our control, we now need to transform it into a format that will work for our application. This process will also ingest the dataset into our analytical database.

5. **Build a Monitoring System**: With a strategy for ingesting the dataset defined, we will deploy an automated monitoring process with notifications so that we can identify any anomalies or errors and address them.

6. **Hand Over Initial Dataset**: We can now get the dataset to end users to assess the dataset for their applications. This step is the first of our delivery milestones and should be delivered as quickly as possible.

7. **Review Process and Feedback Loop**: The final step in our delivery process requires regular feedback from our end users to maintain data quality. We can also improve usefulness over time in response to the feedback that our users provide.

These general steps are common to any data pipeline. But, of course, we do not address every requirement, and there is plenty of flexibility to go outside this process when needed. And not all steps are necessary for every situation; the dataset might be internal and require modification for a new application. However, this provides a reasonable basis for implementing a DataOps project.

Summary

Now that we have our DataOps principles and understand how they work in the three pillars of People, Delivery, and Confidence, we learned the specifics of building a data pipeline with Alteryx and how to implement these principles.

The following section looked at the different processes for accessing data sources on the basis of the DataOps framework. Then, we learned how to transform those datasets with Alteryx and publish them in other storage locations. And finally, we used Alteryx to build reports and visualizations in value extraction processes.

In the next chapter, we will start by accessing internal data sources, whether those data sources are files or database connections. We will then look at how we can access external data sources, either open public or private secured data sources. Then we will look at some of the initial processes for making sure our sourced data is in a raw format for us to use.

Part 2:
Functional Steps
in DataOps

The second part covers the methods to create a data pipeline in Alteryx. You will learn how to access new data sources, how to transform those data sources into analytical databases, and then save them for future use. Then, using the data sources you have created, you will learn how to use Alteryx to analyze the data and how to perform spatial analysis and create machine learning models.

This part comprises the following chapters:

- *Chapter 4, Sourcing the Data*
- *Chapter 5, Data Processing and Transformations*
- *Chapter 6, Destination Management*
- *Chapter 7, Extracting Value*
- *Chapter 8, Beginning Advanced Analytics*

4
Sourcing the Data

The first step of creating a new data pipeline is the process of sourcing the raw dataset. While scoping and defining the dataset are crucial parts of the entire data pipeline project, the framework for extracting the information is well established in general project management and the underlying Agile framework. Therefore, in this chapter, we will begin at the point of having the initial requirements defined and understood.

We will focus on the methods for accessing data sources from both internal sources, freely available public sources, and **application programming interfaces (APIs)** that have security applied.

We will also discuss some methods for validating the data sources you connect to and ensuring that the raw data structure has not changed. If the data source has changed, we will have automated methods to assess those changes.

In this chapter, we will cover the following topics:

- How to connect to different internal data sources
- How to download public files with Alteryx
- How to authenticate against a public API
- Performing the initial cleansing of a dataset for validation
- Constructing a data pipeline in Alteryx Designer

Technical requirements

In this chapter, we will use Alteryx Designer to connect to data and create datasets. Local files are part of the Alteryx Designer installation. The API section will require a Google Cloud account to test the Google Maps Places API. The example workflows can be found in the book's GitHub repository here: `https://github.com/PacktPublishing/Data-Engineering-with-Alteryx/tree/main/Chapter%2004`.

Accessing internal data sources

Internal data sources are any data assets managed by your organization. These data sources could be local files, network files, or organization databases. For Alteryx, any file stored on your PC's hard drive (such as your C drive) is considered a local file, whereas a network file is any file stored on the organization's network storage. In either of these cases, the way you access them in Alteryx is the same. Still, when you start trying to automate them, how they behave on the server depends on specific configurations we will examine in the *Using the Alteryx Input Data tool* section.

The first significant challenge in accessing data sources is locating them. **Alteryx Connect** provides a level of discoverability and organization. It can search across network locations and extract the details of the files' location and their metadata. For example, Connect can pull a list of tables in a database, the columns in those tables, and the tables' metadata.

Connect can act as a central location for requesting access to the data source for both files and databases.

We use Connect to find, share, and connect to data sources, pipelines, and reports in *Chapter 12, Making Data Easy to Use and Discoverable with Alteryx*.

Data source types

The most common file types are Microsoft Excel files, **Comma-Separated Value (CSV)** files, and others delimited or fixed with text files when looking at data source files. In addition, if the data source is internet-based, then the **JavaScript Object Notation (JSON)** files are common, along with **Extensible Markup Language (XML)** files. The following screenshot shows the data connection window of the Input tool. The window includes sections for the different data source types, an area for dragging and dropping files from your Windows environment, and a list of Alteryx optimized file types.

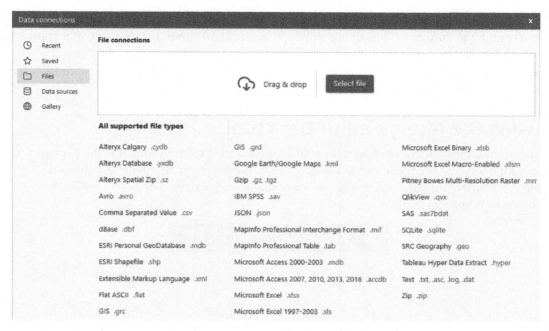

Figure 4.1 – Alteryx File connections dialog window

File-based data sources are usually less organized or planned. These files can be scattered across your organization, and other users in your organization can easily modify them. A more organized location for data is in the company databases. This database could be an open source database, such as **PostgreSQL** or **MySQL** (or the commercial databases built on them), or proprietary databases such as **Oracle** or **Microsoft SQL Server** (**MSSQL**).

The database connections rely on either **Open Database Connectivity** (**ODBC**) or **Object Linking and Embedding Database** (**OLeDB**), a successor to ODBC. These connections can be managed with Microsoft's built-in ODBC Data Source Administrator application or using a connection string specific to each database type.

There are three common methods for connecting to a database in Alteryx. These are as follows:

- **Data Source Name** (**DSN**) connection
- **DSN-less** connection
- **Gallery Data** connection

Each of these methods has pros and cons depending on what you want to achieve. If you're going to automate your data pipeline, I recommend either a DSN-less connection or a Gallery Data connection. These connection types provide a more straightforward setup for any data source user and work in the Alteryx Server and Designer environments. Now, let's discuss the Alteryx Input Data tool.

Using the Alteryx Input Data tool

The first method for connecting to files and databases is the Input tool. It is the primary tool for accessing the common data sources that Alteryx supports. *Figure 4.1* showed the full connection page menu, and in *Figure 4.2*, we can see the details of the different connection options available:

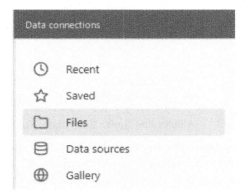

Figure 4.2 – Focused view of the Data connection options in the Input tool

We can see two types of connection creation options from the preceding screenshot. The **Recent**, **Saved,** and **Gallery** options are all pre-saved or used connections. These connections have all configuration information populated from previous use and make it easier to access them from this area. On the other hand, the **Files** and **Data sources** options create a brand-new connection from scratch, which we will use in the next section.

Connecting to files with the Input tool

Connecting to files, either local or on the network, is achieved by selecting the **Files** option in the **Input** tool. We will see an example of this in practice later in this section and in the following screenshot. Once the files selection page is available, there are three ways of choosing the file of interest:

1. **Drag and drop** the file from Windows File Explorer into the connection area.

2. Click the **Select file** button and navigate to the file.

3. Use the **Supported file types** list as a filter. You will still navigate to the file as you would with the **Select file** button, but in this case, the file navigation dialog window filters the files displayed to just that file type.

After you have selected the file, the configuration window has changed. It now has options specific to the file type you have chosen.

In *Figure 4.3*, we can see a CSV file installed with Alteryx as a sample file:

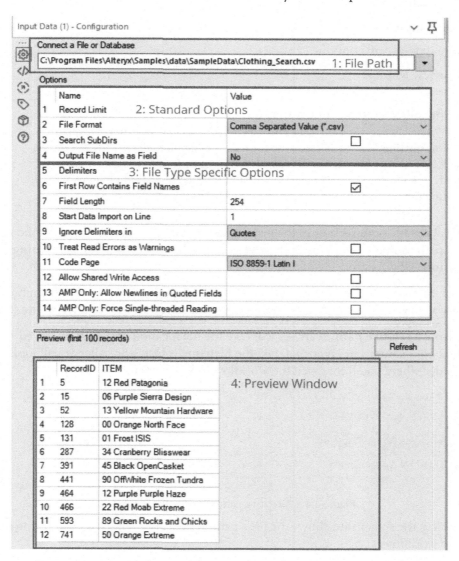

Figure 4.3 – Annotated view of the Input Data Configuration for a sample file

The preceding screenshot shows a file in the `SampleData` folder of the Alteryx installation. By default, you find the Alteryx install folder here:

```
C:\Program Files\Alteryx\Samples\data\SampleData\Clothing_
Search.csv
```

There are four sections in this configuration window:

- File path
- Standard options
- File type-specific options
- Preview window

> **The Alteryx default install path**
>
> When Alteryx is installed, a sample data folder is created with its install information. The default location for this installation folder is `C:\Program Files\Alteryx`. The references to this folder location assume that the default location has been used, but if your installation path is different, you will find the `data` sub-folder in the modified location.

Looking at the file path section in the preceding screenshot, we see the path to the file. This path can be absolute, as in the screenshot, relative, or a **Universal Naming Convention** (**UNC**) path.

As shown in *Figure 4.3*, an **absolute path** defines the file's location starting from the drive letter. If you haven't located the file on this path, you cannot read it in an absolute format.

When using a **relative path,** searches will take the file location based on the saved workflow. For example, in *Figure 4.4,* just the filename is listed. So, Alteryx will look in the folder where you have saved the workflow in this format.

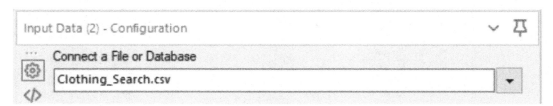

Figure 4.4 – A relative path for using the filename

In *Figure 4.5*, the screenshot shows the file's path in the `data` subfolder where you have saved the workflow:

Figure 4.5 – A relative path with a subfolder

The benefit of using relative paths is when you share workflows with users using the packaged workbook option (**Options | Export Workflow**), you can find all the workflow file dependencies in the other user's environment. If you used an absolute path, the exact file path needs to match all users who want to run the workflow. Often this is not the case. When you save workflows in the **My Documents** folder, the absolute file path will also include your username in the file path.

The last file path option is to use a UNC path. This path is beneficial for network files as the UNC path will be consistent for anyone accessing the network file. A UNC path has a format of \\ServerName\FolderName\FileName. The file can be found in this format even though different persons search for the file with a different drive letter. This formatting is also important when publishing workflows to Alteryx Server; you want to reference the original file rather than a snapshot. When a workflow runs on the server and doesn't see any network drive mappings, it cannot resolve the network drives to a drive letter.

Connecting to databases with the Input tool

Using the **Data sources** option of the Input tool allows us to connect to databases. In the following screenshot (*Figure 4.6*), we can see all the different data sources that Alteryx can natively support:

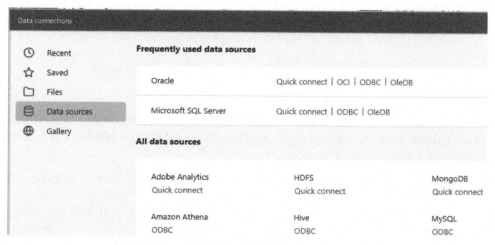

Figure 4.6 – Partial view of the data sources page

The preceding screenshot shows the **Data sources** tab, which has links to the supported data sources, including the relational databases; **MySQL**, **Microsoft SQL Server**, **Snowflake**, and cloud data sources with built-in connector APIs; **Adobe Analytics**, **Amazon S3**, and **Google Analytics**.

For each of the connections, there are two general ways of connecting to the data source:

- **Quick Connect** – Creates a shortcut to a custom connection tool that will replace the Input tool and allow you to provide the required connection information
- **ODBC/OleDB** – Uses the industry-standard communication protocol to connect to the database

The process of connecting with the **Quick Connect** option is unique to each different data source. To connect to a Microsoft SQL Server, the information you provide differs from a Google Analytics connection. If you want to learn more about a specific data type, the Alteryx help pages provide details on how to use each connection at `https://help.alteryx.com/20213/designer/data-sources`.

Selecting the ODBC or the OleDB options will launch the native Windows connection manager filtered for the established connection. So, if you use the ODBC connection option for Snowflake, you will see all the DSN connections for Snowflake.

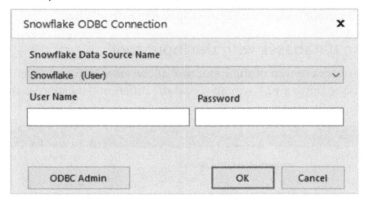

Figure 4.7 – Snowflake ODBC Connection

Figure 4.7 shows an example of connecting to a Snowflake DSN. If you don't already have a DSN configured, you can create a new one through the **ODBC Admin** button found in the bottom-left corner of the dialog box.

While a quick connection is designed to be easily shareable across Alteryx users or published to the Alteryx Server, you need to configure the DSN alias in every environment where you want to use the connection. This configuration means that in addition to the database drivers required for the data source, the DSN alias would need to match the same format (including name case) in every environment where you want to run the workflow.

An alternative to DSN is the DSN-less connection string. A DSN-less connection contains all the information required to connect to the database in the Alteryx Configuration window and bypasses the Windows ODBC manager.

While every database has its own implementation of parameters and configuration, one common format is as follows:

```
Driver={DBDriver};Server=IP
address;Port=DBPort;Database=myDataBase;Uid=myUsername;
Pwd=myPassword;
```

In this string, DBDriver is specific to your database, and you can find it in the **Drivers** tab of the ODBC Connection Manager. For example, the Snowflake DB driver is SnowflakeDSIIDriver, while the Amazon Redshift driver is Amazon Redshift (x64). In both of these drivers, the name must match what is seen in the ODBC Administrator **Drivers** tab, as seen in *Figure 4.8*:

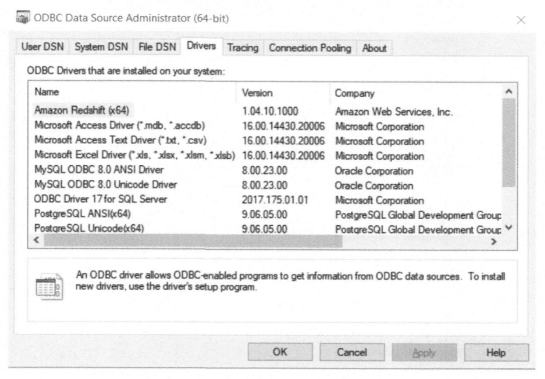

Figure 4.8 – ODBC Administrator Drivers tab

Let's look at in-DB tools in the following section.

Using in-DB tools to offload data processing

While connecting to databases using the standard Input tool works well for small databases or small-scale testing, it is inefficient for larger databases or production. Firstly, moving the entire dataset from the database to Alteryx and back again for publishing will slow the workflow significantly. Secondly, database servers are, in nearly all cases, larger, more powerful computers designed to query your datasets. We can take advantage of these systems by pushing the queries we want to run to the database with **In-DB** tools.

The process for connecting with In-DB tools uses the same ODBC connection fundamentals as the standard tools but accesses those details in a significantly different manner.

The first way of connecting with In-DB tools is to use managed In-DB connections. *Figure 4.9* shows the **Manage In-DB Connections** window where you choose the **Data Source** type, what type of connection (**User** or **File**) it is, and enter the connection details:

Figure 4.9 – Alteryx Manage In-DB Connections dialog window

The connection type is the primary difference when setting up an In-DB connection. This option allows the creation of a local alias for your In-DB connection or the saving of that connection in a file for easy sharing, allowing flexibility in using the connections and simplifying the connection sharing.

An important note about In-DB tools is that all the processing happens on the database; the database, not Alteryx, defines the syntax of calculations. This means that the syntax needs to match the database SQL syntax and has the same calculation limitations as the database.

You will repeat the connection processes when persisting the dataset for later use. For example, saving the dataset to a file follows the same process as connecting to a file. Likewise, saving the dataset to a database also follows the same method as connecting to a database.

But how can you connect to data sources that aren't internally managed but are freely accessible? We can access these data sources using the Download tool in Alteryx.

Integrating public data sources with Download tool use

Public data provides an excellent resource for enriching internal data sources with other supporting data. Government agencies are an ideal resource for getting economic, business, environmental, education, or other national datasets. These datasets often provide information at local levels for planning and are freely available. One such dataset is the **consumer price inflation time series (CPI)** from the UK **Office for National Statistics (ONS)**. You can find this dataset at the following URL:

```
https://www.ons.gov.uk/economy/inflationandpriceindices/
datasets/consumerpriceindices.
```

You will find a regularly updated file and links to old versions archived for reference at this static location. We can easily download files published in this way with the Download tool.

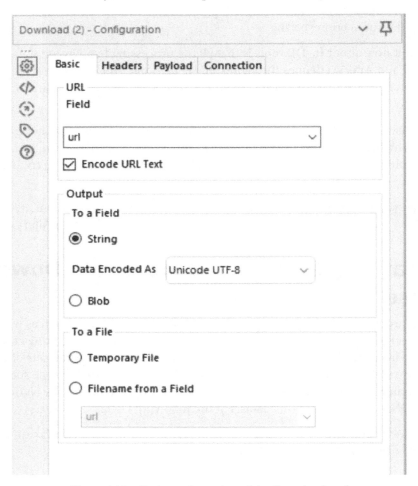

Figure 4.10 – Basic configuration of the Download tool

In *Figure 4.10*, we can see the essential connection details. In the configuration, we need to provide the URL. When connecting to a public data source, this is often the only information we might need.

The URL needs to be the location of the file we want to download (https://www.ons.gov.uk/file?uri=/economy/inflationandpriceindices/datasets/consumerpriceindices/current/mm23.csv) and supplied as a field.

You can add that to a variable called **URL** with a new text Input tool, as seen in *Figure 4.11*. With this tool, the variable name is added to the column where the three dots ... appear, while the value of the field can be populated below it. The row numbers will populate automatically (replacing the three dots in the rows) as values are added.

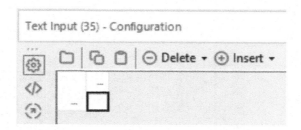

Figure 4.11 – A blank text Input tool ready for adding values

When you have created this new URL field, it can be selected in the **URL** configuration of the Download tool.

The next step is to decide where to download the file. It could be downloaded to a string field for immediate processing, a temporary file, or saved to an internal location. For a data pipeline, it is often valuable to save that file to a local source. So, if you need to recreate a dataset, the raw data source is available internally.

Identifying whether the data structure has changed

Once we have the source data, having a method to determine whether the data structure has changed is a crucial step in data management. We need to be able to monitor whether our dataset changes throughout its life cycle to ensure that what we are providing to our end users continues to fulfill their requirements. If we are not watching how a dataset is changing, it can quickly drift from our original output and stop answering our end users' questions.

This is the first check to make the data reproducible and manage the quality. We discussed these two points in the **Confidence pillar** of DataOps in *Chapter 3, DataOps and Its Benefits*.

The following diagram shows a process for validating the downloaded file against a reference file:

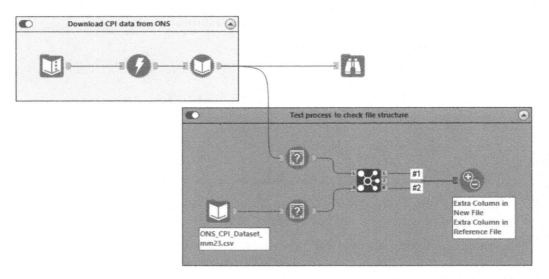

Figure 4.12 – Workflow for downloading CPI data and validating against a reference file

We can create a template structure using a reference file when building the pipeline or provided with the dataset. Then, we can cross-reference both files' metadata with the **Field Info** tool utilizing that template. Finally, once we have the field names and details, we can match the field names of the new file against our reference with the **Join** tool.

Creating our first validation test

Figure 4.12 implemented the logic for finding new or missing columns in the downloaded files. Unfortunately, the join logic on its own wouldn't inform anyone as to whether a new field appeared without manually checking—not a good result for automating the validation.

We can create a way to automatically inform us whether the workflow has failed our logic test by adding the **Test** tool to the workflow. The test tool will take a logic test that you define, such as the number of records that equals a value, as seen in the following screenshot:

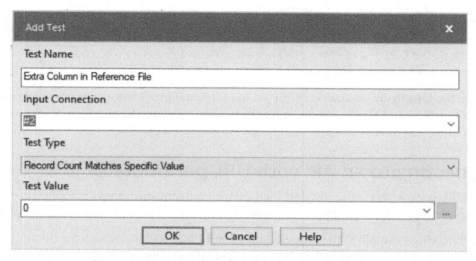

Figure 4.13 – Test tool configuration for an individual test

When the records pass into this tool, it will evaluate the list of tests. Should any tests resolve to `False`, the test will fail and produce an error.

Because the test tool produces an error, the action we take can also be triggered automatically when the workflow is automated. This action can result from the workflow starting an event (which we will see in more detail in *Chapter 9*, *Testing Workflows and Outputs*). The events are defined in the **Workflow Configuration | Events** tab and include sending emails or running a script responding to the workflow error event.

Leveraging external data sources from authenticated APIs

While accessing public datasets gives a basis for a dataset's enrichment, it is limited to publicly available information. Many more datasets available can be accessed both on a subscription and without payment, but require some form of authentication.

The specific authentication method will change from one API to another, but you will find some common themes across the different data providers:

- API URL parameter
- API call headers
- OAuth authorization framework

The **OAuth** authorization framework is the most complex of the three examples. The complexity is because each OAuth provider can customize the process for their application. The URL parameter or call header process follows a more consistent approach across different API providers.

Because the OAuth authorization is unique to individual providers, describing a general process to follow is difficult without tying the process to a specific provider. Additionally, that provider can modify the process, invalidating any process described.

Connecting to an API with URL parameters

Using URL parameters is the simplest method for authenticating an API. This method provides a unique identifying process (often an **API key**) as part of the URL downloaded.

In the following example to the **Google Maps Find Place** API, we search for the formatted_address field of the location *London Eye*. The API key is added to the key parameter, uniquely identifying your account. Because you associate the query with your account, you are served different service levels based on your subscription level. Here's what the link to the Google Maps API would look like:

```
https://maps.googleapis.com/maps/api/place/
findplacefromtext/json?fields=formatted_address&input=London
Eye&inputtype=textquery&key=YOUR_API_KEY
```

> **Creating a Google Maps API Key**
>
> To replicate the API key example, you will need a free Google Cloud account project with an API key that has permissions for the Places API. To create a new Google Maps API key with the required permissions, you can follow the instructions in the Google Maps JavaScript API, as documented here: https://developers.google.com/maps/documentation/javascript/get-api-key.

Create your Google Cloud Console account project by following the instructions in the *Set Up in the Google Cloud Console* section described here: https://developers.google.com/maps/documentation/javascript/cloud-setup.

We need to populate the query location and the API key in the preceding URL query. You can populate the query parameters for the Download tool in two ways:

- Build the complete URL in a Formula tool.
- Build the URL from fields in the Download tool.

Building the URL in a Formula tool is the simplest method as it allows the entire call to be read quickly and tested in other tools if needed. While using the Download tool to build the query affords significant dynamism, troubleshooting a query can be more challenging as external programs must catch the exact query sent to the API.

Connecting to an API in call headers

Some APIs will require authentication information as part of the HTTP header information. In this case, simply adding the API key to the URL will fail. The Download tool has a separate tab for populating header information with the HTTP call.

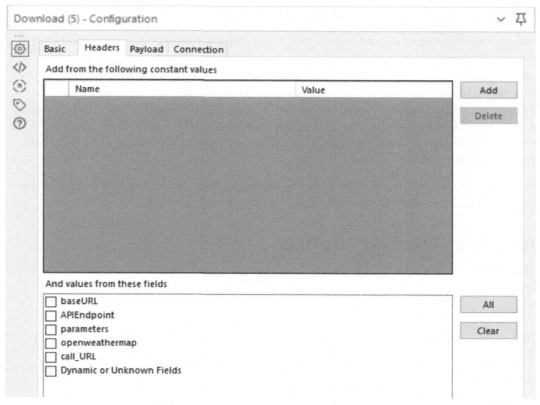

Figure 4.14 – Headers tab of the Download tool

In the **Headers** tab, you can add the header fields manually, which helps set fixed parameters, such as the download format or content-type information, or dynamically from a field.

Both methods send the header information as the field name or the constant name to identify the header with the value. The header will be sent in the following format: `[name]=[value]`.

Once we have populated the header options, we configure the rest of the download configuration in the method as with the *URL parameter* example. Again, we provide the URL for what we want to download, where we want to download to, and the payload is, in our example, left to the default values.

We have our raw dataset from here, and we can begin the initial cleansing process.

Initial cleansing of datasets

We now have an initial dataset, which we can keep as a raw dataset but doesn't otherwise provide a source that our end users can use to extract value. For example, when we investigate the public consumer price inflation dataset (which we downloaded in the *Integrating public data sources with Download tool use* section), all the fields are text fields because the reference is a CSV text file. In contrast, the Google Places API data is a complete JSON file but not arranged into usable tables. In both situations, applying any **statistical process controls** (**SPCs**) is difficult as the data type doesn't allow for the appropriate statistical measure.

To cleanse our dataset, we will use a generic cleansing process. We will take the concepts needed to cleanse a dataset and apply them to our example raw file.

A simple cleansing process

The preview of our dataset in *Figure 4.15* shows four initial problems that we want to address:

- Titles are not user-friendly.
- There are a series of informational lines that aren't part of the dataset.
- The Year column follows different format conventions.
- Empty values are populated as blanks.

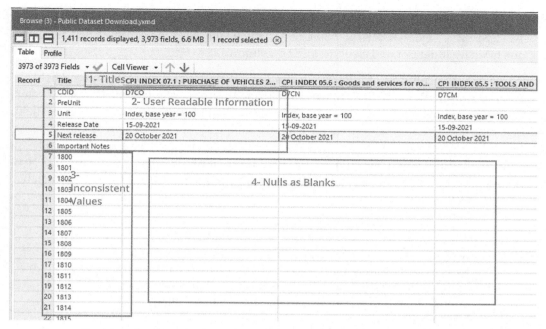

Figure 4.15 – Preview of the CPI dataset with the initial problems annotated

These four issues are problems as they impede the dataset's usability by introducing fields that interfere with analytic processes, such as aggregations. These issues also cause challenges with implementing the SPC for monitoring the dataset as these monitoring processes use the same analytical techniques. Fixing these issues requires the information to be identified in order to retain and present it in a user-friendly readable format.

Title cleansing

Cleansing the titles involves removing the ONS prefix information from each field. These prefixes also identify the three different inflation indexes in this file: the **Consumer Price Index (CPI)**, the **Retail Price Index (RPI)**, and the Consumer Prices Index, including owner occupiers' housing costs (**CPIH**). When processed, these datasets provide different information and should have separate database tables.

Selecting the right columns could be achieved manually with the Select tool, but with 3,973 fields in the dataset, a manual process has a high chance of errors. It also fails to follow the DataOps principle of *Analytics is Code*; a better method is to use the **Dynamic Select** tool.

With the Dynamic Select tool, we can define a condition (StartsWith([Name], "CPI INDEX") OR [NAME]= "Title"), which will select the columns that are part of our first target dataset and also the Title column.

Once we have the columns of interest, we can remove the dataset prefix from each field with the **Dynamic Rename** tool. When configuring this tool, we select the characters after the : in the field name ([_CurrentField_]) for all fields excluding the [Title] field. Using some string manipulation, we have the formula Right([_CurrentField_], Length([_CurrentField_]) - FindString([_CurrentField_], ":")-2), which identifies where the colon is and then takes all the characters to the right of that character. We can now add a second dynamic rename to format the field names to match our target destination's convention.

Should You Keep or Discard the Extra Information?

As we process the initial dataset, we discard the extra document information. We have decided that this information is not valuable to us. In another situation, this information can also provide value and should be retained. It could be in the form of a generated report or saved into a supporting table in your data warehouse.

User-readable information

The next issue to address in the initial cleansing is the initial rows in the dataset. These initial rows provide context information for the user but are not part of the actual data. As such, we remove these rows from the data stream.

The simplest way to remove these records would be to skip them with a **Select Records** tool. However, this option is limited because you are assuming that the number of header rows will not change. It also removes the headers from further processing in a separate stream.

An alternative would be to use a filter tool to identify the records we want to keep. The regular expression REGEX_Match([Title], "^\d.*") in a **Filter** tool formula would look for any record, starting with a digit. This digit signifies a year and is part of the records in our dataset.

Inconsistent values

Now that we only have the records to focus on, we can address the contents of the Title column. The Title column is the date when the inflation was recorded. This column comes in three different formats and needs to be standardized.

The formats we have are as follows:

- A four-digit year

- A four-digit year followed by a three-digit month

- A four-digit year followed by the quarter in Q1 format

We need to standardize the column with these three different formats to do the aggregations when required. The most logical format would be to create a date format with each period set to the start of the period. For example, when the date is just the year, the date would be January 1 of the year. In contrast, if a month is included, the date would be the first of that month.

Formatting the different date values requires three different formulas, and each formula needs to be combined for the final result. We can do this in a single field with each formula operating sequentially, or it could be done in new separate fields and then combined into a final field. This example uses the single column example, as seen in the following diagram of the Formula tool:

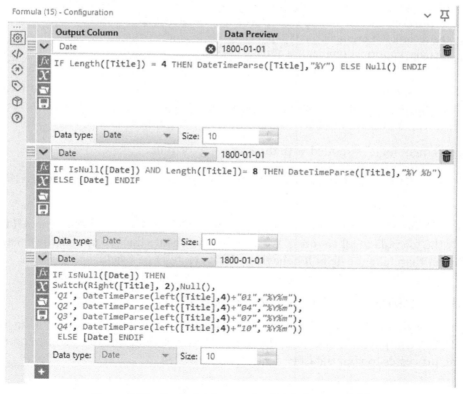

Figure 4.16 – Formulas for standardizing the Date field

The three formulas address the different formats of the date with a condition to identify each format. You can handle the Year and Year Month formats with the standard `DateTimeParse` formula and the associated identifiers for date parts. The Quarter format doesn't have a direct translation from the `Q1` format into a month, so we use a `Switch` statement and text manipulation to translate into a format that `DateTimeParse` will transform correctly.

Nulls as blanks

The final preparation we need to cleanse is that the dataset has many missing records, but they are read as blank records rather than `nulls` when imported. While this might be acceptable for some applications, for a dataset, it is probably better to convert those blanks into `nulls` for later use.

> **What Is the Difference between Blanks and Nulls?**
>
> There is a subtle difference between blank and null fields that changes how Alteryx interacts with those fields. A null record is a record with an absence of any information, and this includes having no metadata associated with the record. A blank field has no value associated with it, but there is metadata for the record. For example, a cell populated with an empty string contains the metadata information that it is a string field.

We can transform fields with a **Multi-Field** formula, which repeats a single formula across multiple columns. To make the substitution, we need to implement the logic to replace any blank field with a null but otherwise return the original value.

The replacement logic is applied with the following formula:

```
IF IsEmpty([_CurrentField_]) THEN Null() ELSE [_CurrentField_]
ENDIF
```

By choosing the **All Types of Fields** option in the Multi-field tool and selecting **All fields**, we apply the formula to all columns. We also need to ensure that we update the existing fields rather than take the default behavior, which creates a new field.

A consolidated cleansing process

An alternative method to applying cleansing manually is to use the Data Cleansing tool. The Data Cleansing tool, as shown in the following screenshot, will apply some common cleansing processes to your dataset:

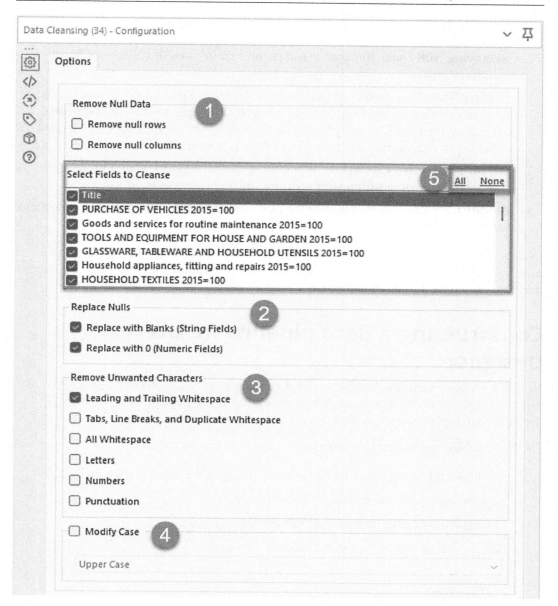

Figure 4.17 – The Data Cleansing tool with annotations

In the preceding screenshot, there are four common cleansing processes and a section for choosing which fields, including **All** or **None** shortcut buttons (annotated button **5**).

The Data Cleansing tool applies the following common processes:

1. **Removing Null Data**: This option will remove entire rows or columns when all values are `null`.

2. **Replace Nulls**: This option acts similarly to the **Multi Field** formula from the *Nulls as blanks* section covered earlier in this chapter. The biggest difference compared with using the Data Cleansing tool is that it updates the `null` values with a fixed value depending on the data type of `String` or `Numeric`.

3. **Remove Unwanted Characters**: When processing string text, you can remove the unwanted characters within your text.

4. **Modify Case**: You can standardize the case of your text fields to provide a consistent format in your dataset.

Using the Data Cleansing tool provides a method for consolidating and simplifying the common cleansing processes. You can then combine this option with any other cleansing steps to create your desired data pipeline.

Constructing a data pipeline in Alteryx Designer

Now that we have a working extraction workflow, we need to convert this into a production pipeline for automation. We need to add the extra documentation and the validation for the workflow to do this.

The steps we will implement in relation to the workflow are as follows:

- Configure the annotations/names of tools, meaning the logs are more helpful.

- Add the initial documentation to the workflow.

- Calculate the first initial statistical values for the dataset.

- Add an output step to persist the processed dataset.

The previous steps are added to the workflow to support the DataOps deployment by building the Confidence pillar. In addition, these steps allow anyone to understand the workflow quickly in the future.

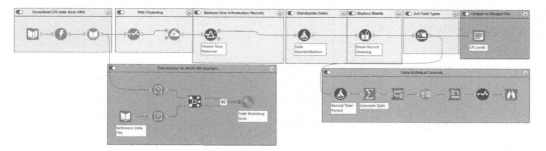

Figure 4.18 – Overview of the entire pipeline

The preceding diagram shows an overview of our example workflow. This workflow performs the following processes:

1. Downloads from the public API

2. Checks that the fields present are what we expect

3. Conducts the initial cleansing of the downloaded file

4. Saves the resulting dataset to a local file

5. Generates the mean and standard deviation for each data field

This process is the basis of our DataOps pipeline, and we have implemented step one in this chapter. The processing steps will be introduced in this section and then extended in *Chapter 5*, *Data Processing and Transformations*, with other steps (such as destination management and value extraction) in the following chapters of this book.

Configuring the annotations and names

In the annotation tab of any tool, there is a default name of the tool type followed by the ID. This name is what appears in the result message log. Updating this tool name can provide more context for your message log by indicating what is supposed to be happening in the workflow.

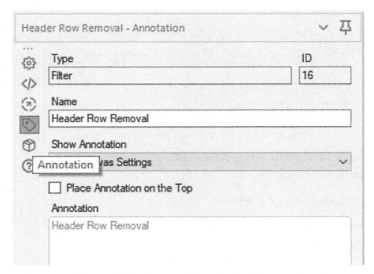

Figure 4.19 – Annotation tab of a Filter tool

Additionally, in the **Annotation** area, you can provide information on the canvas for easy review. Not all tools have a default annotation, but if the annotation is populated, it usually indicates a formula that happens in this tool.

If you have updated the tool name, this annotation will automatically update. However, you can also overwrite any annotation for a manual value. The manual value can provide any context you need for your users to see at a glance.

Adding initial documentation in the workflow

Updating the annotations provides the first part of your extended documentation. Then, using the **Tool Container**, **Comment**, and **Explorer Box** documentation tools, you can add more depth to your documentation.

In the workflow tool, containers extensively group different processes. For example, the **Title Cleansing** container has steps where we perform the modifications to the field titles. You can also use color to highlight the different processes in the workflow; green for input processes or blue for field manipulations. The specific colors used are not important, just that you are consistent with the colors you use across all the data pipelines created across your organization.

You can also use Comment tools and Explorer boxes to provide more text information and explanations that provide more context for why the workflow exists and what assumptions you have made when building it.

Calculating the first set of statistical values

Once we have a working intermediate dataset, we need to apply our statistical process controls. We achieve this by aggregating the data fields and recording how they change. However, at this initial point of creating the dataset, we might not have insight into the expected values. Therefore, more exploratory data analysis would be needed to identify the trends of your dataset and signify an outlier. We will learn the process for creating statistical process controls and exploratory data analysis in *Chapter 7, Extracting Value*.

Saving the processed dataset

Finally, we have a completed dataset, and we need to persist it somewhere. Using an **Output** tool, we can either write the output to a file, as we can see in *Figure 4.20*, or write it into our target database:

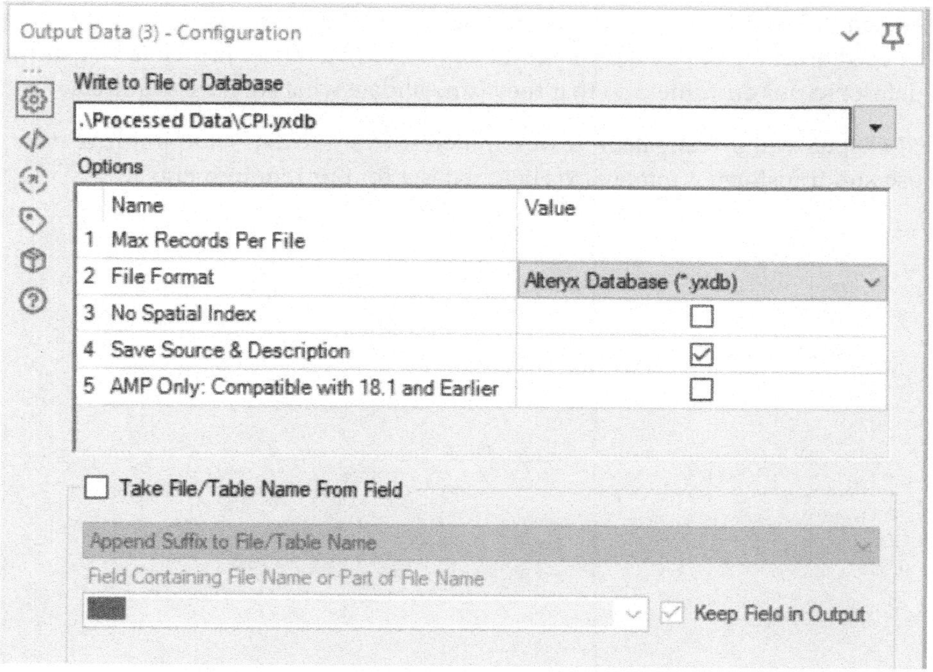

Figure 4.20 – Output configuration to a local .yxdb file

In our output, we are using the `.yxdb` file type native to Alteryx for saving an intermediate file. We save the dataset to a local file in a folder called `Processed Data` found in the same location as the data pipeline workflow. Using the relative path makes the workflow more robust when working with other people. This robustness is because of the specific folder location of the workflow (like the particular user's `My Documents` folder) as the check that is checking the `Processed Data` folder is co-located with the workflow.

We could also use any other file type by changing the filename extension and the **File Format** option.

Summary

In this chapter, we have looked at connecting to different data sources. First, we investigated connecting to local and network files and learned the principles for connecting to databases with ODBC connections. We also investigated enriching our internal data sources with public and authenticated APIs. Finally, we saw how to use the Download tool to access the data resources and download them to Alteryx.

Once we had the data source, we performed some initial data cleansing so that our dataset could be used quickly. We can deliver on the *Improve Cycle Times* principle by getting the initial dataset to our customers so that they can validate what we have acquired.

The next chapter will investigate how we can iterate over the dataset to improve it for better use and transform it into an excellent dataset for our requirements.

5

Data Processing and Transformations

Now that we have our initial raw dataset, we can start transforming data into the final state. When building your data pipeline, this processing and transformation process is the core of the entire pipeline and often requires separation into multiple subsets for different applications.

The core data processing is the simplest part of this process, and it is what we started looking at in *Chapter 4, Sourcing the Data*, where we began the process of creating the pipeline by taking the raw data, cleansing the titles and information headers, and setting the data types. This just provides us with an initial dataset to work with, and not a final dataset for use. When we look at the column headers, we see three different datasets making up the columns. Additionally, the records are shown across multiple different time periods – annually, quarterly, and monthly.

Our next step will be to improve the dataset to provide a more relevant dataset for our end user. In this chapter, we will cover the following topics:

- Core skills for transforming and cleansing a dataset
- Methods for understanding our dataset with data profiling and statistical aggregations

We will apply these skills to build another data pipeline for a dataset of interest.

Technical requirements

This section will use Alteryx Designer to create and modify datasets. The datasets we will use are either part of the Alteryx installation media or will have been downloaded as part of the workflow completed in *Chapter 4*, *Sourcing the Data*. The example workflows can be found in the book's GitHub repository here: `https://github.com/PacktPublishing/Data-Engineering-with-Alteryx/tree/main/Chapter%2005`.

The data cleansing process

The data process is built around identifying the records that are useful for the intended purpose and enriching the dataset with any fields that might be valuable. We can achieve this in two ways:

- By modifying the existing dataset
- Or by adding additional data to the dataset

Of those two options, adding additional data is effectively just an extension of modifying the dataset by combining multiple data pipelines into a single, cohesive pipeline.

When modifying the existing dataset, four primary processes provide an umbrella for the transformations:

- **Selecting** the columns of interest
- **Filtering** the relevant rows
- Creating and modifying columns with formulas
- **Summarizing** the dataset to a more relevant level of granularity

Each of these steps focuses on transforming the dataset according to your use case and solving your data question.

Selecting columns

Selecting the relevant columns in a dataset is achieved either manually with the **Select** tool or dynamically with the **Dynamic Select** tool. For many data engineering applications, the manual configuration of the Select tool makes the most sense as it is a one-off application. However, when building reusable macros that apply a defined logic, using the Dynamic Select tool gives more flexibility on how to create the desired output.

Configuring the Select tool

Basically, configuring the Select tool just requires choosing the fields of interest with the checkboxes in the following screenshot, and then defining what the data type is from the list of numeric, string, datetime, or spatial types. You find the Select tool in the **Preparation** bin of the **Tool Pallet**. Finally, we can manually change the column name and description, as well as the column metadata, for any field.

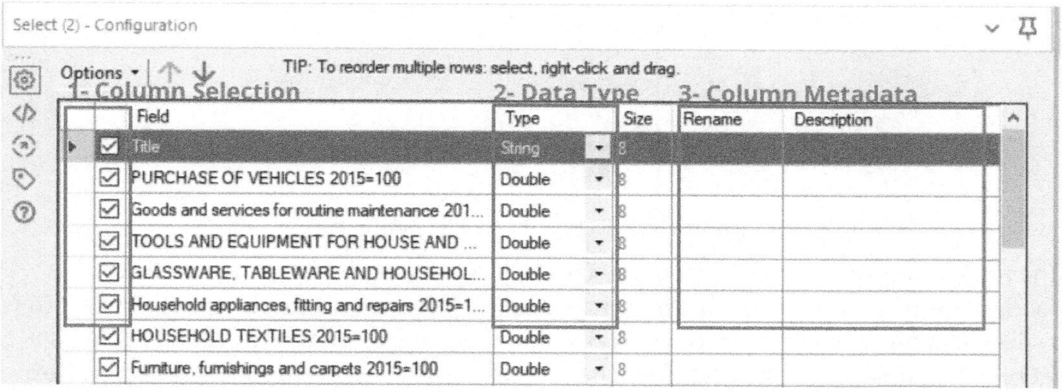

Figure 5.1 – Basic Select Configuration options

After we have the basic manual configuration options, many changes become difficult to manage when dealing with a substantial number of fields. We can address these issues using the additional choices in the **Options** menu (see *Figure 5.2*). In the **Options** menu, we can choose to select all or none of the fields, and we can sort the fields en masse either according to the field type or field name for easier interaction. We can also move columns to the top or bottom of the list. Each of these individual options is about making the list of columns easier to work with in the following tools and processes.

The second set of choices in the options menu is to modify the column names en masse, either by modifying the prefixes or suffixes or by resetting the changes back to the default options. Additionally, any fields that were present previously will appear as missing fields, and these missing fields can be removed from the options menu as well.

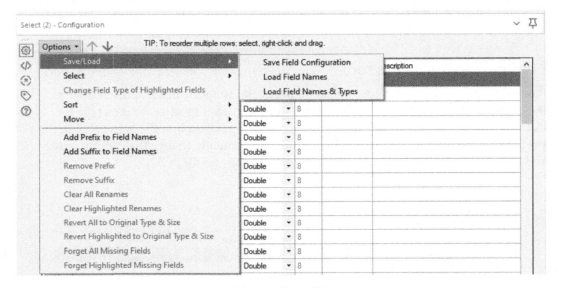

Figure 5.2 – Selecting the tool Options menu

The final process we can leverage in the **Options** menu is the ability to save a field configuration and import it back in at a later stage. This does require that the fields are in a specific order when they arrive, but it does allow for all columns to be set to a defined set of values that are known ahead of time. A use case for the **Saved Field Configuration** option is when extracting a dataset from an API. The download tool that we use to call the API (which we saw used in *Chapter 4, Sourcing the Data*) will return all values as a text type in a specific order. For this example, you can then load field names and types from a known previous field configuration.

Configuring a Dynamic Select tool

The Dynamic Select tool allows you to choose your columns based on two option types:

- The field type
- A conditional formula

These two selection options allow you to choose the fields that match the logic needed for your data pipeline. The **Select Field Types** option, as shown in the following screenshot, is frequently used inside macros where a series of transformations will take place on a data type, and having a data type the macro is not expecting would cause the macro to fail. This option is limited to a standard data pipeline as most pipelines will not be focused on a single data type. It could be used in situations where the different data types might be processed in separate data streams and then recombined later. For example, in *Figure 5.1*, most fields are **Double** type processes; however, if we wanted to change the case of text fields alone, we can dynamically select **String** type fields. The **String** button is shown in the following screenshot:

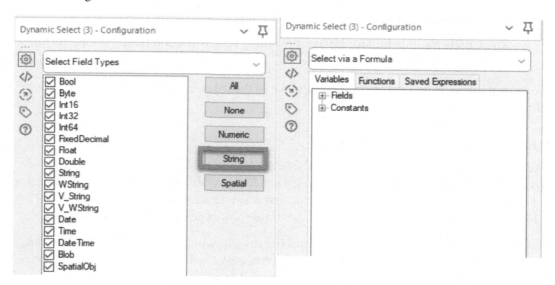

Figure 5.3 – Dynamic Select Configuration options

The **Select via a Formula** option gives more flexibility to your choices of field conditions. The formula option only requires a conditional formula output where the output results in a Boolean `True` or `False` result. This allows you the flexibility to extract any fields using a calculation. To create the formula, any of the existing functions that Alteryx provides and any conditional logic you define can be used to select the columns.

When creating a formula to select the columns, your logic is based on the column metadata: field names, types, size, source, description, or field number. These columns can be combined with multiple conditions using the Boolean operators `AND`, `OR`, and `NOT` to isolate the columns of interest.

Filtering to relevant rows

Now that we have a process for choosing the fields of interest, the next part of the data processing pipeline is to ensure that we have the rows of interest. In *Chapter 4, Sourcing the Data*, we saw the use of the Select Records tool for choosing specific rows, and we can also use a series of different tools for choosing the records for different operations:

- The **Select Records** tool for choosing a specific subset of rows

- The **Filter** tool for choosing records based on some condition

- The **Sample** tool for isolating a set of records based on the groups of row numbers

- The **Random Sample** tool for selecting a randomized number of records

- The **Create Sample** tool for building training, validation, and holdout datasets for data science applications

Each of these tools focuses on a different niche of record selection that is required in different applications.

Using the Select Records tool

As we have seen in the previous chapter, the Select Records tool is for choosing records based on a numerical range. You can choose a single row with a specific number, or a range of rows using the format n-m, where n is the first row and m is the last row. You can also choose records up to a row with the format -m and records after a row with the format n+.

Each of these different options just specifies the rows in which we are interested. If we are interested in a series of different ranges, each extra range is defined on a new line. In the following screenshot, the Select Records tool is used to select rows 4-100:

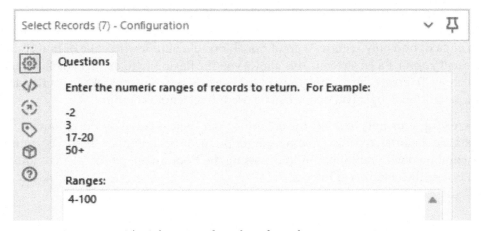

Figure 5.4 – The Select Records tool configured to extract rows 4 to 100

The biggest limitation to using the **Select Records** tool is the fact that there is no flexibility if the format or row counts change. There is no pattern matching included, so if the records of interest move for any reason, they will not be selected. This limitation can be addressed with the Filter tool in the next section.

Using the Filter tool

The **Filter** tool differs from the **Select Records** tool as the rows are split into two streams of data based on a logical condition. The logical condition can be configured using the **Basic** or **Custom** options, as seen in the following screenshot:

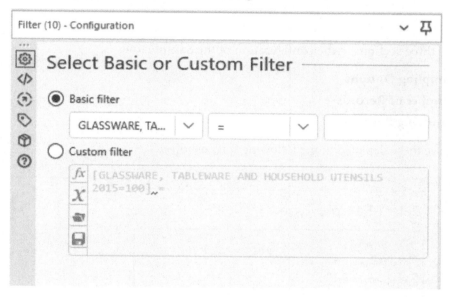

Figure 5.5 – Configuration window for the Filter tool

The basic filter allows you to choose a field and apply standard logical operators such as equals, greater than, and is null, and the result is then compared against your check.

The custom filter provides a bit more flexibility in creating your filter as it gives you access to the full range of functions that can be found in Alteryx. The only limitation in using the custom filter is the fact that the final output of the formula must be True or False.

The output of the Filter tool is two streams of data, one for any record that evaluates as True, the other for False. This gives you the option of processing each stream independently for different results.

Using the sampling tools

The Sample tool provides a method for selecting a defined number of rows from the overall row stream. The Sample tool can be found in the **Preparation** bin of the tool pallet and the icon is shown as follows:

Figure 5.6 – Sample tool icon in the Preparation bin of the tool pallet

There are three sections to the configuration of the **Sample** tool:

- **Sampling Options**
- **Number of Records**
- **Grouping Records**

You can see these depicted in the following screenshot:

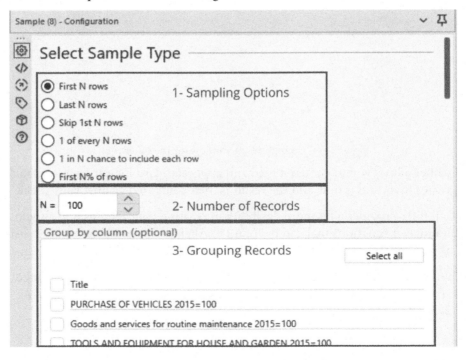

Figure 5.7 – Sample tool configuration

The setup of the sample is relatively straightforward:

1. Configure the sampling options, where you choose which type of record subset you are interested in.

2. Choose the number or proportion of rows to select.

3. Finally, you choose an optional grouping field. The grouping field allows you to restart the sampling for each new entry value in the group field.

Using a Random % Sample tool

The Random % Sample tool allows you to choose either a random number (number **1** in *Figure 5.8*) or a random proportion (number **2** in *Figure 5.8*) of the records. This is useful for managing large datasets when planning and developing the entire process. The following screenshot shows the configuration of the Random % Sample tool:

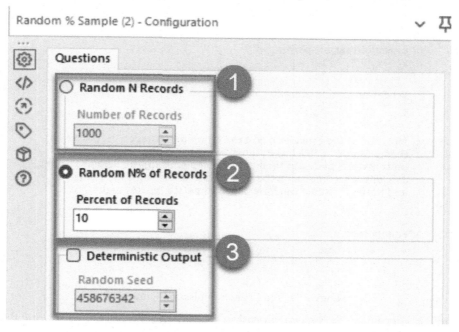

Figure 5.8 – The Random % Sample tool with the configuration annotated

The preceding screenshot also shows the configuration option to create a **Deterministic Output** (number **3**). By selecting a deterministic output, the output will always contain the same records rather than a new random sample with every run. In development applications, this allows for consistency when testing and modifying the process, or can be used to generate randomization between runs to check the output is as expected in all situations.

Using the Create Samples tool

The **Create Samples** tool allows for the creation of estimation samples, validation samples, and holdout samples. This capability is useful for data science and ML.

The tool allows you to define what proportion of the records is used for the estimation data stream, often in building ML models. You also define the proportion of the dataset for the validation data stream. This subset is often used for tuning the ML models during development. The rest of the records are fed out into a holdout data stream. This can be used for final performance testing on the final data ML model that is built. The following screenshot shows the initial configuration of the **Create Samples** tool:

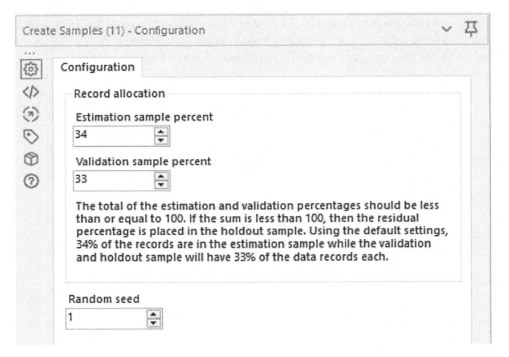

Figure 5.9 – The Create Samples configuration

In *Figure 5.9*, you can see the record allocation section. In this section, you define the percentage of records that go to each of the estimation and validation data streams. If this does not add up to 100%, the rest will go to the holdout dataset. In the screenshot, **34%** of the records would go to the estimation sample, **33%** would go to the validation sample, and the remaining 33% would go to the holdout sample, ensuring the total for all samples sums to 100%.

> **Note**
>
> While Alteryx uses the terms *estimation*, *validation*, and *holdout set* in the sample tool, they are commonly referred to as training, validation, and test sets in data science applications. While the terminology is different here, the application in Alteryx is very flexible and can fit with these other data science applications.

The Create Samples tool includes a **Random seed** generator number. This provides deterministic randomness, meaning the samples are consistent (the same records in each dataset) each time the workflow is run.

These methods allow us to isolate the records of interest. This isolation allows us to focus our transformation processes on the records that will form part of our final dataset. The next process we need to apply when cleansing our dataset is to generate new features or modify records in our fields.

Generating features and modifying columns with formulas

Generating new features or modifying existing fields is commonly achieved with a **Formula** tool. The **Formula** tool (along with the **Multi-Field Formula** and the **Multi-Row Formula** tools we will see later in this section) can be found in the **Preparation** bin of the tool pallet. When you want to apply a calculation or function to a single column (rather than repeating it across multiple columns) and the calculation will be done at the granularity of the current rows, the formula tool is the go-to option. It enables the row-level operations to update the records.

There are five areas of the Formula tool:

1. The column selection
2. Data type confirmation
3. The Formula tool helpers
4. The expression window
5. A preview of the resulting output

As you can see, the following screenshot showcases them all:

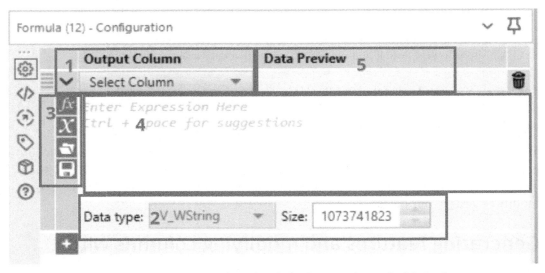

Figure 5.10 – The Formula tool with the functional areas highlighted

When writing a formula, each of these sections represents a step in the formula creation process. First, you can either select a column to update or add a new column. If you add a new column, you then decide on what the data type will be for that new field. In the following table, the different data types are listed below their generic data type role:

Object	Boolean	Numeric	String	Date	Spatial
Blob	Bool	Byte	String	Date	SpatialObj
		Int16	Wstring	Time	
		Int32	V_String	DateTime	
		Int64	V_Wstring		
		Fixed Decimal			
		Float			
		Double			

Table 5.1 – Listing of the data types in Alteryx

Once the data type has been decided, you can build the calculation needed to create your desired field. Part of that involves using the built-in functions, such as **Contains()**, **Trim()**, **ABS()**, or **Floor()** (a full listing of built-in functions can be found in the Alteryx documentation: `https://help.alteryx.com/20213/designer/functions`). Different functions produce different output types, so having a matching field type before trying to apply the function simplifies the process.

You can use the **Formula tool helper menu** to provide access to a full listing of the functions in the *f*x menu, while the **X** menu contains the existing columns and constants available in the dataset. You can also find the Formula tool helper menu by selecting a help tool and pushing the *F1* button on your keyboard. Finally, the disk menu and the folder menu allow you to save and retrieve formulas you use frequently across workflows.

The last two spaces in *Figure 5.10*, the **expression** window and **Data Preview** window are where you craft your formula using the built-in autocompletion functionality and preview the result of the calculation when applied to the first row of data.

While the function writing process is used in many different tools throughout Alteryx, two other key places for creating columns are the **Multi-Field Formula** tool and the **Multi-Row Formula** tool.

Creating special columns with the Multi-Field Formula tool

The Multi-Field Formula tool allows you to define a single formula and loop that formula over a set of columns you define. In *Figure 5.8*, you can see the three sections of the Multi-Field formula tool:

1. The column selection area where you choose what columns to repeat the formula over

2. The formula helper menu, which provides the same information as the Formula tool's helper menu

3.   The expression window, which does not have autocomplete enabled, meaning you
     will need to reference the helper menu more often as you learn your commonly
     used functions

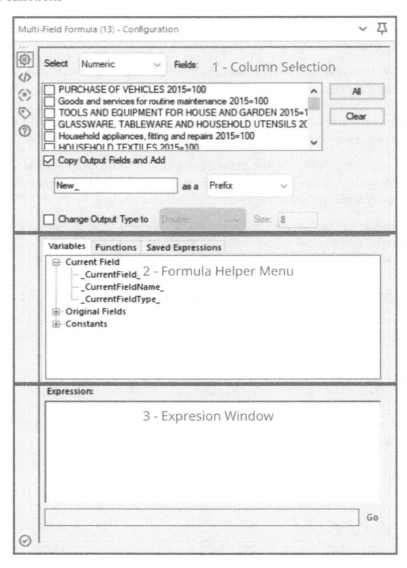

Figure 5.11 – The Multi-Field formula tool

The formula helper menu **Variables** tab has a dropdown for **Current Field**. These fields allow you to do operations based on the selected column. _CurrentField_ references the records in each column. The **_CurrentFieldName_** and **_CurrentFieldType_** columns allow you to check the metadata of the columns and apply conditional logic based on what is returned.

Referencing multiple rows with the Multi-Row Formula tool

By default, all formulas in Alteryx only operate on a single row, and you can reference any column within that row but no other records. The **Multi-Row Formula** tool allows you to reference other records within a formula. You are not able to perform this calculation on multiple columns in the Multi-Row Formula tool.

The different rows are referenced using the Row-N: or Row+N: prefixes on the column name. – references previous rows, while + looks at the following rows and the N number details how many columns prior the calculation will cover.

This row referencing is all based on the incoming record order, and because of this implicit assumption, it is always advised to sort the records just before using the Multi-Row Formula tool.

The cleansing processes we have looked at so far have all operated on each individual row, transforming the values or isolating the records of interest. The next operation we need to perform is to decide whether the granularity of our dataset matches what we need.

Summarizing the dataset

When looking at the granularity of your dataset, it might not be at a level that is useful for the analysis that was requested. Additionally, there may be calculations that you want to make that require the dataset to be at a different granularity for part of the equation. Transforming the granularity of your dataset is most often achieved with the **Summarize** tool, which you can see as follows:

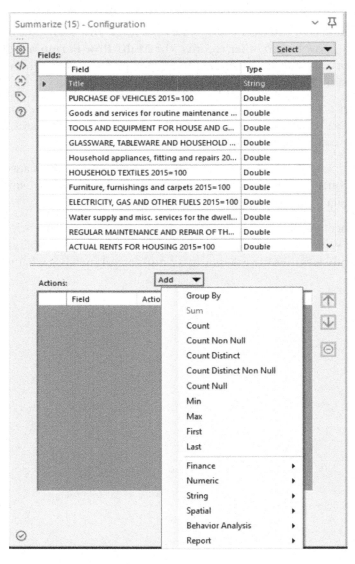

Figure 5.12 – The Summarize tool with the Actions menu expanded

The important section of this screenshot is the configuration choices in the **Add** action menu. In this menu, the first choice is **Group By**, which allows you to select key fields you want to aggregate over.

All other choices in that menu are different options for summarization. The top section shows the most commonly used aggregations – the **Sum**, **Count**, **Min**, and **Max** variations. The bottom section of the **Add** menu contains all other summarization methods grouped together under their process types: **Finance**, **Numeric**, **String**, **Spatial**, **Behavior Analysis**, and **Report**.

The process of choosing the action involves highlighting the field you want from the list, either individually or highlighting a selection of the fields, and then choosing the action you want to apply. This will populate the **Actions** table with the field you want and the action applied. It also lists the column names after the summarization. By default, grouped field names will not change and any summarization fields will be prefixed with the summarization that is applied.

The summarizing process completes the core skill set for cleansing and transforming a dataset. With these skills, we can now prepare a clean dataset for profiling and statistical analysis.

Profiling data with summary and statistical aggregations

Once you have your dataset, getting an idea of what values are in it allows you to understand what the data looks like. Knowing what the data is like provides a reference when you are ready to compare across runs.

In Alteryx, there are a number of ways in which to investigate the range of values that appear in the dataset. In this section, we are going to look at the following three areas:

- What is the variation in the dataset and the size of the range?

- How is the dataset distributed?

- What proportion of your records is missing values?

In each of these areas, Alteryx provides tools for answering the questions quickly and also has methods for those answers to be persisted in your logging systems.

Investigating the variation and size range of your dataset

The first area to investigate is the spread of the data. Understanding the aggregated spread of the records in each field will give you an understanding of what an expected dataset is and you can identify whether the records conform to that expected range.

The simplest way to identify the variation and range of your dataset is to summarize the data to extract that information. Once you have that information, you can review it quickly and reference it against expected values. The visualization of the datasets can be completed in your visualization tool of choice, or you can use the Alteryx visualization and reporting tools found in the **Reporting** bin of the tool pallet.

Figure 5.11 shows the different aggregation options in the Summarize tool. They offer different methods for finding the center of distribution (different averaging options) and the statistical spread information from the standard deviation and variance.

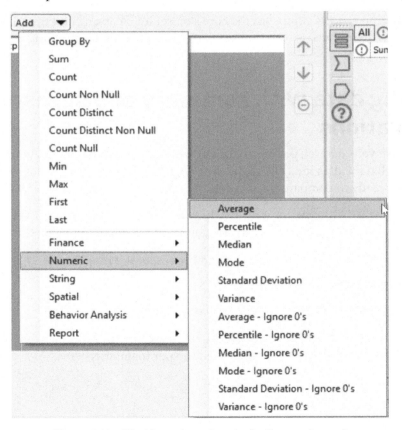

Figure 5.13 – The Numeric options in the Summarize tool

To understand the range and spread of our dataset, we can use the **Min** and **Max** aggregations along with **Standard Deviation** to provide an understanding of the dataset spread. On its own, however, this is not very actionable, nor does it provide any method for quickly understanding what has changed and whether it is expected. To see that, we need to extend the values to a visual format for fast interpretation.

Reporting the statistical profile

Creating a visualization in Alteryx involves preparing your dataset to the granularity of the view you want to see. This means that in order to create the reference information you want to see, you will need to prepare the references and append them to each record before passing that information to either the **Insight** tool (for creating dashboards you can view in Alteryx Server) or the **Interactive Chart** tool (for building reporting parts).

To view each value in a view and compare it to a reference, such as the standard deviation for building a control chart, you would need to create a dataset to have the values of interest, the **upper control limit** (**UCL**), and the **lower control limit** (**LCL**). Finally, you would need an indicator column to indicate whether the value is in the control or outside it. The final dataset would look like the following screenshot:

Record	Year of Measure	Date	Measure	Index Value	Mean	StdDev	UCL	LCL	Indicator
1	1988	1988-01-01	GLASSWARE, TABLEWARE AND HOUSEHOLD UT...	83.4	94.012121	5.559438	99.57156	88.45268	Out of Controls
2	1989	1989-01-01	GLASSWARE, TABLEWARE AND HOUSEHOLD UT...	86.8	94.012121	5.559438	99.57156	88.45268	Out of Controls
3	1990	1990-01-01	GLASSWARE, TABLEWARE AND HOUSEHOLD UT...	91.7	94.012121	5.559438	99.57156	88.45268	In Controls
4	1991	1991-01-01	GLASSWARE, TABLEWARE AND HOUSEHOLD UT...	97.9	94.012121	5.559438	99.57156	88.45268	In Controls
5	1992	1992-01-01	GLASSWARE, TABLEWARE AND HOUSEHOLD UT...	98.3	94.012121	5.559438	99.57156	88.45268	In Controls
6	1993	1993-01-01	GLASSWARE, TABLEWARE AND HOUSEHOLD UT...	97.9	94.012121	5.559438	99.57156	88.45268	In Controls
7	1994	1994-01-01	GLASSWARE, TABLEWARE AND HOUSEHOLD UT...	96.9	94.012121	5.559438	99.57156	88.45268	In Controls
8	1995	1995-01-01	GLASSWARE, TABLEWARE AND HOUSEHOLD UT...	98.4	94.012121	5.559438	99.57156	88.45268	In Controls
9	1996	1996-01-01	GLASSWARE, TABLEWARE AND HOUSEHOLD UT...	99	94.012121	5.559438	99.57156	88.45268	In Controls
10	1997	1997-01-01	GLASSWARE, TABLEWARE AND HOUSEHOLD UT...	98.2	94.012121	5.559438	99.57156	88.45268	In Controls
11	1998	1998-01-01	GLASSWARE, TABLEWARE AND HOUSEHOLD UT...	97	94.012121	5.559438	99.57156	88.45268	In Controls

Figure 5.14 – Prepared dataset for showing the structure needed to create a control chart

Once we have our dataset, we can create our chart with our charting tools. The process for creating the chart is the same in both the Interactive Chart tool and the Insight tool, so our example will use the interactive chart for any image.

When building the visualization, you need to add each component (found in a column) as a separate layer, as seen in the following screenshot:

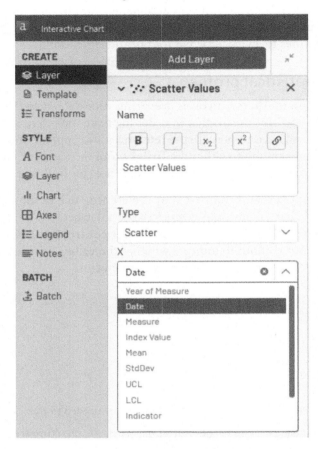

Figure 5.15 – Adding the first layer to the control chart

In the figure, you choose the chart type, scatter for the main values, and what values will appear on the **x** axis (`Year of Measure`) and the **y** axis (`Index Value`).

Once the first layer has been created, you repeat the process for each different column you want to include in the visualization (for example, UCL and LCL).

Next, you will decide whether you want to create a different chart for each measure. For the multiple chart options, you will batch the process according to the column that identifies the column name (`Measure`).

Finally, you can format your chart to your own preferences using the **Style** options. For example, if you want to set the color of the reference lines, you would choose the **Layer** menu and then set the color for each layer you want to modify.

The final result from an Interactive tool (shown in the following screenshot) is a report component that can be viewed in a browsing tool and rendered into a report with the **Render** tool, which will be discussed in more detail in *Chapter 7, Extracting value*:

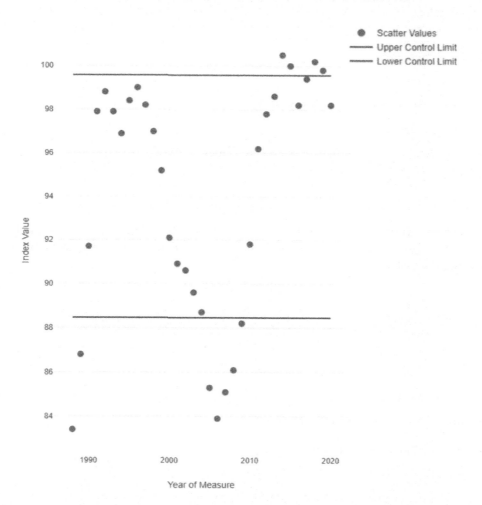

Figure 5.16 – An example control table created using the steps described

The preceding diagram shows an example control table that was created and rendered as an output.

After creating our control chart using the statistical profile, we can check how the distribution varies across our dataset.

Investigating distributions in your dataset

The next aspect of data profiling involves understanding what the distribution of the values is in the data. This can be achieved from the summary information provided in the **Basic Data Profile** or **Field Summary** tools.

The **Basic Data Profile** tool provides the text summary information for the profile seen in the **Browse** tool. This profile includes the summary information relating to the following:

- Field metadata
- Basic data quality
- Check for leading or trailing whitespaces
- Field range
- Standard numeric statistical summary values
- Numeric percentiles

This information can be recorded or used to recreate the browse profile for later reference.

The **Field Summary** tool (seen in *Figure 5.17*) provides the same information (field size, summary statistics, counts, and unique value counts) but adds a visual histogram for observing the distribution:

Figure 5.17 – Field Summary icon from the Data Investigation bin of the tool pallet

This information is output in three ways:

- An interactive browse output
- A static report that can be rendered or saved
- The record values in standard output for saving to a data storage medium

Each of these outputs provides the same information but is used in different applications. The interactive report is for interactive investigation. It is especially useful when investigating a dataset for the first time. The report and output values provide a method for recording the information from the Summary tool for future reference.

Using the Tile tool

Another method for understanding the distribution of your dataset is by creating buckets or binning the records in your dataset. This binning process allows for similar values in your dataset to be grouped together. This grouping reduces the number of unique values in your distribution and reduces the appearance of variation from minor observation errors. These bins can then be visualized to understand the data spread. The following screenshot shows the **Tile** tool:

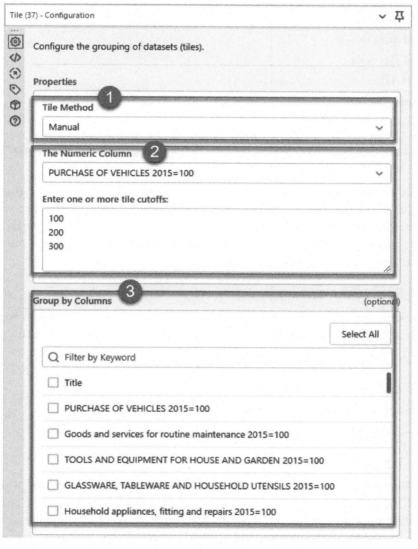

Figure 5.18 – The Tile tool configuration window

In the screenshot, there are three configuration sections:

1. The Tile Method area
2. The method configuration area
3. The optional grouping configuration

When configuring the tool, changing the Tile method will change the appearance of the method configuration, thereby allowing unique changes to be made. The Tile tool provides five Tile methods for configuring your Tile tool:

- **Equal Sum**
- **Equal Records**
- **Smart Tile**
- **Unique Value**
- **Manual**

Each of these options gives a different method for defining the size of the buckets and the associated distributions they create.

There is also an optional grouping configuration that you can apply to any of the tiling options. With the **Group by Columns** option, it will restart the tile set for each new value of the columns. In our data profiling checks, we can transpose the dataset, meaning all the measures are stacked on top of one another, and then use this grouping option so that each measure has its own tile set.

Using the Equal Sum option

The **Equal Sum** option allows for records to be grouped together into buckets so that when all the records are summed together, the result for each bucket is the same.

The process for configuring the Equal Sum option involves the following:

1. Choosing the number of tiles to create
2. Choosing which column you want to create a tile for
3. Optionally identifying which column to sort on for creating the bucket

Using the Equal Records option

The **Equal Records** option is similar to Equal Sum with regard to how it works and is configured. The difference between the two options is that for Equal Sum, the count of records in each bucket need not be the same. The Equal Sum option bins the values by aggregating the values in the column and creates buckets where the sum is the same. This will usually result in a different count of records compared to the Equal Records option.

The configuration options between the Equal Sum and Equal Records options are the same aside from a variation in the **Tile** method. These options facilitate choosing a column to ensure that any records contained in a group are not split across tiles. If this optional configuration is not applied, the tiling split will take precedence.

Using the Smart Tile option

The **Smart Tile** option uses the standard deviation to define the tiles in the dataset. In this option, the central tile of **0** ranges between **-0.5** and **0.5** standard deviations from the mean. Then, each additional tile ranges an additional **1** standard deviation in either the positive or negative direction. This use of standard deviation for defining the tiles means that the most values would be expected in the low numbered tiles, and high numbered tiles would be outlying values that would require exploration. The way the tiles are created is shown in the following screenshot using a **bell curve** as an example distribution:

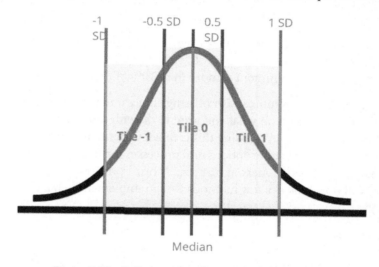

Figure 5.19 – Bell curve distribution with tiles overlaid

Using the Smart Tile option can highlight any values that appear to be extreme compared to the median when compared to a **normal distribution**.

Using the Unique Value option

The **Unique Value** option is a method for creating a unique identifier based on a combination of fields. This is a great way to create keys for database tables and provides a method to define a complete set of unique values.

Using the Manual option

The **Manual** option allows you to define custom tile sizes on a numeric field. To implement the cutoff values, you enter one value per line in the configuration window. The Custom setting allows you to create tiles of varying sizes, for example, to make custom age ranges for your customer profile.

After identifying the distributions within your dataset, you can apply the knowledge gained to interpret what an expected value might look like. With this knowledge, you can process any missing values in your dataset.

Correcting missing values in your dataset

The final processing step we will discuss is how to manage missing values. Missing values can be a problem in data science and analytics applications and knowing how to manage them will help improve the experience of your end users.

The simplest way to identify missing values is with the output from the **Field Summary** tool. In that output, it calculates the `Percent Missing` values. It also has a comment in the `Remarks` field with a comment if more than 10% of the values are missing.

Once you have identified the columns with missing values and the proportion of missing values, you can make a decision on what you want to do with those fields and the associated records. The decision process surrounding this is much wider than can be covered in this book (and you can read about some options and processes for managing missing data in the *Packt* tutorial, *Dealing with a Mess*, at `https://hub.packtpub.com/dealing-mess/`), but we will now look at a few methods we can implement to handle those missing values in Alteryx.

The first way to manage the missing values is simply to remove the missing rows with the Filter tool. The process for filtering records is described in *Chapter 4*, *Sourcing the Data*, and it involve using a filter condition to match the `null` values in the column with the missing records. This process could also have an impact in terms of removing relevant values for other fields and may not be desirable.

The next option would be to remove the entire column. If the number of missing values is high enough, it could be that the column holds no useful information and dropping it would be an effective process. This could be achieved through a combination of updating the column description with a dynamic rename tool and then using that updated description as the logic in a dynamic selection.

In both of these options, a decision to remove potentially valuable information must be made so you will have to make the decision and implement the logic on how to address those situations.

A final situation for removing the columns is if the entire row or field is null. These situations would be found in dirty datasets and removing those entries would not result in any lost records.

Figure 5.20 – The Data Cleansing tool icon from the Preparation bin of the tool pallet

The simplest way to implement this would be to use the Data Cleansing tool seen in the preceding screenshot. *Figure 5.21* shows the **Data Cleansing** tool and the **Remove Null Data** option for removing columns and rows that only contain `Nulls`.

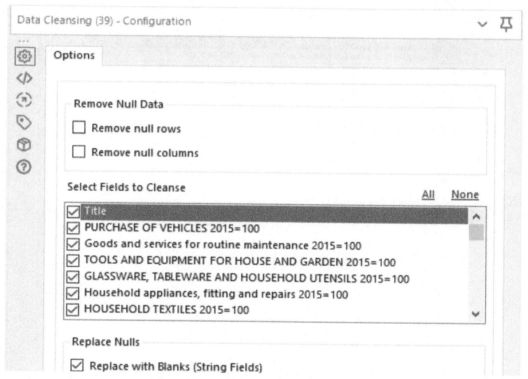

Figure 5.21 – Using the Data Cleansing tool to remove null data

While removing values is a viable method for addressing missing values, it results in a loss of depth in our dataset. One method of adjusting the missing values without removing them completely is imputation.

Correcting missing values by imputation

Once the missing values that hold no value have been addressed, we can then decide how to manage the remaining missing values. The process for populating the missing values with a default is called imputation, and one method for achieving this involves using the **Imputation** tool.

When the Imputation tool allows you to replace a specific value, by default, that value would be NULL, but could also be any value you define. You can then replace those NULL values with a standard average value (the mean, median, or mode) or it could be a different value that you define.

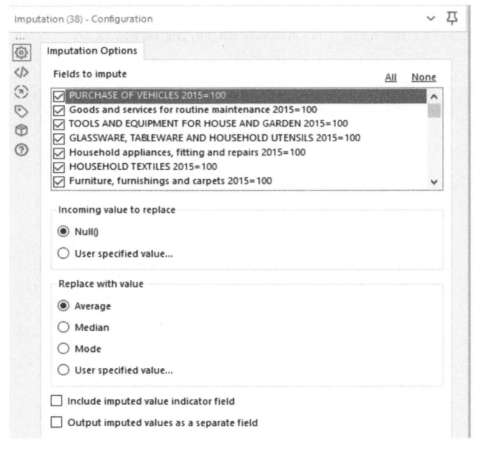

Figure 5.22 – The configuration of the Imputation tool

When you look at *Figure 5.22*, you can see the configuration of the tool that we have already seen. The final two options in the tool are to include an indicator field for when you impute a value, and you can also choose to output the imputed column into a new column. These two options mean you will know if the column has been changed from the default values.

Now that we have investigated common processing and profiling options, we can see the whole process in action.

Transforming our data pipeline

As a reminder, as we did in *Chapter 4*, *Sourcing the Data*, we are downloading the formatted address of the *London Eye* from the *Google Maps Find Place API* (`https://developers.google.com/maps/documentation/places/web-service/search-find-place`). Now we need to transform the JSON output, cleanse it, and perform tests and profiling on the dataset for saving. The API URL we are calling is as follows:

```
https://maps.googleapis.com/maps/api/place/
findplacefromtext/json?fields={return_
fields}&input={place}&inputtype=textquery&key={API_Key}
```

In this call, the parameters we are customizing are as follows:

- `{place}` is the place that you want to search for (the London Eye, UK, in our example).

- `{Return_fields}` is a comma-separated list of the fields that you want to receive from the API. Our example returned the formatted address, but you can get a full list of options in the Find Place API documentation (`https://developers.google.com/maps/documentation/places/web-service/search-find-place`). Our example query returned the values for name, `formatted_address`, `type`, and `business_status`.

- `{API Key}` is set to your personal API key to authenticate to the API.

The response that will be returned by the API is a JSON string that we will need to process.

Transforming the downloaded data

Transforming our downloaded data is achieved by applying the cleansing processes we have learned, as shown in the following steps:

1. Convert the downloaded JSON data into data objects.

2. Isolate the header details from the dataset.

3. Split the data node keys into the identifying parts.

4. Cross-tab the long column of records into a table format.

5. Process the data fields into the appropriate format.

These five steps cover the basics for ensuring that the dataset creates a table from which an analysis can be made. We will now investigate in more detail each step and the tools we use to achieve our data table.

Converting the JSON data

Converting the JSON cell from the download data is a simple process in Alteryx. Because JSON is a very standard data type, a single tool has been created, the **Parse JSON** tool, which will take a single cell of JSON data similar to what is commonly returned by APIs, and separate the key/value pairs into a **JSON Name** column and a **JSON Parse** column. You can see an example of the output in the following screenshot:

Record	JSON_Name	JSON_ValueString
1	candidates.0.business_status	OPERATIONAL
2	candidates.0.formatted_address	Riverside Building, County Hall, London SE1 7PB,...
3	candidates.0.name	lastminute.com London Eye
4	candidates.0.types.0	tourist_attraction
5	candidates.0.types.1	point_of_interest
6	candidates.0.types.2	establishment
7	candidates.1.business_status	OPERATIONAL
8	candidates.1.formatted_address	Riverside Building, County Hall, Westminster Brid...
9	candidates.1.name	London Eye River Cruise
10	candidates.1.types.0	tourist_attraction
11	candidates.1.types.1	point_of_interest
12	candidates.1.types.2	establishment
13	status	OK

Figure 5.23 – Example output from the JSON Parse tool

When you look at the **JSON_Name** field, you can see that each level of the object tree is separated by a dot. If there are nested records, those sub-records will need to have the name parsed into separate columns so that they can be correctly aggregated in a cross-tab tool.

Isolating place candidate records

The API call returns a dataset that contains all the candidate results for your search with additional metadata information for the API call. By isolating the candidate information, we can create a targeted dataset that contains only the places we are interested in.

In *Figure 5.23*, the **JSON_Name** field shows all records containing the word candidates using the Filter tool. The configuration of the Filter tool is shown in the following screenshot:

Figure 5.24 – Filter tool configuration to isolate the candidate records

This filter configuration uses the **Basic filter** option to use the **Contains** operator to isolate the word **candidates**. We will focus our dataset on just the candidate entries to create the table for future analysis.

Splitting the key fields into identifying parts

When we examine the **JSON_Name** field in both data streams, we see that they need to be treated differently. In the header and current records, there is only one level of information. That means that the **JSON_Name** field for those records already identifies the rows and we can cross-tab directly.

The places records are different as they also contain nested records and we need to separate the record identifiers from them. When we look at the `candidates.0.formatted_address` record, we see a pattern common to all JSON objects. When we see a text name, that is describing the key at a particular node. Every number in the record identifies the row in a nested field (using a zero-index counting). What this means is that every time we see a new number, we know there is additional nested information from the following key and we will need to group the records by this number.

For our places records, we see that there is only one number to identify the nested records, so we can split the column using the **Text to Columns** tool and create three new columns.

Transforming our records to a text table with the Cross Tab tool

Now that we have separated the JSON name data into the requisite number of columns, we can reshape the dataset from being a tall, narrow dataset into a wide dataset where each row is one observation.

Figure 5.25 shows the configuration of the **Cross Tab** tool for the places data:

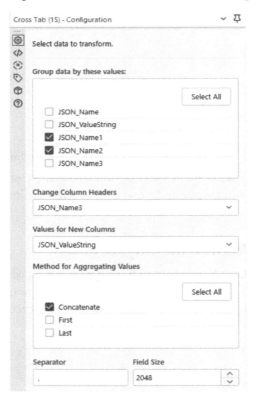

Figure 5.25 – Cross Tab tool configuration for the Places data

In the configuration, we group the records according to our identifying fields – **JSON_Name1** and **JSON_Name2**, where **JSON_Name1** is the dataset identifier (**candidates** in this example) and **JSON_Name2** is the row identifier. We then set the column headers for the new table to be **JSON_Name3**, the key for each node, while the values we populate the table with are taken from **JSON_ValueString**.

Because we have taken the records from a downloaded text field, the field type is a string. This means that the aggregation options we have are for string values. Provided we have identified the records correctly, each cell will be made of one value and no aggregation will be needed. By setting the required aggregation to **Concatenate** with a comma as an identifier, we can use this to search and test to ensure our data quality.

Setting our data types

Now that we have produced a table that matches the format we want to see, we need to set the columns to the appropriate data type. The simplest way to achieve this would be to use the **Auto Field** tool. The **Auto Field** tool will take any string fields and convert that field's data type to the smallest possible data type that will fit all the information. For example, if the longest string in a field is 15 characters, the column size will be set to **15**, but if the field only contained whole numbers, the data type would be set to an integer type.

This is an easy way to convert all the columns, but it does have its limitations. Because every single record needs to be examined before setting the data type (to ensure that no information is lost), it can be a slow process, and this is especially true for large datasets. For our eight-record dataset, the time it takes is not significant, but if more records are returned in any operation, the processing speed may be a consideration. The other consideration is that because the data types are set every time the workflow is run, it could result in unexpected behaviors if a field type changed.

For these reasons, the Auto Field tool is great for development, but it is not advised for use in production. To move into production, it is advised to extract the column type information into a .yxft file and then load it into the **Select** tool.

Profiling our dataset

Now that we have a clean dataset, we want to profile the data and implement some additional tests using that information.

For this dataset, we want to create a summary report that will display the business operational status, especially if there is no business that is OPERATIONAL in our search. We also want to confirm we have an entry for formatted_address and the place name.

So, the conditions we want to apply are as follows:

- Is at least one of the places from our search OPERATIONAL?
- Is the formatted_address field populated with an address?
- Is the Name field populated with a place name?

The outputs we want to create from these conditions are log notifications for any missing records in the Name or formatted_address fields, while the operational business check will throw an error if none of the places from our query are operational.

Confirming our record accuracy

Because the operational business check is a failing condition, where the condition is not met, the workflow will error and stop processing, so we will make that check first. We will use the **Message** tool for this as we want the check to happen in line with the dataset (rather than as a parallel process). Including this accuracy check as part of our data pipeline instead of a separate process allows immediate feedback on the dataset every time the workflow is run. It means the data quality can be assessed before it is fed into other systems and applications.

To make this check, we will concatenate all the business_status records into a single row and append this concatenated field back onto the main data table so the check can happen inline.

Next, we want to configure the Message tool, as can be seen in the following screenshot:

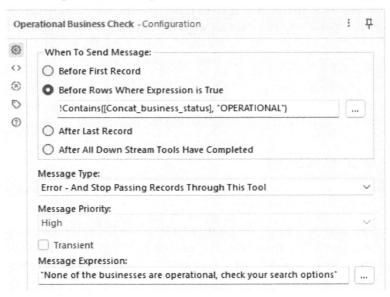

Figure 5.26 – Configuration of the business operational error check

In this tool, we have configured a check to confirm that at least one `business_status` field (as found in the `Concat_business_status` field created by summarizing the business status with no **Group By** set) contains an entry for OPERATIONAL. To trigger the error message, we want our check to return a `True` result when none of the records contain the word OPERATIONAL.

Next, the message type we want to generate is an error and to stop processing.

Finally, we return the following message any time none of the `business_status` fields are operational:

```
"None of the businesses are operational, check your search
options"
```

This message includes the call to action to check your search.

Generating our data profile report

For our data profile, we want to check the `name` and `business_status` fields for null fields. We will also check those fields to ensure that the text is not *blank*. For different applications, we will likely want to examine the other string fields' quality, but our current check is only interested in the quality of the target fields mentioned.

To isolate our target fields, we will use a dynamic select and choose the **Select via a Formula** option with the formula `[Name] in ('business_status', 'name')`. This configuration is shown in the following screenshot:

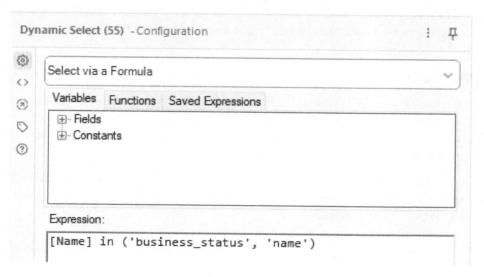

Figure 5.27 – The configuration of the Dynamic Select tool

We will then pass these targeted columns into the basic profile tool, which provides the information we need to validate the field contents.

The Basic Data Profile tool provides a large amount of information that is useful for other applications, but we will not be applying it in this chapter. The important fields for our checks are the **Blanks** and **Nulls** columns. These columns indicate whether there are missing or blank values in our target fields.

Applying our conditions

The final step in our checks is to apply our conditional checks to the data profile and manage our data quality. The checks we are going to apply are as follows:

- Confirm the business status is OPERATIONAL.

- Ensure there are no null values for the name or business_status.

These two checks will output the message as a warning to the logs and will prompt us to investigate the records and ensure they are acceptable. Because we will only be running these on the name and business_status fields, we will first filter the basic profile output to where the Field Name column contains either business_status or name.

Creating the messages will require two message tools. Each message tool will output the warning message type of normal priority. The message priority option is for controlling the passing of a message out of a macro into a workflow.

The message condition will be that our logic checks the value of business_status equals OPERATIONAL or there are null values that return a TRUE result. When either of these events happens, a message will be created and entered into the logs.

Summary

In this chapter, we have investigated several ways in which to process a raw dataset to produce a functional output for our end users. We have also learned about some different methods for profiling our dataset and how we can use that information to ensure the quality of our data.

After learning these skills, we then applied those skills in a practical example, taking the Authenticated API from *Chapter 4*, *Sourcing the Data*, and turning that dataset into a useful data table for our application.

In *Chapter 6, Destination Management,* we will investigate the different ways in which we can output data and different methods to manage those connections.

We will also look at some methods for managing our data connections across different environments so we can be secure in the way we use our data for development and apply it to production.

Finally, we will publish our datasets in an analytical database and leverage the capabilities of Alteryx to upload our dataset for the benefit of our end users.

6

Destination Management

After creating a dataset, we need to persist it to a location. The simplest place to save a dataset is as a local file, often an Excel or CSV file, but in business environments, storing the dataset in a database is a better solution.

In this chapter, we will explore the output options. We will investigate saving to a data source from the local Designer testing and what the differences are when publishing to the server.

In this chapter, we will cover the following topics:

- Connecting to destinations locally
- The process for integrating workflows across environments
- Completing an example process to publish to a Snowflake destination

Technical requirements

In this chapter, you will need Alteryx Designer to create workflows and the content that we have been using throughout the process. The example workflows and supporting code can be found on GitHub: `https://github.com/PacktPublishing/Data-Engineering-with-Alteryx/tree/main/Chapter%2006`. If you want to use an alternative database, the processes would be the same with the connection modified for your alternative. If you want to complete the publication to Snowflake, you will need a Snowflake account. You can create a new Snowflake trial account, which will allow you to follow along with the chapter. Specific requirements for a Snowflake connection and the reasons why this database was chosen are described in the *Publishing the external data to a Snowflake destination* section.

You can follow the instructions for creating a Snowflake trial account described here: `https://docs.snowflake.com/en/user-guide/admin-trial-account.html`.

Writing to destinations

The requirements for managing the destinations are similar to those for connecting to internal datasets described in *Chapter 4*, *Sourcing the Data*. Managing the destinations falls into three categories:

- Writing to local files
- Writing to databases
- Custom connection tools from Alteryx Gallery

Managing these three categories on a local machine is relatively simple, but should be done in a manner that works for other people or environments (such as your Alteryx Server). In this section, we will look at the default way in which you connect to local files and how we can make that connection process more robust, why those changes fit with our DataOps processes, and how we can leverage these changes for collaboration.

Writing to files

Saving files to a location on your computer is a good way to persist data during a pipeline development. When you do save the file, it is often saved as a full path, such as `C:\Users\username\project\output_file.csv`.

This location is easily found on your Windows computer in File Explorer. However, continuing to use the location when collaborating with other people causes errors as any new person is unlikely to have the file located in the same place on their computer. Any other people you collaborate with are unlikely to have the same username as you, and Alteryx will be unable to find a file in this location. This failure to find the file location breaks two of the DataOps principles, *making it reproducible* and *disposable environments*.

The issue with using the local location is that if there is any external modification to the file output location, you will not be able to reproduce the workflow and the output. It could also have downstream side effects where other processes that depend on the created output are unable to work. You would also produce an error when trying to run the workflow in a new location, meaning that the environment is not disposable.

Fortunately, there are simple methods to prevent this from being an issue:

- Reference files with relative paths.
- Reference files with a **Universal Naming Convention** (**UNC**) path for network locations.
- Embed a snapshot of the file when publishing and sharing.

Each of these options has different methods for implementation and shares fundamentals with the processes for input files. We will learn how to use these methods in the next section.

Creating relative paths to output local files

When saving files locally, using a relative path allows you to identify the location based on where the workflow is stored. The simplest case for this is to store the output file in the same location as the workflow. The following screenshot shows an example of saving a file to the same folder:

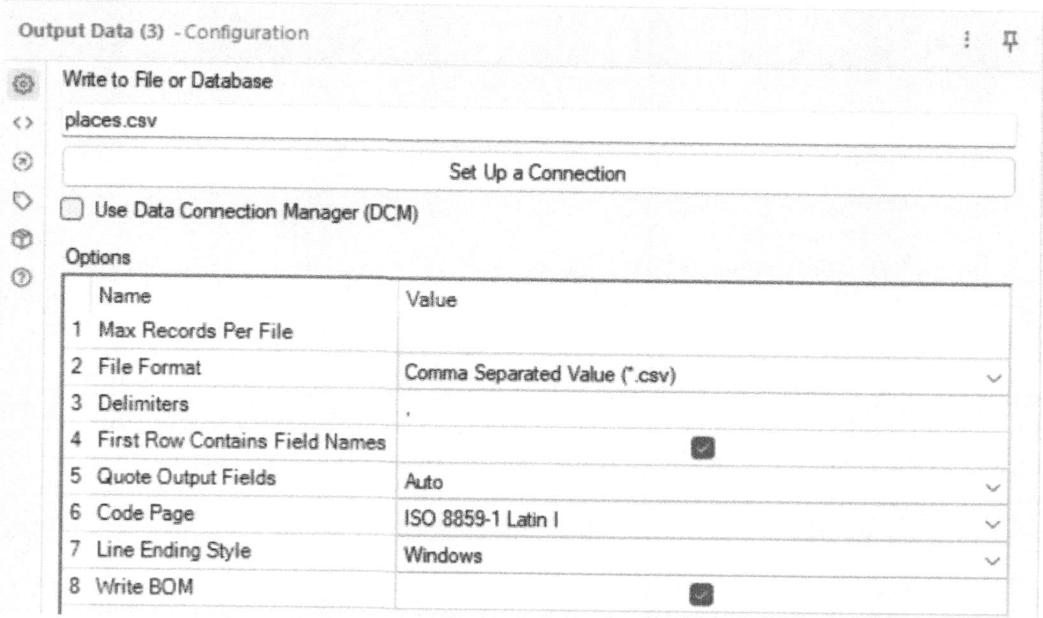

Figure 6.1 – Saving the places dataset to the same folder as the workflow

What we see is that the path is entered as just the filename, in this example, `places.csv`. Because the file location (`C:\Users\username\project\`) has not been defined, Alteryx will auto-populate the location with the internal variable `[Engine.WorkflowDirectory]`. This variable returns where the workflow is located. By defining the file save location to the same location, there will never be any problems when saving the output of that folder.

Saving your output file to the same folder is a common and simple option. However, it limits your flexibility in structuring your project; for example, if you wanted to use dedicated data folders for all data files while workflows or supporting documentation are located in a separate folder in the project.

We can accommodate this desired flexibility by extending our relative paths down into child folders or up into parent folders. The following screenshot shows the use of a relative path to save the file to a `Data` subfolder:

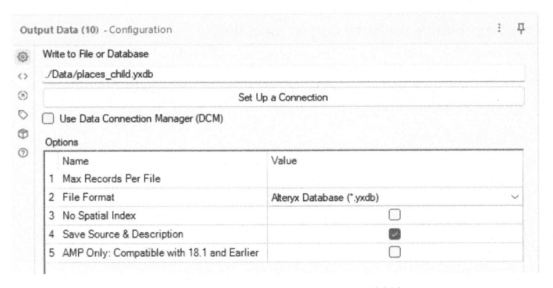

Figure 6.2 – Saving the places dataset to a child folder

In this example, the file path starts with a dot forward-slash (`./`) combination. This combination indicates a path relative to the current working directory. In the same manner as the file location (with `[Engine.WorkflowDirectory]`) is added to the main folder example, `./` is replaced with the same variable. If we look at the entire path, we can expand out the location where the output file will be saved:

`./Data/places_child.yxdb`

In this path, we start in the same folder as the workflow and navigate to the `Data` child folder, where we save the `places_child.yxdb` file. We can navigate further down the child folder paths by adding additional folders before the filename. For example, `./Data/intermediate_data/places_child.yxdb` would save the file to an additional child folder called `intermediate_data`.

The final method for using relative paths is to navigate up into parent folders. In this case, rather than starting in the current location and navigating down the file path, we want to move back up the path. When we use a path that starts with two dots and a forward slash (`../`), it tells Alteryx to navigate up one folder. The example file path below moves up one folder from the workflow location and then navigates across to a folder called `Raw_Data`:

`../Raw_Data/places_child.yxdb`

All other configuration is the same as seen in the following screenshot. If you need to navigate up additional folders, add additional double dot forward-slash (`../`) combinations to the file path.

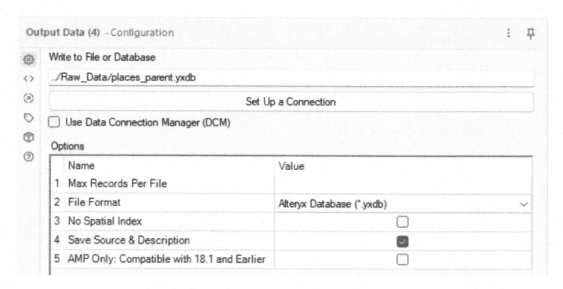

Figure 6.3 – Saving the places dataset to a parent folder

Defining relative paths only works for files that are local to your computer. Any file that is stored on a network drive (often mapped to a drive letter) cannot be found when publishing workflows to Alteryx Server. UNC paths provide a method for robustly locating the files on network drives.

Creating UNC paths to output network files

Relative paths are useful for locations that are associated with the computer you are working on. Network locations need a different method to make them portable. When we use network locations in Alteryx, they are often referenced by a mapped drive such as R:\places_mapped.xlsx.

In this example, the mapped network drive is represented by the drive letter R, but this could just as easily be any other letter. The problem is that other machines might not have that drive or the specific location mapped to the same letter. Additionally, when a workflow is published to Server, Alteryx does not see any mapped drives at all.

The best method for referring to network locations is to use the **Universal Naming Convention** (**UNC**) path. We looked at UNC paths in *Chapter 4, Sourcing the Data*, to connect to a file, and the principles for outputting a file are the same. The path is created with the format \\ServerName\FolderName\FileName, where ServerName is the host or IP address of the server, and FolderName represents the folder structure where the file is stored.

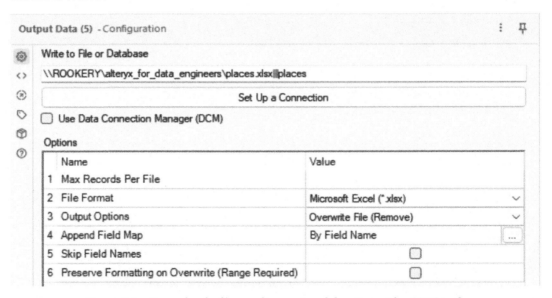

Figure 6.4 – Example of a file saved to a network location with a UNC path

You can see an example of this in the preceding screenshot, where the path is \\ROOKERY\alteryx_for_data_engineers\places.xlsx|||places, and ROOKERY is the server name, while Alteryx_for_data_engineers is the folder where the file (places.xlsx) is saved. The path also has an additional segment, |||places, that identifies what table or sheet the data is being written to.

Embedding a snapshot of the file

The next option for making a workflow transferable is to export a snapshot of the file with the workflow. Because the workflow will be recreated when the workflow is run, this option is less important for output files. The output files will also need an output location to be created with a relative or UNC path.

When sharing the workflow directly with another person, embedding any required files is achieved with the export workflow option. You will find this option on the menu toolbar: **Options** > **Export Workflow**. This option will package the workflow and dependencies into a `.yxzp` file that can then be imported and run by your colleagues.

When publishing to an Alteryx server, the packaging option is contained in the **Workflow options** > **Manage workflow assets** submenu, as shown in the following screenshot:

Figure 6.5 – Gallery Save Workflow assets submenu

In this submenu, we can see which assets (input files, output files, and local macros) are packaged with the workflow when it is published to your Alteryx Server.

Managing workflow dependencies

While each of these methods for managing your output files makes sharing a workflow possible, most of the time, when you start building a workflow, you will use the file path that Alteryx creates. This format is the normal absolute path that you would see.

When you are ready to publish your workflow to a server or want to share it with another person, you will need to convert all your existing file paths to a shareable format. This can be achieved by using the **Workflow Dependencies** settings window.

This window shows all the dependencies that are present in your workflow. An example of this is seen in *Figure 6.6*:

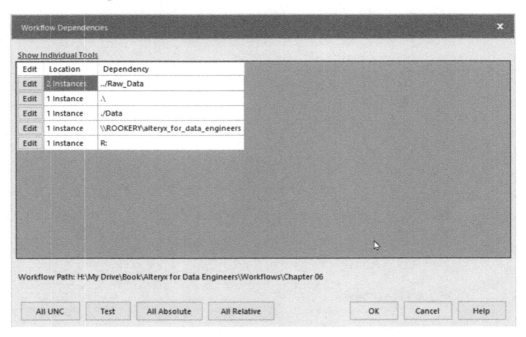

Figure 6.6 – Workflow Dependencies settings window

The **Workflow Dependencies** window lists all the dependencies in your workflow. If you want to manage a dependency related to a specific tool, you can switch the view to sort it by the individual tools.

From the workflow dependency window, you can manage the dependencies collectively and change all dependencies at the same time. Using the buttons in the bottom-left corner, you can convert all the dependencies to **All UNC, All Absolute,** or **All Relative.** There is also a **Test** button to check whether the dependencies are working. Alternatively, you can click on the **Edit** button next to each dependency and change just that path.

Now that the methods for managing local files have been addressed, we can now share our workflow with our team or publish and run it on the server. The next connection output type we need to address is our database connections.

Managing database connections

When outputting files to a database connection, there are additional considerations regarding how we will manage the process. Commonly, the development workflow will connect to a sandbox or development database instance before connecting to the production instance when published. You also have to consider how the **Open Database Connectivity (ODBC)** connections will be synchronized across the local and server environments. You also have to consider the implications of the type of output connection, either standard or bulk loading, that you use.

Using standard connections

The standard output connections in Alteryx make use of the standard INSERT statements to load data into a table. You can leverage any of the ODBC connection properties and capabilities in the same way that you can leverage them when connecting to a data source from an input tool. You also have the same limitations when sharing the workflows with **Data Source Names (DSNs).**

If you do use a DSN for your connection and leverage the Windows ODBC manager, then you will need to ensure that the configuration of the connection is consistent across environments. This means you will need to confirm that all the properties match, especially if any performance tuning has been implemented.

You can also leverage the DSN properties for changing database environments in different locations. As I mentioned earlier, it is common to develop a workflow in a sandbox environment, while the server operates in a production environment. In this situation, your user desktop environments can have their DSN identifiers, such as the server hostname or database name, set to the sandbox location, while the Alteryx server has those properties configured based on the production environment. With this configured, you can set all the other properties to be identical in both environments.

To create a new connection with the DSN configuration, you need to add the new database settings to the ODBC manager in the server environment. This process could be time-limited if it requires some manual intervention for implementation. While it is likely that you can automate this process, it might not be a good use of resources to implement this when testing new connections, as additional requests to IT would be required for a data source that might not work. For situations where a new data source requires faster access, a **DSN-less connection** is ideal.

A DSN-less connection is where the database connection information and all the connection settings are contained within the Alteryx output tool. The connection will have the following format:

```
odbc:Driver={Driver}; Server=localhost; Database=myDataBase;
User=myUsername; Password=myPassword
```

In this connection, all details of how to connect to the database are defined in the connection. If there are any other connection parameters you need to add, such as defining SSL, they can be appended to the string with a *key-value* pair.

This same connection can also be used in the **Data Connections** manager in Alteryx Server. In the Data Connections manager, you can define a central location for connection information and share a centralized connection with users and groups throughout your organization.

The connection string for a data connection is the same one you would use in a local DSN-less connection. It does require that all workflows with this connection use the same authentication permissions. This could have data security implications if row-level security has been applied for individual users. Row-level security is managed and controlled by your database, so implementing and assessing any impacts would require the assistance of your database administrator.

Whichever connection type you decide to use, a standard output tool provides a flexible way to modify existing records. In the following screenshot, you can see the options for outputting to a Snowflake database table:

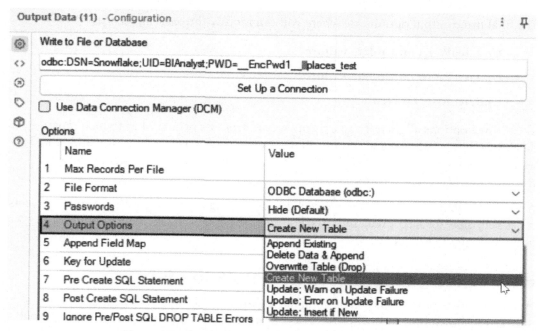

Figure 6.7 – Output options for a Snowflake database table

In the output options, there are a total of seven different choices. The first four are for writing new records to the database table:

- **Append Existing**: Where the new records are added to the bottom of an existing table.

- **Delete Data & Append**: In this option, all the records are deleted from the table, but the schema is kept.

- **Overwrite Table (Drop)**: The entire table is removed, including all schema information, and a new table is created in its place.

- **Create New Table**: This option will create a brand-new table with the schema information being fed from the Alteryx field metadata. This is the default option when an output tool is created.

All these options are row-by-row insert statements. The performance of the uploads can be tuned with the transaction size parameters, but it still requires one SQL statement to be executed on the database per row of data.

The final three output options are where you can modify the existing records:

- **Update: Warn on Update Failure**
- **Update: Error on Update Failure**
- **Update: Insert if New**

These three options all identify an existing record from its primary key (which most database tables will have) and modify all the records to the data stream. The difference between each operation is how update errors are managed and what Alteryx will do with any newly created records.

A standard ODBC connection works well for modifying exiting records and small datasets but is very slow for larger data imports. For these situations, a bulk loader connection provides better performance.

How to load data faster with bulk loaders

While all update operations can be completed with a standard ODBC connection, a transaction-based upload is where records are written one at a time. This upload method will result in performance losses. This is where the Alteryx bulk loader connection allows for increased upload performance on compatible databases.

The compatible databases are as follows:

- Amazon Athena
- Amazon Redshift
- Amazon Redshift Spectrum
- Microsoft SQL Server
- Microsoft Analytics Platform System
- Microsoft Azure Data Lake Store
- Microsoft Azure SQL Data Warehouse
- Microsoft Azure SQL Database
- Oracle
- PostgreSQL
- Snowflake

Each of these different databases has its own mechanism to bulk load the data. However, the underlying database import process allows you to load entire datasets with a single database transaction. In some cases, the file can also be compressed as part of the upload to improve performance further.

To enable the connection to be shared across different environments, you can also leverage the connection strings for each of these connections thus removing the dependency from the Windows ODBC manager.

In most data loading situations, the standard ODBC and bulk loader connections will provide all the functionality you require. However, you may find an edge case where you need to run custom SQL code. In this situation, you can leverage more of the database's functionality with custom tools.

Leveraging a database's custom tools

The final option for interacting with a database is to leverage the command-line tools if your target database has any available. A great example of this capability is shown in the Snowflake starter kit that you can find at `https://www.alteryx.com/starter-kit/snowflake`.

In the starter kit, you can generate the SQL script with Alteryx **Formula** tools and aggregations that will run on your database. The script that you generate can be parameterized, allowing for any standardized parts to be populated based on your configuration requirements.

This process allows you to leverage the different capabilities in your database SQL client to use any **data definition language (DDL)** or **data manipulation language (DML)** commands.

When you create your SQL script, they are executed using the *Run Command* tool. This tool calls a Windows Command Prompt instance and executes the script or command. You can then use the results of the command by streaming them back into Alteryx and continue your processing.

Accessing more data sources with custom connections

When outputting your data, you may want to save it in a web application. Usually, this is not possible with file output or ODBC connections. If the web application does have an API, there is the option to load data by calling the API directly. You can use some of the skills mentioned in *Chapter 4, Sourcing the Data*, using the **POST** HTTP verb.

For many web services, such as Google Sheets and Tableau Server, Alteryx has created custom connectors for interacting with these services. Below is a screenshot of Alteryx Gallery, a community collection of Alteryx-curated connections:

Figure 6.8 – The Browse by Category pane of the Alteryx Community Gallery page

On the Alteryx **Community Gallery** page, the top section shows the featured tools created by the community. Below that, and identified by box **1** in the screenshot, is a series of links to curated tool categories. By selecting the **Data Connectors** link in the **Capability** list, you have the available connectors for expanding your capability.

In *Figure 6.8*, data connectors are shown with annotation **1**. By contrast, annotation **2** highlights technology partners, such as Microsoft and Google, who have custom connectors available for their product offerings.

Now that we understand the different methods for saving data, we can investigate some methods for working across different environments.

Integrating data pipelines across environments

When considering how to integrate your workflows across environments, there are two major factors to be aware of:

- **Connection compatibility**
- **Target environment**

The connection compatibility consideration is about whether the environments will recognize the connections. We have spoken about connection strings as the first method for managing the connection across environments, but it is a simple method for ensuring that the connection will work across the environments.

The target environment consideration is about how you target different database connections across the desktop, development, and production environments. Commonly, you will have a production environment that is the primary system that supports your company. To make changes to your production environment directly is very risky if you do not test the impact the changes might have. Those impacts may concern the sequencing of other processes or how the overall performance of the production environment is affected.

Managing these factors requires consideration of how the output is referenced. For files, if we apply the methods described in the *Writing to files* section, the connection capability will be maintained, and you can publish or share your workflows freely. For databases, we need to extend our methods to incorporate the changes to the environment.

Two methods we can apply to environment management are as follows:

- **Using a secret file or environment variables**: With this option, we use an external source that contains the connection information needed for our data source, with connection files that can be read using a standard input tool. The environment variables can be extracted using a command-line call with the **Run Command** tool. Once these variables have been imported, they are used to output data by dynamically changing the destination information for the output.

- **Using Windows ODBC manager**: For multi-database environments, the connection manager provides an effective method for providing environment-specific connection information. Using PowerShell commands, you can create new DSNs for users in an automated process.

We will now look at how to employ both a secrets file and Windows ODBC manager for controlling our output environment.

Using a secrets file or environment variable

A secrets file is a locally stored file holding the variables you want to use in your desktop development environment. The file will hold the connection information for the development environment, while on the server, you use the connection information for the production environment.

The process for using a secrets file requires the implementation of a custom macro. This macro provides the dynamic control for your output destination by updating the connection string based on the parameters you enter.

Using a file or environment variable to hold the parameters for your connection means this becomes an external dependency related to where you are running the workflow (on your local computer or from the server environment) and will deploy the data to the right environment.

There are two steps for creating the dynamic output. The first step is to create a macro that will update the target connection string. The following screenshot shows a simple batch macro that will update the table that is being written with a new table for production:

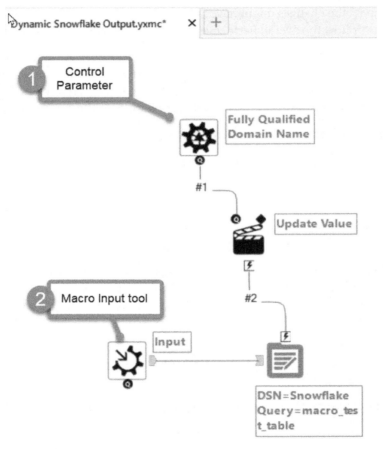

Figure 6.9 – A dynamic output macro that updates the output table

In this macro, the **Control Parameter** (number 1 in the preceding screenshot) updates the target table. When this new table name is a **Fully Qualified Domain Name** (**FQDN**), it includes the schema, database, and table information, allowing the environment to be defined in the parameter. The **Macro Input** tool is where our workflow dataset will pass the records that we want to publish to the database.

The second step is to import the secrets file or environment variable to be used in the control macro.

Reading the secrets file

Reading the secrets file is a process of reading a file that is isolated from the individual machine from where the workflow is being run. This file can be a simple CSV file that is placed in a secure, universal location on your machine, such as a `C:/Environments` folder that can also be replicated on the server. Once this file has been read into your workflow, you can perform any transformations required, such as concatenating separate schema, database, and table fields into a single FQDN that the macro is expecting. This implementation is seen in the following screenshot:

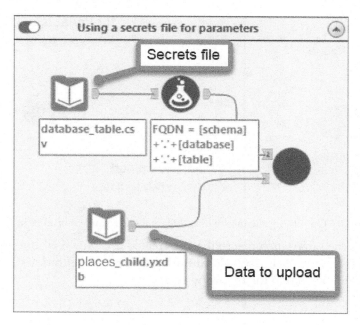

Figure 6.10 – Outputting a dataset with a dynamic macro and secrets file

In the screenshot, we have a secret file held as a CSV file that contains the target table information and is connected to the control parameter input. Our dataset is read into the workflow the same as in any other situation and connected to the macro input.

Importing environment secrets

We can define the output database destination in Windows environment variables. You find the environment variables in the **System Properties** > **Advanced** > **Environment Variables…** settings menu in your Windows operating system. These variables would need to be created in every instance where Alteryx is going to be run, but it allows for the same workflow to output to different locations depending on the environment where it is run. In this case, we would use a batch command or PowerShell script. This script could be static for the workflow or created dynamically, depending on your requirements.

The following screenshot shows an example of how to create and read the variables:

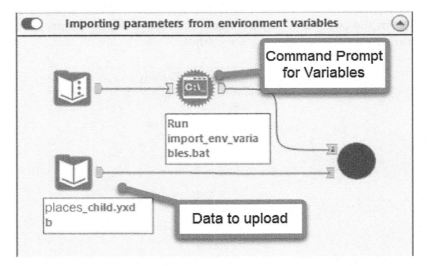

Figure 6.11 – Outputting a dataset with a dynamic macro and environment variables

The process uses the same batch macro that we created in *Figure 6.10*, but the control parameter field is created in the **Run Command** tool. The configuration of the Run Command tool can be seen in the following screenshot:

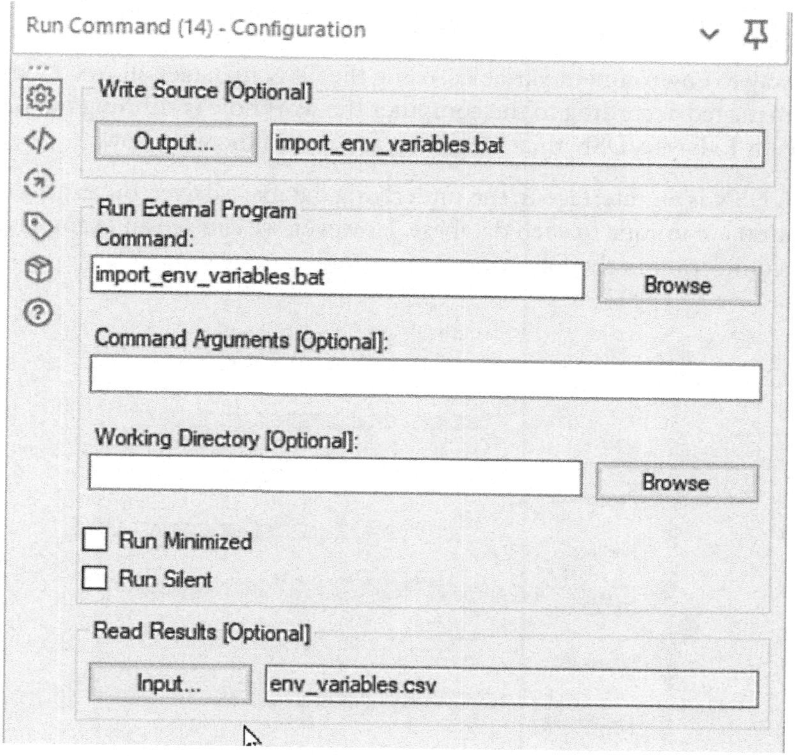

Figure 6.12 – Configuration of the Run Command tool to import the environment variables

In the screenshot, the batch file, import_env_variables.bat, is run from the containing folder. The result of the batch file is then read back into the Alteryx workflow from the env_variables.csv file that is created.

The script is the two-line command as follows:

```
echo "FDQN" > env_variables.csv
echo %SCHEMA%.%DATABASE%.%TABLE% >> env_variables.csv
```

This script first writes the field name FDQN to the env_variables.csv file. It then uses the echo command to append the SCHEMA, DATABASE, and TABLE variables to the same file. These variables would need to be defined before the Alteryx workflow is run.

Because the variables are defined on the computer where the workflow is being run, Alteryx server can use a different production server. These variables can also be applied to the server host as part of a bootstrap script in cloud environments or a maintenance script in desktop environments.

Creating a DSN in the Windows ODBC manager

In a similar way to environment variables, using the DSN manager allows the database target to be managed according to the computer the workflow is running on. Each computer needs to have a DSN matching what appears in the workflow.

Because each DSN is an interface to the underlying database driver, the exact details of its configuration are unique to each database. However, we can see an example of creating a Snowflake connection in the following screenshot:

Figure 6.13 – The Windows ODBC Snowflake driver creation window

In the screenshot, box **1** outlines the required inputs. These inputs are used to identify the server and to test the connection. In other applications, the user and password are also accessed from here. For Alteryx, the user and password are required as part of your workflow.

Box **2** shows the optional parameters specific to the Snowflake driver. These additional options all define the default connection parameters for the database, including what compute warehouse is used and what user role the connections are executed as. These options can all be modified in the Alteryx workflow when needed.

Once we have defined the connection properties allowing us to access our database, we can customize the connection to improve performance or functionality.

Getting the most from a connection

Once you have an output connection established, you can modify the connection properties to improve performance. This can be done in collaboration with your database administrator to get the best results, but an example of some tuning options can be seen in the Snowflake bulk load connection as follows:

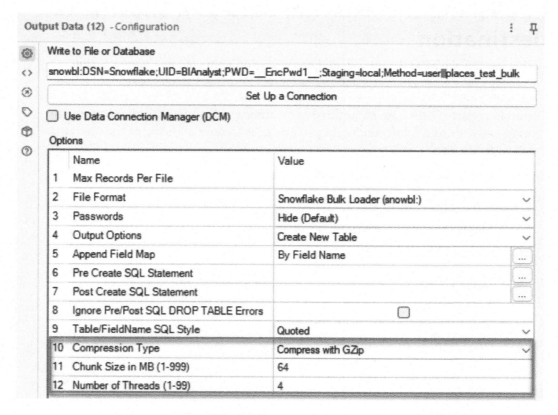

Figure 6.14 – A Snowflake bulk loader with tuning options highlighted

In the preceding screenshot, the final three options are highlighted as parameters that can be tuned to improve the performance of the output. In this case, the file is compressed, which might be inefficient for many moderate-sized uploads. You can also tune the chunk size and number of threads used for the upload process.

You also have the option of appending driver parameters directly to the connection. In this case, you would add the parameters in a key-value pair that is supported by the driver.

Now that we have an understanding of how we can manage output connections and we have seen the similarities they have to input connections, we can use them to upload our dataset into a database. In this example, I will use a Snowflake database for the connection. You can use any database that you are familiar with. The steps and process will be the same.

Publishing the external data to a Snowflake destination

In this section, we will take the places data that we downloaded in *Chapter 5*, *Data Processing and Transformations*, and upload it to a Snowflake database using the bulk loader. We chose a Snowflake account for two reasons. First, as a Premier Alteryx Technology partner, they are committed to creating and maintaining connections and tools to use with Alteryx. Secondly, they offer a trial account allowing anyone to try the database for free and have an account set up in minutes.

To achieve this, we will need to do the following:

- Ensure we have the drivers for our database installed.
- Configure the DSN connection.
- Configure the output bulk load options.

These three are all that we need to complete the upload of our places dataset.

Installing the drivers

The drivers for Snowflake can be found in two ways. The first way is from the Alteryx **Data Sources** page seen in the following screenshot and which can be found at the following URL: `https://help.alteryx.com/20214/designer/data-sources`. This page contains a listing of all the currently supported data sources. While you are not limited to these data sources and file formats, any connections outside this list would require the creation of custom connectors.

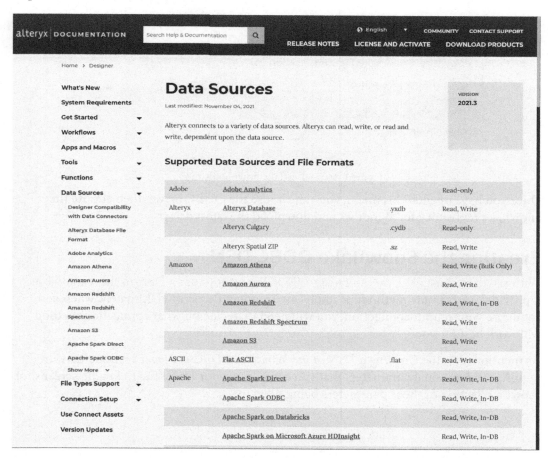

Figure 6.15 – A screenshot of the Alteryx Data Sources web page

Included in this list is the Snowflake connector. When you view the Snowflake details page, it includes a link to the drivers. The second way is to download the driver directly from your Snowflake account. In the top-right corner of the page, once you have logged in to your Snowflake instance, you can select the **Help** menu and check the downloads. This is shown in the following screenshot:

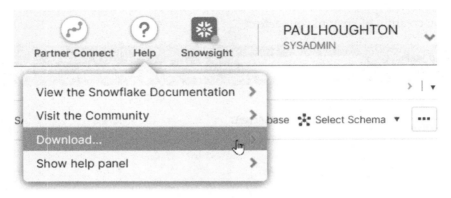

Figure 6.16 – Snowflake downloads menu

Once you have opened this menu, you can choose the ODBC driver, then choose the Snowflake repository for Windows and download the latest driver.

Creating the Snowflake ODBC DSN

With the driver installed, we can create a DSN. We want to use a DSN in this example as it provides an example method for multi-environment decisions. Ultimately, when you configure your output connection, you will need to decide on what connection method will work best for you.

As mentioned in the *Creating a DSN in the Windows ODBC manager* section, there are required and optional parameters that you can add to your DSN. The following screenshot shows a selection of those parameters being filled in:

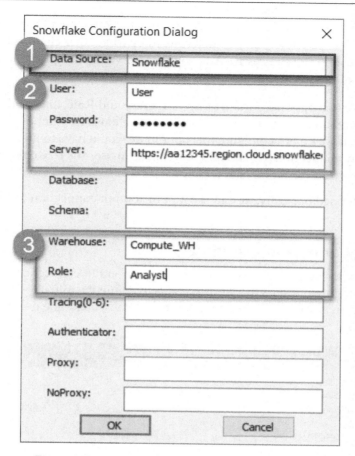

Figure 6.17 – An example DSN in a Snowflake database

In this example, box **1** is the DSN, Snowflake; this is what we will refer to the connection as in Alteryx. When we publish this workflow to our Alteryx server, this DSN name will also need to exist on the server in order for the workflow to run.

In box **2**, we have configured the **User** and **Password** parameters with our login details. The server is the URL you would sign in to when interacting with Snowflake from the browser. The URL is in the format https://aa12345.region.cloud. snowflakecomputing.com/.

In this format, the parts that will change are the following:

- aa12345: This is the account identifier for your Snowflake instance.

- region: When you were configuring your Snowflake account, your account owner decided on the cloud region where your data would be held.

- `cloud`: This is the cloud provider you decided to use as the infrastructure provider. This decision is usually determined by what other cloud resources you might be using. The choices are Amazon Web Services, Google Cloud Platform, or Microsoft Azure.

In box **3**, we have two optional parameters, **Warehouse** and **Role**, that we decided to configure. The warehouse option is what compute warehouse we want our workflows to default to using. If we do not configure this option, we would have to include a preSQL statement on any connection to define the warehouse to use. The role option allows us to decide what Snowflake permissions role to use.

Once we have defined our DSN, we can use it in the output connection tools and save our data source.

Configuring our bulk load output

The final step in our output process is to configure our output connection. There are two steps to configure our bulk loader. The first is to define the initial connection. In the following screenshot, we add our configuration details, including our user and password details.

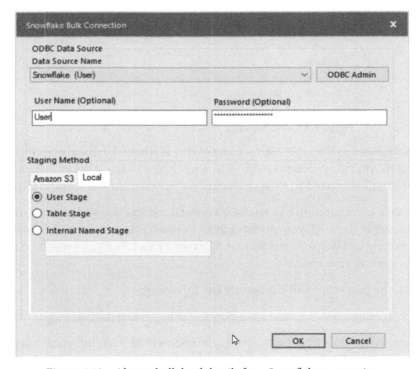

Figure 6.18 – Alteryx bulk load details for a Snowflake connection

We also need to define the staging method. The staging method is where the temporary CSV file is uploaded before being imported into a table. Every user gets access to **User Stage**. This is an upload location specifically for your user. You also have the option of using a customized stage or a stage associated with your cloud provider.

The second stage is to make customizations to the upload process. In the following screenshot, the annotation **1**'s box shows customizations related to the table that is created while the annotation **2**'s box highlights the customizations for the file to be uploaded:

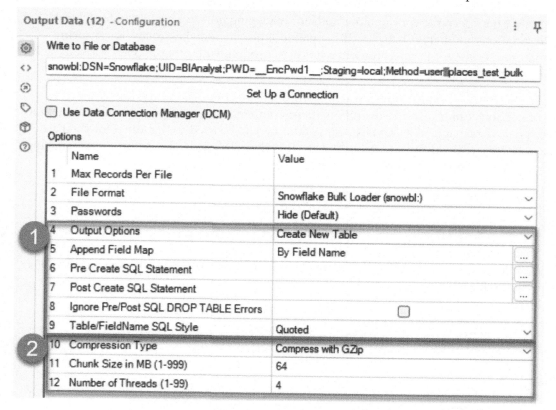

Figure 6.19 – Alteryx bulk load connection customizations for a Snowflake connection

In this example, box **1** defines how we will write the records to Snowflake. Because we are creating our initial table, the **Create New Table** option is appropriate for our connection. If we wanted to use this workflow as a scheduled process, trying to create a new table would error in each subsequent run.

Box **2** shows the optional configurations we can apply. Using these options, we customize the connection for any performance gains. Deciding on what changes to make and keep would require optimization testing. However, in most situations, the default settings would not need to be changed as the gains would be minimal.

Summary

In this chapter, we have investigated several methods for saving our datasets for future use. We have seen the common methods for managing how to save files to both local destinations and network drives. These methods also included a process for ensuring that the workflow will not error when it is either shared with other people or saved to an Alteryx server.

We also investigated methods for managing database connections and how those connections can be used across different environments. We saw how the different methods of variable management and DNS connections could be used so that different databases can be targeted in different environments. This ability is especially useful when managing separate development and production environments.

Finally, we implemented these principles to save our places dataset to a Snowflake database table. We implemented the DSN connection so that when publishing to our server, a separate destination can be used in production.

The next chapter will investigate how we can extract value out of our datasets with Alteryx. We will see how we can complete analytic investigations and present those investigations in repeatable reports.

7
Extracting Value

In previous chapters, we developed a data pipeline to collect datasets from external locations and transform them into a data source to extract organizational value. However, we have not yet attempted to gain any insight or leverage the advanced analytical capabilities that Alteryx provides.

This chapter will help you to enhance your knowledge of how to complete an **exploratory data analysis** (**EDA**) process. This process involves a common set of investigative methods that are also used in other analytic projects.

We will also learn the skills required to build reproducible reports. We will assemble the text, visual, and context components required for an Alteryx report. With the components available, we will compose a report layout and render the report for our end users.

We will cover the following topics in this chapter:

- Exploratory data analysis in Alteryx and surfacing the datasets for BI tools
- Using Alteryx to deliver standard reports

In these topics, we will cover how to get analytic insights directly out of an Alteryx workflow. We will also see how we can leverage the Alteryx Server gallery to provide automated insights and extract these insights in an automated manner.

Technical requirements

In this chapter, you will need access to Alteryx Designer for creating workflows. We will also see how to output to other BI tools, such as **Tableau** and **PowerBI**. This output is not core to the Alteryx experience, but can extend the capabilities into an interactive visual analysis platform. You can find the example workflows in the book's GitHub repository here: `https://github.com/PacktPublishing/Data-Engineering-with-Alteryx/tree/main/Chapter%2007`.

Finally, the datasets we will be using for this section are all part of the Alteryx install. You can find them in the Alteryx sample data folder. By default, it is located at `C:\Program Files\Alteryx\Samples\data`.

The other way to find the folder location is by navigating to the **Help** option in the menu bar of Alteryx and clicking on **Sample Datasets**, which you can see in the following screenshot:

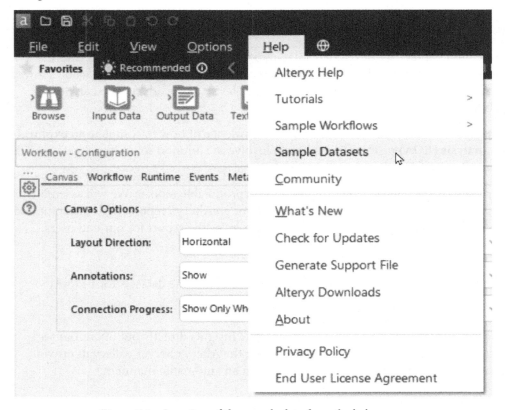

Figure 7.1 – Location of the sample data from the help menu

Let's get started!

Exploratory data analysis in Alteryx and surfacing the datasets for BI tools

To extract value from your dataset, you need to perform **Exploratory Data Analysis (EDA)**. EDA is the process of finding patterns and anomalies in your dataset. It is also a method for testing any assumptions or hypotheses you may have. Typically, you will create visualizations to find the insight and confirm the assumptions and hypotheses. You can also create statistical summary tables to get an overview and general understanding of the metrics in your data.

A general process for EDA would cover the following areas:

- Identifying whether any fields are missing values and summarizing their properties
- Understanding the distribution of the fields in your dataset
- Finding any significant relationships between fields in your dataset
- Searching for any outlier values in your dataset

Each of these steps will explain what your data represents and provide a strong starting position for further analysis. Such advanced analysis is often performed in Alteryx, but you can also use other visualization tools to develop additional interactive dashboards and reports.

Identifying missing values and summarizing fields

Missing values in your dataset are an essential element to analyze. They can represent a potential issue in your data collection process or, when preparing your data for further machine learning, they can skew your modeling.

In *Chapter 5, Data Processing and Transformations,* one of the profiling steps involved checking for null values and correcting those values with imputation. In this chapter, rather than updating the values, we will summarize what fields contain missing entries. This summary information provides us with the context of how many `nulls` are present in our dataset that allow for informed decisions about the impact of `nulls` to be made.

The example dataset with null values is the `CalgaryLoadSampleData.yxdb` dataset from the sample data folder. We can create a simple workflow, as seen in the following figure, in which we use this sample file with the **Basic Data Profile** tool.

Figure 7.2 – A workflow for investigating the Basic Data Profile tool results

We can identify fields with null values using the **Basic Data Profile** tool. You can locate the **Basic Data Profile** tool by navigating to the **Data Investigation** tab of the tool palette. This tool provides basic summary information about the field contents. The summary reflects the data type, so a string field has string summary information, such as field lengths and the most common value. In contrast, numeric fields have summary information such as mean and percentile values.

One summary detail in common for all fields is the count of nulls and non-null values. We can use this information to identify which columns have a significant proportion of missing values and decide how to process these columns.

Basic Data Profile requires no configuration. It will take the data stream you provide and generate the profile. The output of the basic data profile is a list with three columns, which we can see in the following screenshot:

Record	FieldName	Name	Value
1	CONAME	Name	CONAME
2	CONAME	Data Type	V_String
3	CONAME	Size	254
4	CONAME	Source	File: W:\Products\AlteryxSource\RuntimeData\Sa...
5	CONAME	Description	[Null]
6	CONAME	OKs	1500
7	CONAME	Nulls	0
8	CONAME	Non-Nulls	1500
9	CONAME	Blanks	0
10	CONAME	Values with Leading Whitespace	0
11	CONAME	Values with Trailing Whitespace	0
12	CONAME	Values with Both Whitespace	0
13	CONAME	Average Length	19.9
14	CONAME	Longest Length	30
15	CONAME	Longest Value	FORENSIC FINANCIAL INVESTIGTNS
16	CONAME	Shortest (Non Blank) Length	3
17	CONAME	Shortest Value	BTL
18	CONAME	Minimum	202 SUNOCO
19	CONAME	Maximum	ZERO MANUFACTURING
20	CONAME	Uniques	1471
21	CONAME	Unique Values	[Null]
22	ADDR	Name	ADDR
23	ADDR	Data Type	V_String
24	ADDR	Size	254

Figure 7.3 – A snippet of the Basic Data Profile output showing the results from the first field

The screenshot shows the three fields that are output from the data profile for the first column in our original dataset:

- **FieldName**: The name of the original column
- **Name**: The name of the summary output field
- **Value**: The contents of the summary information

The data profile information represents the most general summary information that you will need for EDA. The output structure from the basic data profile is shaped for use in Alteryx internal processes and can be leveraged by other analysis applications; however, we need to reshape the dataset for our current investigations and create a null profile and summarize fields.

We will explore the reshaping process by focusing on the null value analysis; the steps we undertake to reshape and prepare the data profile output will also apply to summarizing any other fields.

Reshaping the basic data profile

To reshape the dataset for our summary, we need to complete three steps:

1. Crosstab the dataset to create one row per **FieldName**.
2. Change the data type of the `Null` and `Non-Null` columns.
3. Create the null value proportion calculation.

These three steps will make the data structure required for our null profile.

We use the **Cross Tab** tool to pivot the data. In this tool, we need to set the following:

1. Which fields we want to group
2. Which fields hold the headers and column values
3. What to do if there are duplicate values for a particular cell

The following screenshot shows the three configuration requirements. In the screenshot, you can see the highlighted step number:

Figure 7.4 – Configuration of the Cross Tab tool to reshape our data profile

We want to group our values according to the **FieldName** field, which represents the field names in our data profile for our reshaping. Then, the **Header** column is the **Name** field, which represents the names of the summary information. Finally, we populate the values for the new columns from the **Value** field.

The next step in our process is to change the record data types from string values to the most appropriate data type for each field.

Setting our data types

When we look at the **Metadata** output of the **Cross Tab** tool (this is found in the **Results** panel by clicking the **Metadata** button in the top-right corner of the window), shown in the following screenshot, every column is a V_WString field. The single data type is because the **Basic Data Profile** tool compresses information into text summaries.

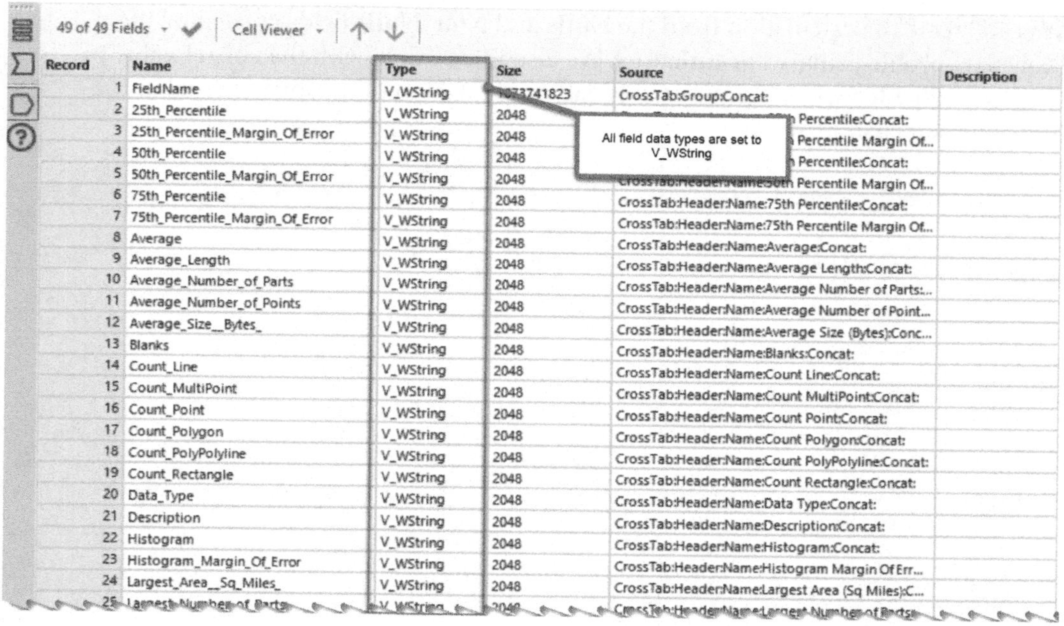

Record	Name	Type	Size	Source	Description
1	FieldName	V_WString	1073741823	CrossTab:Group:Concat:	
2	25th_Percentile	V_WString	2048	Percentile:Concat:	
3	25th_Percentile_Margin_Of_Error	V_WString	2048	Percentile Margin Of...	
4	50th_Percentile	V_WString	2048	Percentile:Concat:	
5	50th_Percentile_Margin_Of_Error	V_WString	2048	CrossTab:Header:Name:50th Percentile Margin Of...	
6	75th_Percentile	V_WString	2048	CrossTab:Header:Name:75th Percentile:Concat:	
7	75th_Percentile_Margin_Of_Error	V_WString	2048	CrossTab:Header:Name:75th Percentile Margin Of...	
8	Average	V_WString	2048	CrossTab:Header:Name:Average:Concat:	
9	Average_Length	V_WString	2048	CrossTab:Header:Name:Average Length:Concat:	
10	Average_Number_of_Parts	V_WString	2048	CrossTab:Header:Name:Average Number of Parts:...	
11	Average_Number_of_Points	V_WString	2048	CrossTab:Header:Name:Average Number of Point...	
12	Average_Size__Bytes_	V_WString	2048	CrossTab:Header:Name:Average Size (Bytes):Conc...	
13	Blanks	V_WString	2048	CrossTab:Header:Name:Blanks:Concat:	
14	Count_Line	V_WString	2048	CrossTab:Header:Name:Count Line:Concat:	
15	Count_MultiPoint	V_WString	2048	CrossTab:Header:Name:Count MultiPoint:Concat:	
16	Count_Point	V_WString	2048	CrossTab:Header:Name:Count Point:Concat:	
17	Count_Polygon	V_WString	2048	CrossTab:Header:Name:Count Polygon:Concat:	
18	Count_PolyPolyline	V_WString	2048	CrossTab:Header:Name:Count PolyPolyline:Concat:	
19	Count_Rectangle	V_WString	2048	CrossTab:Header:Name:Count Rectangle:Concat:	
20	Data_Type	V_WString	2048	CrossTab:Header:Name:Data Type:Concat:	
21	Description	V_WString	2048	CrossTab:Header:Name:Description:Concat:	
22	Histogram	V_WString	2048	CrossTab:Header:Name:Histogram:Concat:	
23	Histogram_Margin_Of_Error	V_WString	2048	CrossTab:Header:Name:Histogram Margin Of Err...	
24	Largest_Area__Sq_Miles_	V_WString	2048	CrossTab:Header:Name:Largest Area (Sq Miles):C...	
25	Largest_Number_of_Parts	V_WString	2048	CrossTab:Header:Name:Largest Number of Parts:...	

All field data types are set to V_WString

Figure 7.5 – Metadata output from the Cross Tab tool

We need to change the data to make these fields useful for analysis. We can do this manually using a select tool, and it is probably the best option for modifying one or two fields. To make all of these fields useful, an **Auto Field** tool (which we first used in *Chapter 5, Data Processing and Transformations*) is most straightforward. This tool will update the data types for every string field (all columns in the example) and set it to the smallest field type possible. For example, the auto field output will update any field containing only numbers, such as our Nulls and Non Nulls counts, to a numeric field type that we can use to create our proportion column.

After running the **Auto Field** tool, we have reshaped our dataset to complete our summary analysis, and we can use this table for our summary field analysis.

Creating our Nulls proportion column

The next step in identifying the nulls is to calculate what proportion of the records are null values. Having nulls in your datasets can highlight issues in data collection or earlier processing. It can also cause errors when creating machine learning models or calculating analytic metrics.

We can create the calculation from the **Nulls** and **Non_Nulls** fields created by the basic data profile using a **Formula** tool. We also want a field with the cut-off value to automatically identify fields. We can see the configuration of the formula tool in the following screenshot:

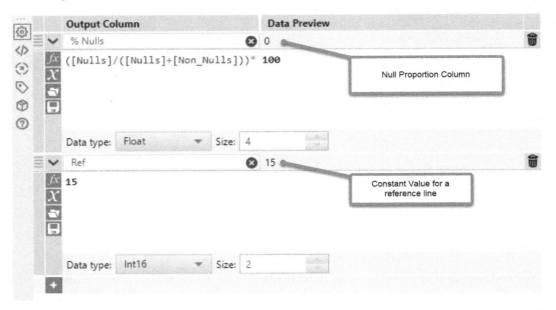

Figure 7.6 – Calculation for identifying the proportion of null values

We have created two new fields; the **% Nulls** field, which is the proportion of null values in a column, and the **Ref** field, which is a constant value that we have set for identifying columns with too many nulls. You can decide the **Ref** value based on your own dataset composition and the impact nulls will have on your analysis. In our example, we set this to **15** to highlight which fields are impacted by null values. The calculation we have used for calculating our proportion is as follows:

```
([Nulls] / ([Nulls] + [Non_Nulls])) * 100
```

This calculation is a standard proportion calculation and converted to a percentage. Therefore, we can use this calculation to identify the columns with high proportions of null values that we will need to process.

Seeing the Null proportions visually

Once we have created the Null proportions, we need to quickly identify which columns need to be processed to manage the null values. As we have already seen (*Chapter 5, Data Processing and Transformations*), we can replace the nulls with imputed values when they are a small proportion of our dataset. Alternatively, the field doesn't contain enough information for further analysis if there is a significant proportion of null values; therefore, we can remove it from our dataset.

One way to process these values is to use a cut-off calculation that checks whether the proportion of nulls is greater than a set proportion. In *Figure 7.6*, the **Ref** field was created and set to **15**. We can use this value to create a cut-off check between the proportion value and the reference:

```
[% Nulls] > [Ref]
```

This calculation check identifies any columns where the percentage of nulls is greater than the reference value. Using this check, we can isolate any columns that match that cut-off and process them, as covered in the *Correcting missing values by imputation* section of *Chapter 5, Data Processing and Transformations*.

Instead of creating a new field, we can create a visualization with the **Interactive Chart** tool from the **Reporting** tool pallet. We can see the **Interactive Chart** tool in the following diagram, and the configuration of the interactive chart is shown in *Figure 7.8*:

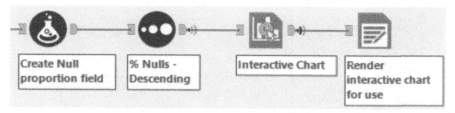

Figure 7.7 – The Interactive Chart tool as part of a workflow snippet

The **Interactive Chart** tool allows us to build a visualization by applying each metric we want to view as a new layer to the chart. Finally, we display these layers in either a **Browse** tool (which we first used in *Chapter 1, Getting Started with Alteryx*) or written to a file with the **Render** tool (which we will learn about in the *Using Alteryx to deliver standard reports* section).

Once we have added the interactive chart to our workflow, we can click on **Configure Chart** to configure the layers for that view. For example, the following screenshot shows the **Layer** configuration:

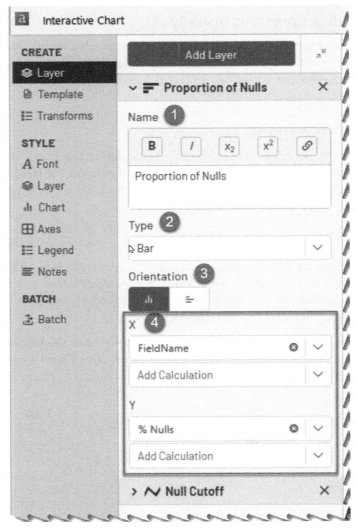

Figure 7.8 – Configuration of a layer in the Interactive Chart tool

When configuring the layers, there are four separate areas to configure. These have been marked in the preceding screenshot and match each list item below:

1. Setting the **Layer** name: This is the title of the layer and is what appears in the legend. It also helps identify the different layers when configuring the Interactive Chart tool. We have chosen the name `Proportion of Nulls`, as shown in the preceding screenshot.

2. Choosing the **Chart** type: You can decide on the chart type from the following options:

   - **Area**

   - **Bar** – This is the chart type selected in the screenshot.

   - **Box and Whisker**

   - **Heatmap**

   - **Line**

   - **Scatter**

   - **Pie**

3. Configuring the **Chart** type: They have slightly different configuration options for each unique chart type. For the bar chart in the screenshot, we can choose the orientation of the bars; we have selected vertical bars.

Choose the fields to fill out the chart: Finally, you need to select the fields that will appear in your chart. Depending on the chart type, you will have different choices for where fields appear. First, we identify the labels for each bar that will appear across the visualization for our bar chart. In this case, we have chosen the field name from the options created by the basic data profile. We have also chosen what field will populate the height of the bars using the `% Nulls` field that we created.

These steps will allow us to build a basic visualization to display in our view. When you run the workflow, the layers of the interactive chart tool are rendered based on the sorted order fed to the **Interactive Chart** tool. Therefore, if you want to have a specific sorting in your visualization, you will need to order your data with a **Sort** tool before the **Interactive Chart** tool. For example, to create a bar chart sorted in descending order, the largest value must be passed to the interactive chart first, followed by the next largest.

At this point, we have added a reference to our visualization by adding a layer. The reference line was added with a second layer to indicate the cut-off for the Null proportion and a title describing the visualization.

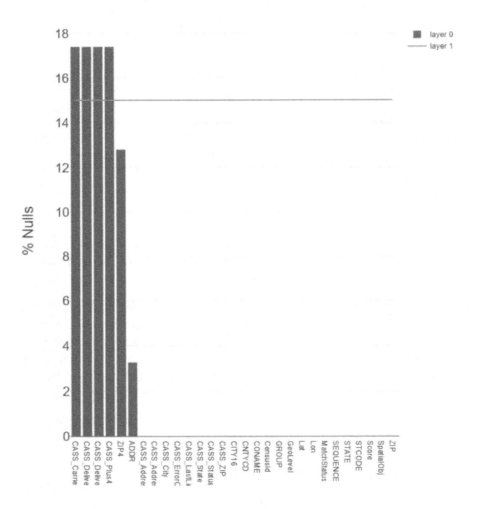

Figure 7.9 – Visualization of Null proportions

With the basic chart showing the null values, we can repeat the process to view the different summary metrics for the fields in our dataset. The profile tool creates different summary information for each data type.

The summary information for each data type is listed as follows:

- **Numeric**: Percentile values, percentile margin of error, average, minimum, maximum, sum, standard deviation, variation, histogram values
- **String**: Average length, longest value, shortest value, longest length, shortest non-blank length, maximum, minimum, values with leading or trailing whitespaces, or both leading and trailing whitespaces
- **DateTime**: Minimum, maximum, date histogram
- **Spatial**: Count of point, multipoint, polygon, line, polyline, and rectangle objects, the average number of points or paths, the average size in bytes, largest number of points or parts, largest size in bytes
- **All Data Types**: Nulls, non-nulls, unique values, and Oks, size, source

With this combination of summary information, we can build visualizations to show our field summary information and deliver it as a report.

Now that we understand the missing values and have explored the field summaries, we can examine the distribution of values and apply any normalization we might need to use.

Understanding your value distribution

Understanding the distribution of values becomes a crucial part of knowing your dataset and its applications. To investigate the relationship between values, we will be using the `HousingPricesTestData.yxdb` dataset in the `SampleData` folder.

We start analyzing the value distribution with the **Field Summary** tool in the **Data Investigation** tab of the tool pallet, which you can see in the workflow snippet in *Figure 7.10*:

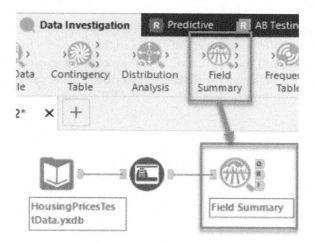

Figure 7.10 – A workflow snippet showing the Field Summary tool

This tool gives us the same summary information from the basic data profile and creates a series of histograms for each field. The following screenshot shows the interactive output report of the **Field Summary** tool:

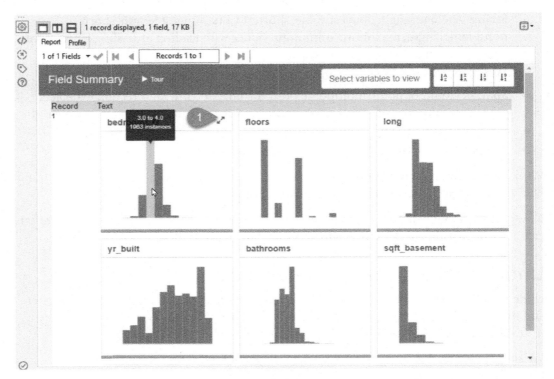

Figure 7.11 – The interactive output report from the Field Summary tool

In the preceding screenshot, there is a trellis of multiple small charts. This view gives us our first indication of the distribution of values in the form of a histogram. Each histogram is interactive, and the tooltip will show the counts for each bar band. Additionally, if you click on the expand button (indicated by the callout button labeled **1**), you can investigate the summary details for that field. The following screenshot shows the summary details:

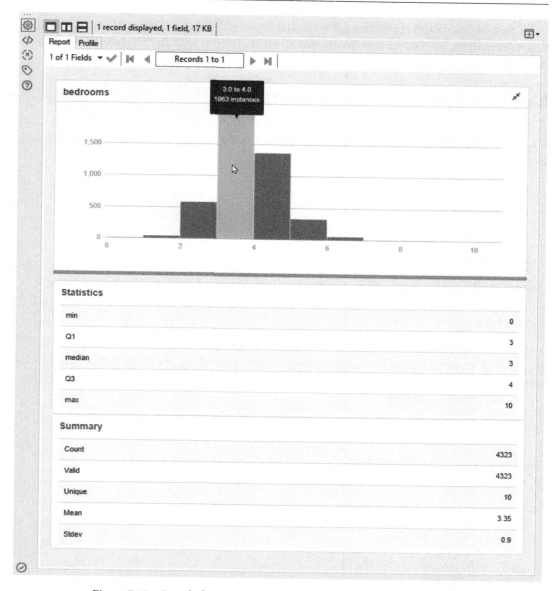

Figure 7.12 – Details for the bedrooms field from the Field Summary tool

With this summary detail, we can get an initial understanding of the distribution. Using this information, we can further investigate the distribution with the **Distribution Analysis** tool.

Running a distribution analysis check

A distribution analysis check tries to identify which distribution fits the data the best. Using the **Distribution Analysis** tool, Alteryx will apply four different distribution tests to the field:

- Normal
- Log-Normal
- Weibull
- Gamma

The tool will return a report that overlays the distributions for the field selected, along with tables showing the goodness of fit, estimated quantiles, and distribution parameters for the field.

We can run the distribution analysis on the **sqft_living** field from the `HousingPricesTestData.yxdb` dataset. After converting the field from a string to an integer with the Select tool (as we saw in *Chapter 5, Data Processing and Transformations*), we get the following output:

Distribution Analysis of sqft_living

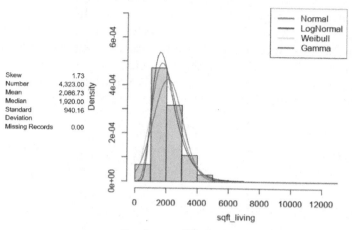

Skew 1.73
Number 4,323.00
Mean 2,086.73
Median 1,920.00
Standard Deviation 940.16
Missing Records 0.00

Goodness-of-Fit Statistics

Type	Test	Statistic	Significance
Normal	Anderson-Darling	1.#INF	< 0.005
LogNormal	Anderson-Darling	0.576	0.1395
Weibull	Anderson-Darling	1.#INF	< 0.01

Type	Test	Statistic	Significance
Normal	Chi-Square	766.173	0
LogNormal	Chi-Square	37.395	0.6731
Gamma	Chi-Square	102.040	0
Weibull	Chi-Square	445.861	0

Type	Test	Statistic	Significance
Normal	Cramer-von Mises	11.656	< 0.005
LogNormal	Cramer-von Mises	0.083	0.198
Weibull	Cramer-von Mises	6.853	< 0.01

Type	Test	Statistic	Significance
Normal	Kolmogorov-Smirnov	0.080	> 0.15
LogNormal	Kolmogorov-Smirnov	0.012	> 0.15

The Chi-Square Significance value is the strongest indicator that a distribution is a good fit. With a value >0.05, the data may likely fit the distribution. The higher the significance the better the distribution fit.

Estimated Quantiles

n	var.quant	estvar1	estlogvar1	estweibvar1	estgamvar1
1%	720	-100	708	320	594
5%	940	540	946	648	882
10%	1,090	882	1,105	886	1,071
25%	1,420	1,453	1,430	1,370	1,449
50%	1,920	2,087	1,906	2,006	1,965
75%	2,540	2,721	2,539	2,710	2,593
90%	3,280	3,292	3,288	3,377	3,259
95%	3,749	3,633	3,837	3,785	3,706
99%	5,040	4,274	5,129	4,561	4,644

Distribution Parameters

Type	Mean	Std Dev	Threshold	Scale	Shape
Normal	2,086.726	940.165	0	0.000	0.000
LogNormal	2,083.897	931.198	0	7.553	0.426
Gamma	2,089.262	878.132	0	368.125	5.669
Weibull	2,083.709	958.486	0	2,351.531	2.305

Figure 7.13 – Distribution Analysis output for the sqft_living field

Using this analysis in our dataset, we can see the bathrooms overlaid with the distribution types. We can determine which distribution type fits our dataset best by looking at the **Goodness-of-Fit Statistics**, magnified in the following screenshot. When we focus on the chi-square values, we see a chi-square statistic of **766** for the normal distribution. This high value indicates that the **sqft_living** field values are not normally distributed. We see a similar situation when looking at the Gamma and Weibull distributions. Finally, checking the Log-Normal distribution, we have a statistic of **37**, a much lower value, indicating that this is the distribution we should use.

Goodness-of-Fit Statistics

Type	Test	Statistic	Significance
Normal	Anderson-Darling	1.#INF	< 0.005
LogNormal	Anderson-Darling	0.576	0.1395
Weibull	Anderson-Darling	1.#INF	< 0.01
Type	Test	Statistic	Significance
Normal	Chi-Square	766.173	0
LogNormal	Chi-Square	37.395	0.6731
Gamma	Chi-Square	102.040	0
Weibull	Chi-Square	445.861	0
Type	Test	Statistic	Significance
Normal	Cramer-von Mises	11.656	< 0.005
LogNormal	Cramer-von Mises	0.083	0.198
Weibull	Cramer-von Mises	6.853	< 0.01
Type	Test	Statistic	Significance
Normal	Kolmogorov-Smirnov	0.080	> 0.15
LogNormal	Kolmogorov-Smirnov	0.012	> 0.15

The Chi-Square Significance value is the strongest indicator that a distribution is a good fit. With a value >0.05, the data may likely fit the distribution. The higher the significance the better the distribution fit.

Figure 7.14 – A magnification of the Goodness-of-Fit Statistics from the distribution analysis

To transform the **sqft_living** field into a log-normal field, we need to create a formula for the transformation. Using the following formula:

```
Log([sqft_living])
```

Alteryx will apply the natural log to the **sqft_living** field. Then, we can check it for normality using this transformed field by running a second distribution analysis on that field. Following the transformation, the Normal distribution statistic is **37**, and the significance is **0.67**, showing we have transformed the field to a normal distribution.

We can now repeat this process for any other field to understand the distribution. Depending on the application for which we want to use our dataset, there may be relationships between fields that we can account for and reduce the number of fields we are analyzing. Let's understand this in the following section.

Finding relationships between fields

When we have many fields in a dataset, relationships between fields may be identified where the behavior of one value is very similar to another. Finding these similarities in multiple fields can add complexity to your dataset without additional information for analysis or machine learning.

These relationships might allow us to reduce the complexity in our dataset with **dimensionality reduction**. The relationships might represent a causal relationship that requires investigation to identify which factors we can change to achieve specific results.

Identifying the relationships between fields is achieved with the **Association Analysis** tool (shown in the following figure). This tool will apply **Measure of association** between all selected fields and produce a report (both interactive and static) for viewing the relationships.

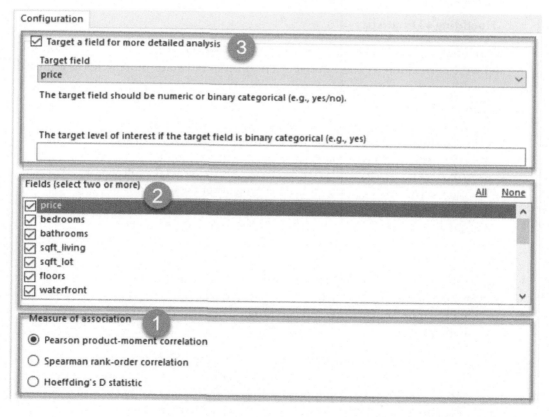

Figure 7.15 – Configuration of the association analysis tool

The preceding screenshot shows the configuration of the association analysis tool. The configuration has three sections:

1. **Correlation type**: The correlation type is the algorithm that is used to determine the relationship between the fields. Three different correlation types can be applied and will provide different insights based on the particulars of your dataset. The most common association is the Pearson product-moment and this will result in something between a positive and a negative number. A positive number indicates a positive correlation (when one value increases, the other also tends to increase). In contrast, negative numbers show a negative correlation. The three options for the correlation are as follows:

   - **Pearson product-moment correlation**
   - **Spearman rank-order correlation**
   - **Hoeffding's D statistic**

2. **Which fields to compare**: The second section allows you to choose which fields to apply the correlation to. You can select a minimum of two or more fields as required.

   > **Common Error Note**
   >
   > If you have enabled the **Alteryx Multithreaded Processing (AMP)** engine in the **Workflow – Configuration | Runtime** menu, you will see an error from the association analysis tool. The error : `Internal Error in RecordReader::ReadFields: Too many fields` will appear. You can resolve this by turning off the AMP engine for the workflow.
   >
   > It is advised to use a separate workflow for the association analysis so that the performance benefits of the AMP engine can still be used for all other processes.

3. **Optional detailed summary for a specific field**: The final configuration is to choose a particular field for detailed analysis. This field is often a target variable for machine learning applications and can provide detailed insights between that target and all other fields.

Once you have configured the association analysis tool, you will create two reports. The first is a static report recording the dataset associations and looking up specific associations. The second report is an interactive view where you can investigate areas with a strong relationship and immediately view the associated scatter plot (shown below).

Correlation Matrix with ScatterPlot

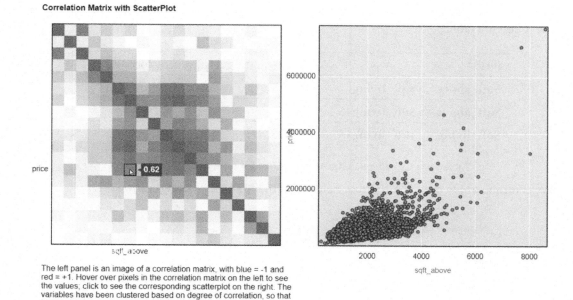

The left panel is an image of a correlation matrix, with blue = -1 and red = +1. Hover over pixels in the correlation matrix on the left to see the values; click to see the corresponding scatterplot on the right. The variables have been clustered based on degree of correlation, so that highly correlated variables appear adjacent to each other.

Figure 7.16 – Association analysis output with the relationship between Price and sqft_above selected

The interactive output shows a correlation matrix where positive numbers are red and negative numbers are blue. The darker the color is, the closer the value is to 1. When any specific value is selected, the visualization on the right will populate a scatter plot for that correlation point. For example, the figure shows the scatter plot when the **Price** and **sqft_above** fields are selected.

Applying dimensionality reduction

We can reduce dimensionality to simplify the dataset for machine learning applications with the association fields found. Alteryx has a **Principal Component Analysis (PCA)** tool, which identifies the principal components between selected fields and outputs the number of principal components selected. Using this tool, we can reduce the complexity of our dataset, shown in terms of the number of fields, without reducing the richness of the data contained in the dataset.

From our association analysis, we can see a strong association between the fields shown in the following table:

Field	Person product-moment correlation
Sqft_above <> sqft_living	0.88
Sqft_above <> sqft_living15	0.74
Sqft_living <> sqft_living15	0.75

Table 7.1 – Closely related fields identified for dimensionality reduction

We can then apply the PCA to these fields with the following configuration:

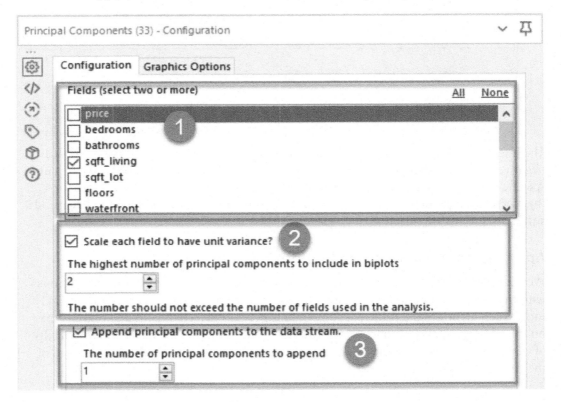

Figure 7.17 – PCA tool configuration

This tool can produce the PCA for the fields selected in area one. These fields are the three we have identified in our association analysis.

Next, we can choose the scaling and biplot options. The scaling configuration will transform the values to the same range. This scaling removes any skewing of the output results caused by any field's absolute value being different from the others.

Finally, we can choose how many principal components to append to the final output. When we look at **Scree Plot of the Component Variances** from the PCA report output (refer to the following diagram), most of the variation is contained in principal component one for this combination of fields. With this insight, we can consolidate the information from the three fields into a single principal component.

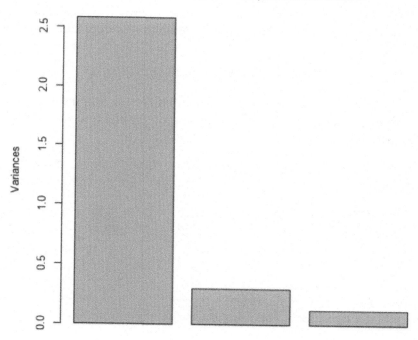

Figure 7.18 – PCA scree plot of component variances

We can continue to identify relationships between different fields and process them into other components where appropriate. In addition, we can reduce the number of columns in our dataset through this process, allowing machine learning processes to be more straightforward in future steps.

Identifying any outliers in the dataset

Now that we have an understanding of the relationships between fields, we can look at the values within fields to identify any outlier values. An outlier is a value that is an extreme distance from all the other values in the field. The extreme nature of outliers means they are not representative of the dataset and, when used in analyses, can skew statistical calculations such as the mean.

There are many different ways to define an outlier, and this can be done either visually using box plots or scatter plots. Alternatively, you can apply a formula and create a flag appended to each record.

We want to start with a programmatic method to identify whether a value is an outlier for our dataset. The identifier we will apply is the **Median Absolute Deviation (MAD)**, calculated as follows:

$$MAD = median\ (|Y_i - median\ (Y_i)|)$$

This formula calculates the median of the values and then finds the absolute median deviation between the value and the overall median. We created this calculation with the following workflow snippet:

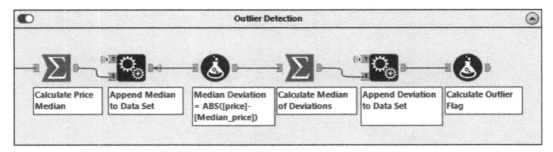

Figure 7.19 – Workflow snippet to identify price outliers

This snippet has six steps:

1. Calculate the overall median with a summarize tool.

2. Append the median back to the primary data stream.

3. For each record, calculate the MAD with the formula tool and the Alteryx formula:

   ```
   Abs(Yi - median(Yi))
   ```

4. Take the average of the MADs to set the variation.

5. Append the MAD that we calculated in *step 4* to the dataset created from *step 2*.

6. Create your outlier flag using the following formula:

```
[Price] > [Median Price] + ([MAD] * x) OR
[Price] < [Median Price] - ([MAD] * x)
```

In this calculation, `[Price]` is the original price field, `[Median Price]` was calculated in *step 1*, `[MAD]` is the median deviation calculated in *step 4*, and *x* is an adjustment constant that accounts for the distribution in your data.

For the example, we set the adjustment value *x* to be 3.5, which resulted in the following table:

5 of 24 Fields | Cell Viewer | 4,323 records displayed

Record	id	price	Median_price	MAD	Outlier
1	7237550310	1,225,000	445,000	145,500	True
2	1321400060	257,500	445,000	145,500	False
3	1175000570	530,000	445,000	145,500	False
4	5101402488	438,000	445,000	145,500	False
5	8562750320	580,500	445,000	145,500	False
6	0461000390	687,500	445,000	145,500	False
7	7231300125	345,000	445,000	145,500	False
8	7518505990	600,000	445,000	145,500	False
9	4217401195	920,000	445,000	145,500	False
10	1516000055	650,000	445,000	145,500	False
11	9558200045	289,000	445,000	145,500	False
12	1189001180	425,000	445,000	145,500	False
13	1274500060	204,000	445,000	145,500	False
14	1802000060	1,325,000	445,000	145,500	True
15	5104520400	390,000	445,000	145,500	False
16	2599001200	305,000	445,000	145,500	False
17	1332700270	215,000	445,000	145,500	False
18	3422049190	247,500	445,000	145,500	False
19	5200100125	555,000	445,000	145,500	False
20	7214720075	699,950	445,000	145,500	False
21	3134100116	470,000	445,000	145,500	False
22	8732020310	260,000	445,000	145,500	False
23	2331300505	822,500	445,000	145,500	False
24	7853210060	430,000	445,000	145,500	False

Figure 7.20 – Outlier detection results using the MAD calculation

In the screenshot, we see the columns we have created, **Median_price** and **MAD**, to build the **Outlier** column.

Understanding the difference between the Interactive Chart tool and the Insights tool

Alteryx has two tools for creating visualizations. We have used the **Interactive Chart** tool from the **Reporting** tab of the tool pallet to build a simple visualization for analysis. A second tool called the **Insights** tool allows you to make an entire dashboard for reporting on Alteryx Server.

To use the Insights tool, you will feed the dataset you have created, with all the details you want to see, in a single stream of data. You can then create multiple independent visualizations with the same layering process from the Interactive Chart tool.

Finally, you can add context with the text modules and add universal filters that will apply to all charts that you have added to the Insights tool.

The Insights tool is an excellent addition for creating monitoring dashboards. In *Chapter 10, Monitoring DataOps and Managing Changes*, we will create an insights dashboard for monitoring the datasets as they arrive. We will also build an insights view for the Alteryx Server processes to monitor system health.

Making our datasets available for other BI tools

When we created and processed our datasets in *Chapter 6, Destination Management*, we discussed the different output methods of files and databases. For others leveraging the analytical capabilities of Alteryx in other **Business Intelligence** (**BI**) applications, they can directly access the files that we have created.

When we save a dataset to a database such as Snowflake, the external BI applications can ingest these datasets directly. Alternatively, outputting a local file, such as CSV or XLSX, can be used directly for local processing.

Certain BI tools, such as Tableau, have their own proprietary data format that requires specific processes for creating a dataset. For example, the Hyper file type that Tableau uses has an **Extract API** for interacting with those files. Alteryx has implemented access to these file types directly into the **Output** tool save options in these applications, which you can see in the following screenshot:

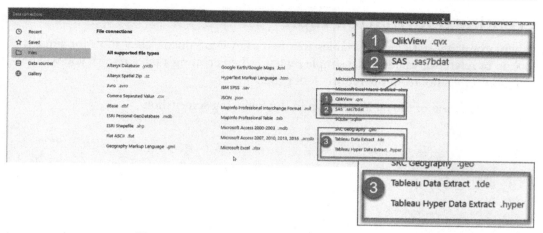

Figure 7.21 – External BI application output file types

The highlighted options 1, 2, and 3, are for **QlikView**, **SAS**, and **Tableau**, respectively. This integration allows you to leverage the best of Alteryx for your analytics and the BI tool for visualization.

Now that we have an understanding of how to undertake exploratory data analysis, we can further leverage the power of Alteryx with spatial capabilities.

Using Alteryx to deliver standard reports

When building reports in Alteryx, you can create and configure the individual reporting components, like a table, chart, or text block, and then combine them into a single layout to render to output.

In this section, we will discuss the following topics:

- Creating a formatted table
- Adding visualizations to the report
- Adding styling to the report
- Outputting the report for consumption

These individual pieces will show how we can build the parts for our report. Then, of course, we can add additional reporting pieces, such as maps or screenshots, but the process will be the same. There will be some tool-to-tool variation, but the logic will remain.

Creating a formatted table

When producing static reports, tables are often a key component. They allow for a quick lookup of reference values and a simple review. When creating a table report, you will be using the *Table* tool from the reports tool pallet.

The configuration of the table is shown in the following screenshot:

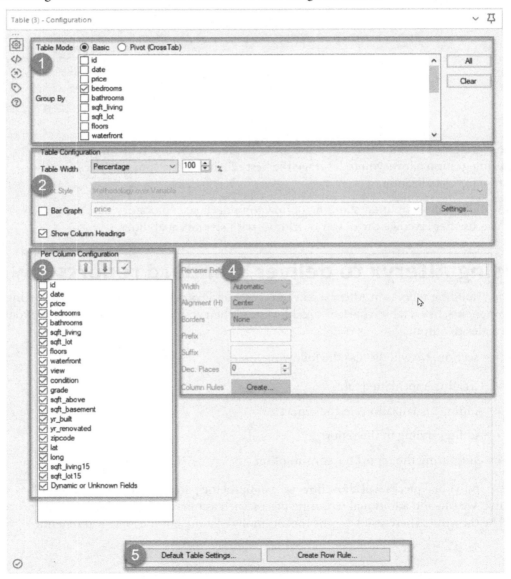

Figure 7.22 – The configuration options for the Table tool

In the screenshot, there are five areas where you need to configure the Table tool:

1. **The Table Mode and grouping**: The table mode defines the creation of a basic or pivot table. You will typically produce a basic table from most data streams. However, you can build a pivot table if you have taken a data stream from a cross tab tool. The main difference between a pivot table and a basic table is the fact that in a pivot table, the new headers will not be selectable for grouping, and the prefixes from the cross tab aggregations are cleansed from the titles.

2. **The table configuration**: In this section, you configure the output of the table. The **Table Width** selection lets you define the width of each grouping selection and whether it will change across each group. The **Bar Graph** option enables you to add a column that contains a bar indicator showing the proportionate size of the field selected.

3. **Column choice configuration**: The Column choice configuration manages which columns are output into your table. You are also able to reorder the columns for your final result.

4. **Column formatting**: This section allows you to define the default formatting for each column. Additionally, you can add a column rule, which will apply conditional formatting to that particular column. By default, a column rule will override any other table defaults and conditional formatting you apply.

5. **The record and table defaults**: The record and table defaults allow you to apply overall formatting to your table and complete rows. For example, if you have a cell with conflicting row and column rules, you can optionally define the row rule to overwrite a column rule.

The tool will create a record for each group in the table group with the configuration created. The output data type is a report type (seen in blue text in the results window) and needs to be rendered by a Browse tool to view the result. You can repeat this process on each table you create and each combination report component you need.

Adding visualizations to the report

In the *Identifying missing values and summarizing fields* section, we discussed creating visualizations with the Interactive Chart tool. The charts created typically assume you will want to interact with them when exploring their content. This interaction isn't always required, and you can design the chart so that it isn't needed. When no interaction is necessary, you can use the output in a report stream to add additional context to your report.

The method for creating the chart is the same as what was explained in the *Seeing the Null proportions visually* section. The advance in this process is to match the grouping you are trying to apply to your report. For example, we have created a series of tables based on table size. We want to have a visual that would provide the same context information.

To achieve this grouping in a chart, you need to **batch** your visualization. For example, the batch menu in the following screenshot shows two sections once the batching option is selected. To find the menu, you will choose the **Batch** button (highlighted as 1), and then toggle the **BATCHED CHARTS** option to **On** (highlight 2).

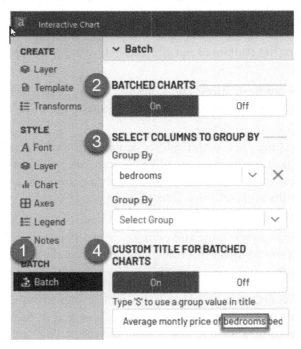

Figure 7.23 – The batching menu in the Interactive Chart tool

Once you have opened the batched charts menu, you get two new options:

- **SELECT COLUMNS TO GROUP BY**: This is how to define the grouping you want to apply to each chart. The combination of fields you select in this section will create a new chart for each unique combination of records selected.

- **CUSTOM TITLE FOR BATCHED CHARTS**: If selected, every chart will use the title added in this custom title. When using a custom title, typing $ will allow you to add a grouping field as a value placeholder. For example, the bedrooms entry in the box is a placeholder in the screenshot. It is worth knowing that the only time you see a placeholder is when you add the field.

With the batching option enabled, you will get one record per chart defined by the grouping. This means you can align your report records between the tables and the charts. We can then start adding the context and style for your report.

Adding styling to the report

You can add styling to your report by creating context fields with text or screenshots. Getting screenshots and text into your report is done with the **Text** tool and the **Screenshot** tool, respectively. An example of the text and screenshot is shown in *Figure 7.24*:

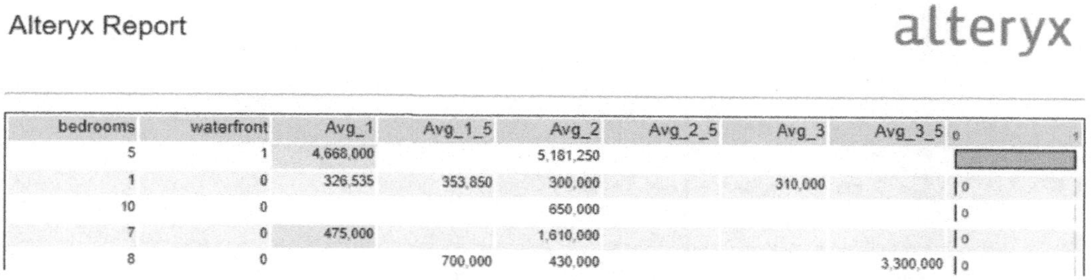

Alteryx Report   alteryx

bedrooms	waterfront	Avg_1	Avg_1_5	Avg_2	Avg_2_5	Avg_3	Avg_3_5	0	1
5	1	4,668,000		5,181,250					
1	0	326,535	353,850	300,000		310,000		0	
10	0			650,000				0	
7	0	475,000		1,610,000				0	
8	0		700,000	430,000			3,300,000	0	

Figure 7.24 – An example screenshot with header text and a logo

You can also add style to the report with a report header and report footer, which we will see in the *Adding headers and footers to your reports* section, later in this chapter.

Adding text to your reports

When you add text to your reports, you can create a new stream with the text you want to add. This new stream provides practical explanations or information text that do not require any specific information from your data to create. Alternatively, you can stream your dataset into the Text tool and provide those fields for use in the text you are crafting.

The following screenshot shows the configuration of the Text tool. The selections in block one allow you to define how to add your new text to your workflow. For example, you can add a new field or, if there is already a report field in your data stream, it can be attached to the existing field and positioned where you want it.

The second block is where you add the text copy and format it how you want. You can apply any text formatting you want, including color, size, or emphasis. You can also insert a field from your data stream using the **Available Fields** menu.

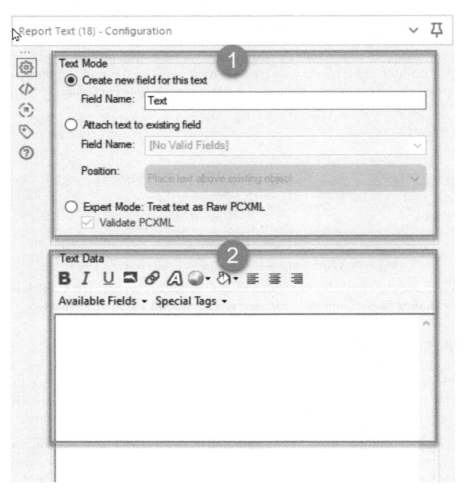

Figure 7.25 – A blank configuration for the Report Text tool

If you have fed a data stream into the Report Text tool, you will replicate the text you add for each record. If you have added a field to your text, the only part of it that will change is the value of the record that will be substituted.

Adding screenshots to your reports

Adding screenshots is usually achieved by creating a new field with the **Screenshot** report tool. This tool lets you use a screenshot in a report by importing it in one of three ways:

1. **Retrieve Image From Disk At Runtime**: Retrieving the file from disk means that the image can be maintained and updated as a standard file and always have the most recent version available for your report. You can also import a different image for each record in your dataset by having the image location information contained in a field in your workflow

2. **Store Static Image In Workflow**: If your image does not change, keeping it as part of the workflow removes an external dependency in your workflow and makes it more robust. For example, this image will not change if the original is updated, but the workflow will not fail because the image has moved or produced an inaccurate result because the picture changed.

3. **Get Image From Binary Data In Field**: If you have binary data included in your workflow for an image, it can be transformed into an image for your report. Using binary data is one method for downloading an image from the internet that you want to use in a workflow, but don't necessarily want to save the image for your use.

You can look at the **Image** report tool in the following screenshot:

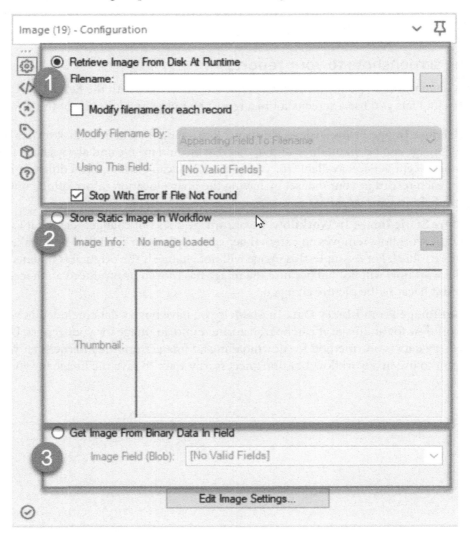

Figure 7.26 – Configuration window for a Screenshot tool

Each of these options adds style and content to your reports. For example, the retrieve image at runtime option can add an image of a product the report is about, while often, the static image option adds logos and background images to the report.

These options add color to your reports and allow better engagement with your end users.

Adding headers and footers to your reports

Many reports will require some context information that will appear on every page of your report. For example, the headers might be the letterhead for a printed report, while the footer might contain the author and page information. This information can be added to every report page using the Report Header and Report Footer tools.

The Report Header tool

The Report Header tool lets you append a new report field to each record. This new record can contain three pieces of information:

- **The Report Title**: This field will create a title across the first page of your report.

- **An optional report date**: This is updated at runtime and added using the format you choose.

- **An optional image:** This image is often a logo and is an alternative method for importing images if used in the header.

When creating the header, it will have a report title and date stacked on top of each other on the left-hand side of the header, while the image will appear on the right side of the image.

The Report Footer tool

The Report Footer tool allows you to add two items of text:

- **Copyright information**: The copyright information text appears on the left of the footer; it is commonly used for the copyright, but is not restricted. The field does add the contextual entry for the current year in the output at runtime.

- **General information**: The general information adds more text to the right side of the footer. It can also add the page number to your footer.

The footer tool configuration is pretty simple, allowing you to add the text to every report.

After building these configurations you will have a component ready for a report. The final step in the report building process is to arrange the components into the design for your report and then render the report for consumption.

Outputting the report for consumption

Once you have created all your report parts, you need to assemble them into your report and render them in your final output. To make your report, you will use the **Layout** tool, which is found in the **Reporting** tab of the tool pallet. With this tool, you can choose the fields you want to combine and whether you want to arrange them horizontally or vertically. You can also chain layout tools together, meaning that some parts of your report can be laid out horizontally and then stacked vertically on top of other elements. For example, your visualization and the text explanation are arranged side by side. Then you can stack the resulting object with the summary table that you want to include, which can be put underneath the visualization.

The layout tool configuration is shown in the following screenshot:

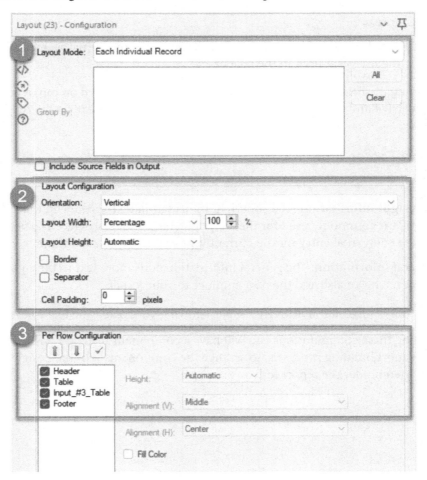

Figure 7.27 – The layout configuration for assembling a report

In the preceding screenshot, the three configuration areas are outlined in a box. The configuration is built by defining the three areas to show:

1. **Layout Mode**: This configuration defines how individual records will be handled by the Layout tool. In this part of the configuration, you can choose to merge all records into a single report or output individual reports for each record.

2. **Layout Configuration**: This area defines how each of the report items (the report items that exist in each column) will be arranged in the final report. You use this section to decide on a **Vertical** or **Horizontal** arrangement and any formatting in that arrangement.

3. **Per Row Configuration**: Setting the per-row configuration will allow you to define the order of the report components. Additionally, this section is where you define the column alignment for each component.

When configuring your report, you can decide to have one new report object per record. So, if you have been batching records or grouped tables, each report will keep to its own time. Next, you decide on the orientation of the layout that you want to see.

Finally, you choose the fields you want to include in the layout object and the order in which you want them to appear.

Once you have created your final object, you will need to output the report object. Unlike when creating datasets, you do not use an output tool; you need to use either the Render or Email tool. Both of these tools are found in the **Reporting** pallet. Using a standard output tool will record the text you see on the Results page rather than the report you have created.

The Render tool

The Render tool creates a file that you can save as one of the following types:

*   PDF document
*   RTF document
*   Word 2007 document
*   Excel 2007 spreadsheet
*   HTML file
*   MHTML file
*   PowerPoint 2007 presentation
*   PNG image

These types are all listed as temporary files useful for development work, so you don't have many testing reports to manage. However, when your workflow is ready for final publication, you will likely need to change the output type to be a specific file. This will then need to be a location that can be accessed when published. This filename will follow all of the file-saving recommendations made in the previous chapter.

Finally, you can decide on the paper size you wish to use and the orientation of each page.

> **Rendering Headers and Footers**
>
> Using the Render tool is also where you will add any headers and footers that you have added to your report workflow. If you try to add the header or footer earlier using the Layout tool, it will not appear on every page, only at the top and bottom of the report.

The Email tool

The Email tool contains all the fields required to create and send emails. These fields include the *from* email address, addressees (both the primary and secondary addressees), and subject fields. In addition, all of these email options can be taken from a field, so you can create a mail merge for sending reports across different user groups.

Next, you can add any attachments; for example, if you have rendered the report to a temporary file, you can add this to the email as an attachment.

Finally, you define the report body. In the body, this is the actual content you wish to send. For example, this could be the report you created and sent directly as an email rather than attaching it as a file.

At the top of the configuration, you also need to define the mail server you will be using. In addition, you will need to know the SMTP details and port for sending emails and, if authentication is required, you add that as well.

At this point, you will have created a report that you can save as a completed file or email directly to your end users.

Summary

In this chapter, we learned how to investigate our dataset. We learned about some of the processes required when completing exploratory data analysis. We used some common investigation questions, such as identifying missing values, to apply the exploration skills we would need.

We also learned how to create a report and bring together the analysis and insights that we have learned. We also saw the two methods for exporting the report and rendering it into a final file or email.

In *Chapter 8, Beginning Advanced Analytics*, we will extend our analytic capability to use **spatial tools** and acquire the initial skills required for a machine learning analysis.

8
Beginning Advanced Analytics

In *Chapter 7*, *Extracting Value*, we developed our skills for analyzing your data and producing a report to consume your insights. In this chapter, we will extend our capabilities to complete a **spatial analysis** and start a **Machine Learning (ML)** project.

Using the spatial capabilities of **Alteryx**, we will learn about how we can generate spatial information in our dataset and use that spatial information to find the geographic relationships that are present.

Next, we will investigate the different options for building an ML project. We will investigate three levels of control for deploying an ML model built from a fully automated process to get complete control of all processes.

These topics will cover how to gain analytic insights directly from an Alteryx workflow. We will also see how we can leverage the Alteryx Server gallery to provide automated insights and extract these insights in an automated manner.

We will cover the following topics in this chapter:

- Implementing spatial analytics with Alteryx
- Beginning the ML process in Alteryx

Technical requirements

In this chapter, you will need access to Alteryx Designer with the predictive tools installed for creating workflows. The install process is discussed in the *Building workflows with R-based predictive tools* section later in the chapter. The predictive tools require a separate Alteryx install package but do not have any additional licensing cost associated with them.

The Using the *Intelligence Suite* section requires the **Intelligence Suite** add-on to the designer package. This add-on is separately licensed to the main Alteryx Designer package and therefore, to complete that section of the exercises, you will require access to that license. The example workflows can be found in the book's GitHub repository here: `https://github.com/PacktPublishing/Data-Engineering-with-Alteryx/tree/main/Chapter%2008`.

Finally, the datasets we will be using for this chapter are all part of the Alteryx install. You can find them in the Alteryx sample data folder. By default, it is located at `C:\Program Files\Alteryx\Samples\data`.

The other way to find the folder location is by navigating to the **Help** option in the menu bar of Alteryx and clicking on **Sample Datasets**, as you can see in the following screenshot:

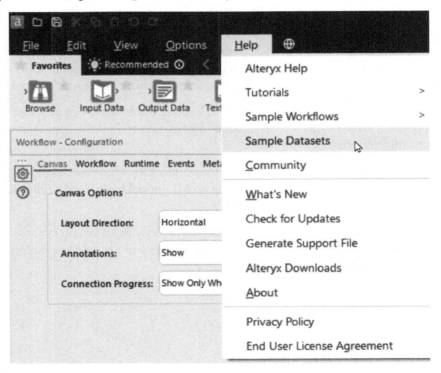

Figure 8.1 – Location of the sample data from the Help menu

Using the sample datasets, let's learn how to perform spatial analytics with Alteryx.

Implementing spatial analytics with Alteryx

Spatial analysis is about taking the geographic location of something and finding patterns related to its geographic location. In Alteryx, you can perform a spatial analysis by leveraging the **Spatial Tool Pallet** and creating a spatial object. To achieve spatial analysis using spatial tools, you need to create a spatial object. The essential spatial object type is a spatial point.

Creating a spatial point

The primary way of creating a spatial point is by using the **Create Points** tool. This tool will take two coordinate fields to assign one to the **X** coordinate point and the other to the **Y** coordinate point. For example, the following screenshot shows the configuration:

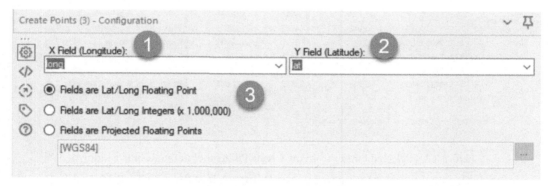

Figure 8.2 – Configuration of the Create Points tool

We will be using the HousingPricesTestData.yxdb dataset, which contains long and lat fields. The long field contains longitude information (*step 1* in the screenshot), while the lat field holds the latitude information (*step 2* in the screenshot). Finally, you can change the projection type. We have decimal values for the latitude and longitude for our data, hence the first option (**Fields are Lat/Long Floating Point**). The other options are for when your latitude and longitude are integers or using a different projection system. The different projection systems are developed and maintained by external standards organizations, but are available in the **Fields are Projected Floating Points** menu.

The resulting output from the **Create Points** tool is a new spatial object field. This field appears in green text in the **Results** window with an identifier of the spatial object type. This is highlighted in the following screenshot with a box:

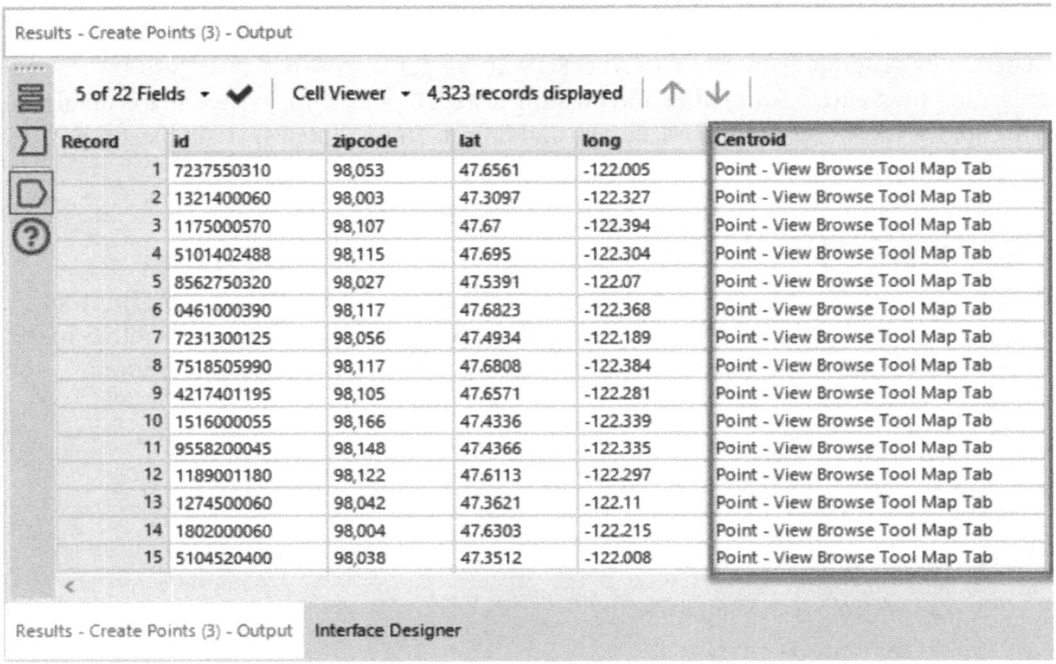

Results - Create Points (3) - Output					
5 of 22 Fields ▼ ✔		Cell Viewer ▼ 4,323 records displayed	↑ ↓		
Record	**id**	**zipcode**	**lat**	**long**	**Centroid**
1	7237550310	98,053	47.6561	-122.005	Point - View Browse Tool Map Tab
2	1321400060	98,003	47.3097	-122.327	Point - View Browse Tool Map Tab
3	1175000570	98,107	47.67	-122.394	Point - View Browse Tool Map Tab
4	5101402488	98,115	47.695	-122.304	Point - View Browse Tool Map Tab
5	8562750320	98,027	47.5391	-122.07	Point - View Browse Tool Map Tab
6	0461000390	98,117	47.6823	-122.368	Point - View Browse Tool Map Tab
7	7231300125	98,056	47.4934	-122.189	Point - View Browse Tool Map Tab
8	7518505990	98,117	47.6808	-122.384	Point - View Browse Tool Map Tab
9	4217401195	98,105	47.6571	-122.281	Point - View Browse Tool Map Tab
10	1516000055	98,166	47.4336	-122.339	Point - View Browse Tool Map Tab
11	9558200045	98,148	47.4366	-122.335	Point - View Browse Tool Map Tab
12	1189001180	98,122	47.6113	-122.297	Point - View Browse Tool Map Tab
13	1274500060	98,042	47.3621	-122.11	Point - View Browse Tool Map Tab
14	1802000060	98,004	47.6303	-122.215	Point - View Browse Tool Map Tab
15	5104520400	98,038	47.3512	-122.008	Point - View Browse Tool Map Tab

Results - Create Points (3) - Output   Interface Designer

Figure 8.3 – Selected output from the Create Points tool in the Results window

You can see that each record in the image has **Point – View Browse Tool Map Tab**. For example, when you display the spatial object in the **Browse** tool, you see the points on a map, as seen in the following screenshot:

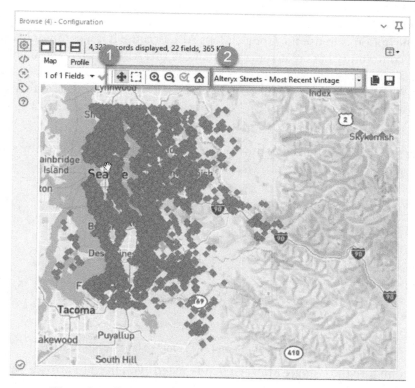

Figure 8.4 – Browse tool map tab for the spatial points created

When viewing the **Map** tab in the **Browse** tool, you can navigate the map using the zoom and selection buttons highlighted in box **1**. Additionally, you can assign what base map you wish to view. The default configuration for Alteryx is to display no base map. By selecting the dropdown in box **2**, you can set one of the other base map options. Any map with **Most Recent Vintage** appended to the map name will query the Alteryx map provider, **MapBox**, for any map image changes. All other map options will use a locally cached version of the base map you have selected.

Geocoding addresses to make spatial points

If you have addresses in your dataset but not the latitude or longitude coordinates, you cannot map the location using only that information. To create a spatial object, you need to geocode the records first. This is where address records are converted into latitude and longitude to create a spatial object. For example, if you have the **Alteryx Location Insights** dataset (which requires an additional add-on license), you can use the macro provided to cleanse and standardize addresses from the United States and Canada. Then you can geocode using the tools provided from that dataset.

If you don't have the Location Insights dataset, you can use one of the geocoding APIs available. One option is to use the Google Maps API. Because it is a commonly used method, the community has created macros that call this API, which are available on the Alteryx Community gallery (`https://community.alteryx.com/gallery`). In addition, Alteryx ACE James Dunkerley has released an excellent macro that you can download from the gallery (`https://community.alteryx.com/t5/user/viewprofilepage/user-id/3554`).

When using this macro, you need to provide two fields, as seen in the following screenshot:

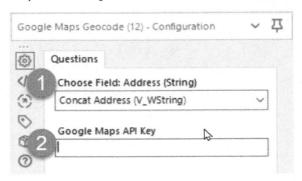

Figure 8.5 – The configuration for the Google Maps Geocode macro

When you configure the **Google Maps Geocode** macro, you need to provide two pieces of information:

1. **The location you want to geocode**: This location can be a building name, business name, or address. Essentially, you can geocode anything you might search for in Google Maps with this tool.

2. **An API key for Google Maps**: The API key needs to have the permissions for the Geocoding API. The information on how to use the API can be found in the Google Maps API documentation (`https://developers.google.com/maps/documentation/geocoding/overview`), including how to configure and create the API key.

With these two fields populated, you can query the API and return a geocoded output with the complete address information as well as `lat` and `long` fields for use with the **Create Points** tool.

Generating trade areas for analysis

Once we have a spatial point, we can perform additional analytics and find the relationships between different spatial objects. When working with spatial analysis, you often have areas of influence for individual points. For example, if you have a retail store, you would expect most of your customers to be from a radius around the store; this area is called a **trade area**. The tool is found in the **Spatial** tab of the tool pallet and the icon is shown in *Figure 8.6*:

Figure 8.6 – The Trade Area icon from the Spatial tab of the tool pallet

You create a trade area around a spatial point with the **Trade Area** tool. There are three highlighted parts in the following screenshot that you need to configure:

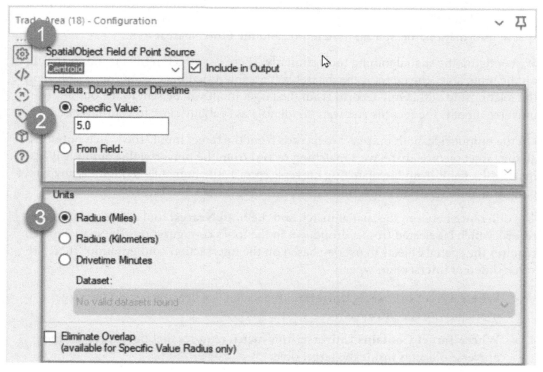

Figure 8.7 – Configuration of the Trade Area tool

When you configure the trade area, you will follow these steps:

1. Choose the spatial object you want a trade area around.

2. Define the size of the trade area you want. This trade area can either be a fixed value or customized from a field in your data. If you use a specific value, you can enter a comma-separated list and create a trade area for each value. When making a trade area, the first value you enter will be placed on your view first, with each following trade area stacked one on top of the other. So, if you put the largest trade area at the end, that will be the only area you see.

3. Finally, you can define the units for the trade area from the choices of **Miles**, **Kilometers**, or, if you have the **Location Insights** dataset, **Drivetime Minutes**.

Once you create the trade area, you will find other relationships in the geographic information in your data.

Combining data streams with spatial information

We can merge the multiple datasets based on their spatial features with the trade area created and the addresses geocoded. Two tools can match data streams together with their spatial information, the **Spatial Match** tool, and the **Find Nearest** tool.

We configure the spatial joining tools similarly. There is a target input and a universe input on the input side. The target is the dataset you are interested in keeping and establishing the relationship with. Only records from the target input will be sent to the output. The universe input is the records you want to identify as spatially close to your targets.

On the output side, both outputs are records from the target input. The match output is all the target records that have a matching record from the universe; this output will also include the fields from the matching universe record. The unmatched output is any target records that do not match the universe.

The difference between the spatial match and the **Find Nearest** tool defines a matching record, which is selected from a dropdown in the tool's configuration. The spatial match requires the spatial objects to overlap based on the intersection configuration. There are seven different intersection types:

-   **Where Target Intersects Universe**: This match is when any part of the target overlaps with the universe.

-   **Where Target Contains Universe**: This match requires that the entirety of the universe object is inside the target object.

- **Where Target Is Within Universe**: This is the reverse of the **Where Target Touches Universe** option and means the entirety of the target object is contained inside the universe object.

- **Where Target Touches Universe**: This match is where an edge, or boundary, of the target and universe objects share an exact location. It also requires that neither object has the same internal space.

- **Where Target Touches or Intersects Universe**: This match type combines the features of both the **Where Target Touches Universe** and the **Where Target Intersects Universe** options.

- **Bounding Rectangle Overlaps**: A bounding rectangle is drawn around both the target and universe objects in this match option. This bounding rectangle has edges touching the maximum distance along each cardinal direction. Using the bounding rectangles, a match is created based on any overlap between these bounding boxes.

- **Custom DE-9IM Relation**: The **Dimensionally Extended 9-Intersection Model (DE-9IM)** describes the relationship between the target and the universe. If you understand the DE-9IM relations, you can use a custom value with this option.

The Alteryx documentation has a great set of visual descriptions for each of the spatial matching types (`https://help.alteryx.com/20213/designer/spatial-match-tool`).

Once you have created a spatial matching between the target and the universe, you can use the output information for further analysis. For example, the Find Nearest tool adds the distance between objects and the direction they are from each other.

Both matching tools combine all the fields from the target and universe that match them, just like a standard join tool. With records that have more than one possible match between the target and the universe, your output will have duplicated records for the target, meaning all suitable matches are seen.

Summarizing spatial information

Once you have processed your spatial information, you may want to summarize the spatial information in each spatial object. In other cases, spatial information is just a method for creating geographic relationships and can be discarded. You will need to do some tidying of the spatial objects in either case.

There are two standard methods for summarizing spatial information:

- The **Spatial Info** tool will take a spatial object and provide summary information, such as the area of a spatial polygon, the length of a polyline, or the spatial object type based on your selection. This tool can extract information relating to a spatial object without retaining the spatial object.

- The **Summarize** tool has five options for summarizing spatial objects but retaining the data for mapping. These five options (seen in the following screenshot) allow you to combine multiple records with spatial objects into a single record and retain that spatial object:

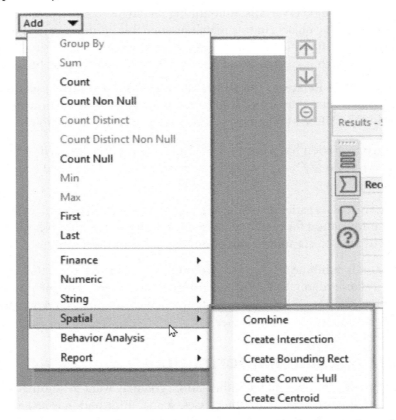

Figure 8.8 – Options for spatial object summarization in the Summarize tool

The final option is to drop the spatial fields manually, with a **Select** tool, or dynamically, with *dynamic select*, and remove the spatial field types.

Now that we can process the spatial information in our dataset, we can extract additional value from our dataset with ML models and analysis.

Beginning the ML process in Alteryx

ML is the process of building mathematical models to extract relationships or predict outcomes from a dataset. These models will take your input data and train the model to isolate the insight you are searching for. There are two broad categories of ML: unsupervised learning, which focuses on finding the relationships between values in your dataset, and supervised learning, which takes a target field and attempts to find the connections that can predict that target value.

This chapter will focus on how you can implement a supervised learning model in Alteryx. This focus is because all the methods for building an ML model in Alteryx focus on building supervised models. However, you can also produce unsupervised models in Alteryx using R-based predictive tools or by creating custom Python or R scripts according to the same methods we described for the supervised models. The only difference is the model algorithm you choose to deploy.

There are three different methods for creating ML models in Alteryx:

- Using Intelligence Suite
- Using R-based predictive tools
- Using custom-built Python or R scripts

Each of these options provides increasing levels of control over the ML process, but requires increasing levels of expertise when applying the techniques.

Using the Intelligence Suite

Alteryx Intelligence Suite is a series of Python-based ML tools and includes the **AutoML** tool (with the icon shown in the following screenshot) to help speed up your initial model development. It is an additional license to your Alteryx Designer product but can improve the speed when modeling ML applications.

Figure 8.9 – The AutoML icon from the Machine Learning tab of the tool pallet

This suite of additional tools is built using the Python language and leverages the most current data science research.

Using the `HousingPricesTrainData.yxdb` dataset, we can see how the AutoML tool and the Assisted Modeling tool can initiate your ML project.

Configuring the AutoML tool

The **AutoML** tool automates the initial creation of an ML model from four different algorithm choices. When configuring the tool, there are two sections you need to configure – the required **Target** section and the optional **Advanced Parameters**; both are highlighted in the following screenshot:

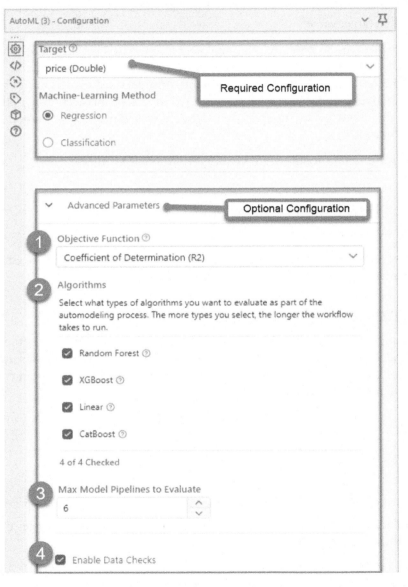

Figure 8.10 – Configuration of the AutoML tool

In **Required Configuration**, you select what your target field is. For our dataset and model, we are targeting the **Price** field. The tool will then default to the ML method of either **Regression** or **Classification**, based on the target field's data type. Of course, you can override this default option.

Optional Configuration is hidden in a collapsed menu. Once you have expanded the **Advanced Parameters** menu, there are four sections you can modify:

- **Objective Function**: You target this function to decide which model performs the best. Depending on whether you complete a regression or classification analysis, you will get a different outcome. Each of these metrics has its own benefits and drawbacks, but using the default value is good for beginning your ML model building.

- **Algorithms to test**: There are four models that Alteryx will test as part of the AutoML process. These models provide a common starting point for building your model, which you can choose to train or exclude. The algorithms you can apply are as follows:

  - **Random Forest**

  - **XGBoost**

  - **Linear**

  - **CatBoost**

- **Max Model Pipelines to Evaluate**: Part of the process will involve a series of data transformations, such as **one-hot encoding**. This option will allow you to tune how many different pipelines you want to test and then build your model.

- **Enable Data Checks**: Alteryx Designer can apply the default data checks from the **EvalML** Python package released by Alteryx. You can find the documentation for EvalML at `https://evalml.alteryx.com/en/stable/user_guide/data_checks.html`.

Once you run the AutoML tool, it will return a single record with the model that performs the best based on your objective function, along with the associated performance metrics. You will then connect the output to a **Predict** tool, along with the dataset you want to predict with the model.

The AutoML tool only provides the model for use in a subsequent step or another Alteryx workflow. It does not return any details about the creation of the model or tuning in the model for building further with that model as the starting point. Nevertheless, this model is great as a baseline for further testing.

Configuring an Assisted Modeling workflow

The **Assisted Modeling** tool is a more guided analysis than a black-box approach. With the Assisted Modeling tool, you will get feedback on the process and what is happening at each step in the model building process. Then, when the modeling is complete, the tool will output each pipeline model for use with a **Predict** tool (in a similar manner to the AutoML tool).

When using the Assisted Modeling tool, you are first prompted to choose between an **Assisted** or **Expert** process. The **Expert** process asks you to choose the **Target** field in your dataset to try and predict. With this option selected, you can use the other ML tools to create an ML workflow.

The second option to choose is the **Assisted** process. After selecting the **Target** variable, you can then choose the amount of interaction you will have in the pipeline creation. The **Step-by-Step** option allows you to review any transformations and recommendations in the Assisted Modeling tool, while the **Automatic** option will apply all recommendations and generate the leaderboard for you.

Before you exit the tool, you view the leaderboard, where you can see the performance comparisons between each tested model. The comparison metrics include **Accuracy**, **Balanced Accuracy**, and other accuracy metrics depending on whether the model is a classification or a regression model. Finally, you see the recommended model from this view and you can select one or more of the models as an Alteryx pipeline snippet.

The Assisted Modeling tool is an excellent method for continuing your ML project. It provides more feedback regarding the model you are building and more flexibility in creating future iterations of the ML model.

Building workflows with R-based predictive tools

In cases where the guided process of Intelligence Suite is not adequate, or you don't have access to Intelligence Suite, you can use R-based macros. R-based macros require a separate install, with the installer taken from the same download location as the Alteryx Designer install. This second install is required due to the license for the R language but has no additional cost associated with its use.

Installing R-Based Predictive Tools

If you need to install the R-tools for predictive analysis, you can access the installer directly from `https://downloads.alteryx.com` or by following the link in the navigation to the **Options** menu in the menu bar of Alteryx and clicking on **Download Predictive Tools**.

Once you have installed the R tools, you can start building a workflow using the R-based predictive tools. These tools will require a better understanding of the process you are applying.

The first step when using the R-based tools is to train the model. The training process requires configuring each model you want to create, such as a linear regression model or a boosted model. Each model has its own configuration parameters that you can tune and explain in a separate book. Therefore, when using the R-based tools, you must understand what model you are creating and what each parameter can do.

Each model tool has a consistent set of outputs:

- **The Object output (O)**: This output is the R model the scoring tool uses to make predictions.

- **The Report output (R)**: This output has a static report with the performance metrics and configuration of the model. This report is what you need to examine to understand the performance of each model.

- **The Interactive output (I)**: Some of the R-based models also have an interactive output (I). This output contains an interactive version of the report generated by the model tool, making exploring the performance of that model configuration easier to undertake.

When building an ML pipeline, you need to make multiple models and evaluate which performs the best. You will have to decide what model to use with your expertise and manually compare each workflow's performance. You can make a comparison by using the **Model Comparison** tool, and this can be downloaded from the community (`https://community.alteryx.com/t5/Public-Community-Gallery/Model-Comparison/ta-p/878736`).

This tool will allow you to take the trained R models from multiple tools. The models need to be unioned into a single field for the model comparison to generate predictions for each option. The models can be from different algorithms, for example, comparing a random forest model with linear regression, or from the same algorithm with different configurations, such as changing the tree pruning depth in a random forest. As mentioned, these different configurations will be unique to each tool, but will give you the flexibility to customize the algorithm for your application.

Creating a custom Python or R script in a workflow

The final method for creating an ML pipeline is to use custom code tools. The ability to implement your scripts within Alteryx allows you to take the results of any methods we have already discussed and customize them even further for your application. Alternatively, you can create a unique model using different R and Python data science communities.

The R tool and the Python tool implement the scripting functionality in different processes based on when they were created.

Using the R tool

The R tool was the original predictive tool created by Alteryx and uses a more straightforward text editing scripting process, with the ability to add standardized Alteryx-specific snippets to the code. The following screenshot shows the **Insert Code** menu with the different options available:

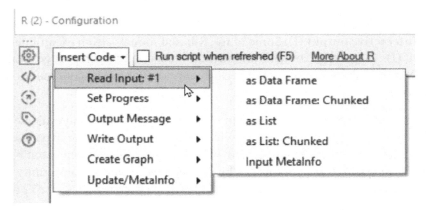

Figure 8.11 – R tool Insert Code menu

The R tool will take any R code available and process that with the data you feed into the tool. It allows you to leverage the analytical capabilities of Alteryx and then extend that capability with the expertise and packages in the R community. A limitation of the tool is that it does not do any code checking while you are writing the script; it is only evaluated at runtime. Additionally, you must run your entire workflow to run the code. If you have any slow upstream processes, they will run every time you test a code section. The simplest solution to this is to output an intermediate dataset as a .yxdb file and run the R code on only that dataset (without the processing with every test).

If you want to use any non-standard packages, the best method for installing them is to use the *Install R Packages* tool from the community (`https://community.alteryx.com/t5/Public-Community-Gallery/Install-R-Packages/ta-p/878756`). This tool will install the new packages into the R instance that Alteryx uses and place them in the library for you to use in the future. Alternatively, you could install the packages directly in the R console with the `install.packages()` function or any alternative method you might use in your R application.

If you want to use any custom package in a server application, you will need to run the same process on your server to make it available there.

Using the Python tool

The newer Python tool uses a Jupyter notebook instance for the Python editor. This method gives the advantage of having a cell-based code editor, thereby allowing the easier running of code snippets during your Python development.

The following screenshot shows the initial Python tool window before you add any code:

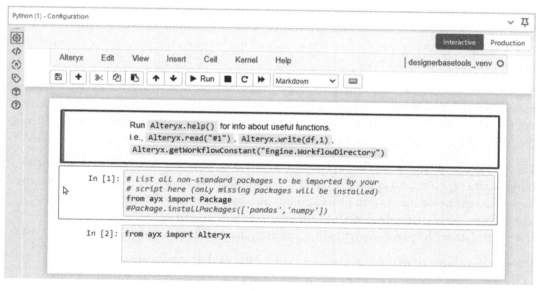

Figure 8.12 – Initial loading view of the Python tool

In this view, there are three initial cells created. The first is a markdown cell with information on how to access the Alteryx-specific Python functions, such as `Alteryx.read("#1")`, for importing the dataset from connection #1.

The next two cells are Python code cells, showing how to import and install packages for the Python tool. The Alteryx module from the `ayx` package is required to access the Alteryx data engine from the Python code in the Python tool. The *Packages* module lets you install a new package in the Alteryx workflow.

We now understand the three methods for creating an ML project in Alteryx. You can start with a hands-off process or a guided method using Intelligence Suite. You can then customize the pipeline more with the R-based Python tools. Finally, you can take complete control of the code with the R and Python tools. This progression shows how Alteryx can leverage the no-code, low-code, or code-friendly development options for creating your workflow.

With this understanding, we can learn the method for building standardized reports and reporting objects for delivering your insights.

Summary

In this chapter, we learned how to perform advanced analysis on our dataset. We took the skills learned in *Chapter 7, Extracting Value*, and extended our analysis to acquire a more in-depth understanding of the data. We started with spatial analysis and learned how to create spatial objects before finding the relationships between the geographic information that appear in your data.

Next, we learned the different methods for creating ML models with Alteryx. We found how to develop black-box and guided models for quickly beginning a data science project. We then saw the different methods for gaining control over the data science process using the R-based tools and taking complete control with the R or Python tools.

This chapter also concludes *Part 2, Functional Steps in DataOps*. First, we learned how to build a data pipeline and apply the DataOps method to create workflows. Then, we learned how to access raw datasets and process them into valuable final datasets. We have also learned how to manage the output of the created datasets. Finally, we extracted value from our data with spatial analytics, ML models, and building reports.

We will learn how to manage and govern your Alteryx data engineering environment in the next part. The next chapter will focus on applying tests to your workflows and enhancing this with continuous integration practices. We will also build a monitoring insight report to ensure that our data quality remains high.

Part 3:
Governance
of DataOps

The final part of the DataOps framework entails the processes needed to monitor the entire pipeline. This process includes testing the workflows before production, monitoring the workflows in production, managing access to the Alteryx environment, and making sure all the processes are discoverable and usable.

This part comprises the following chapters:

- *Chapter 9, Testing Workflows and Outputs*
- *Chapter 10, Monitoring DataOps and Managing Changes*
- *Chapter 11, Securing and Managing Access*
- *Chapter 12, Making Data Easy to Use and Discoverable with Alteryx*
- *Chapter 13, Conclusion*

9
Testing Workflows and Outputs

In the data pipeline that we have created, we have focused on acquiring datasets and extracting some value from them. Therefore, this part of the book will now focus on managing the Alteryx data pipeline created in *Chapter 5*, *Data Processing and Transformations*, as well as managing the DataOps process.

This chapter will be applying workflow tests and methods to monitor the data outputs that we created. The following topics will be covered:

- Strategies for adding tests and messages to your workflows
- How to validate your data outputs in the context of a regularly run workflow
- Methods for centralizing your monitoring with Insights

Each method allows you to establish confidence in your datasets and monitor how well the workflow performs in production.

Technical requirements

To complete the examples in this chapter, you will need access to an Alteryx Server with the permissions to publish workflows and insights. The example workflows can be found in the book's GitHub repository here: https://github.com/PacktPublishing/Data-Engineering-with-Alteryx/tree/main/Chapter%2009.

Workflow tests and messages

When you are trying to test your workflow, there are two tools for executing the checks:

- A **Message** tool
- A **Test** tool

These tools take a validation check that you create to confirm an expected operation. This validation will produce a `True` or `False` result, which you use to define the action to take. Once you have this output, you can manage your systems and react to workflow failures.

Monitoring workflows with the Message tool

The Message tool creates inline messages in your workflow log. The messages respond to a Boolean test result, or they can be a fixed commentary for your workflow.

The following screenshot shows the configuration for the **Message** tool:

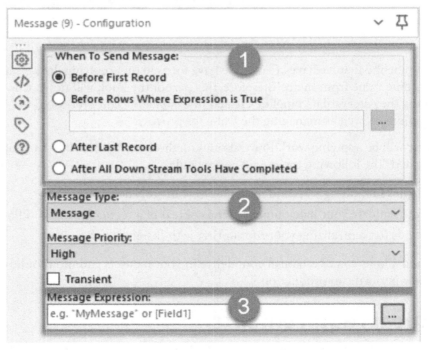

Figure 9.1 – The configuration window for the Message tool

The preceding screenshot highlights the three sections in the **Message** tool configuration:

- **When to Send Message**. This section (highlighted as box **1**) defines when a message is generated. It can be at a fixed time, such as before the first record, or based on a conditional statement. This conditional statement is how you would make the message respond to a test statement.

- **Message Type**. This section (highlighted as box **2**) manages the message level that Alteryx generates. The message types change the highlighting in the results window and provide additional options when processing the message. The message types are as follows:

  - **Message**

  - **Warning**

  - **Field Conversion Error**

  - **Error**

  - **File Type Message**

  Alteryx treats each of the different message types with different importance. For example, messages and conversion errors are primarily for logging context for the workflow. Warnings are used when something unexpected has happened in the workflow, but isn't a failure. Errors are failure events in your workflow that require some interaction. Finally, file-type messages provide context when a workflow interacts with files and needs reporting in the logs.

- **Message Expression**. The message (highlighted as box **3**) expression is the information that will appear in the workflow logs. This field is a formula input box and can be edited directly in the window or by selecting the **...** (ellipsis) button on the right-hand side to access the function and variable tabs.

The three sections in the Message tool allow you to script when and where a message appears in your logs. It also defines what the message is.

If the tool is in a macro, the **Message Priority** dropdown in the **Message Type** section defines whether you will see the message in the primary workflow:

- A **Normal** priority message will only appear in the workflow with the tool or if the **Show All Macro Messages** checkbox has been selected in the **Workflow Configuration** window in the **Runtime** tab.

- A **Medium** priority message will appear when the workflow is one level down in a macro. This means that if you open a macro and see the Message tool, that message will appear in any workflow that uses the macro.

- A **High** priority message will appear no matter how many levels deep the Message tool is. This means that even if the Message tool is inside multiple nested macros, the message will always appear.

- A **Transient** message updates itself for every new message created by the same Message tool. So, for example, if you are running an iterative training of an ML model, each iteration provides a transient update that gets overwritten with every run.

Monitoring workflows with the Test tool

The **Test** tool provides pass or fail errors in a workflow. Additionally, you can have a single Test tool check multiple streams. Once you have connected the streams, you can define tests against each stream and likewise compare numerous streams.

In the following screenshot, you can see a blank **Test** tool configuration:

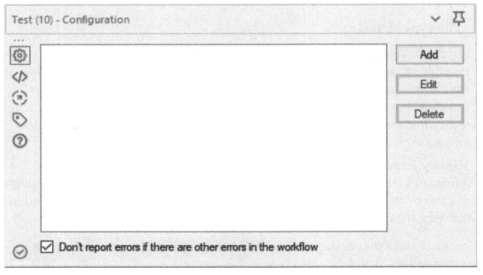

Figure 9.2 – A blank Test tool configuration

The preceding screenshot shows the simple configuration of the Test tool. **Add**, **Edit**, and **Delete** buttons are located on the right-hand side for managing the tests you create. At the bottom, there is a checkbox for turning off reporting tests when another error appears in the workflow.

When you select the **Add** button, you will get a new window to define a new test (shown in the following screenshot):

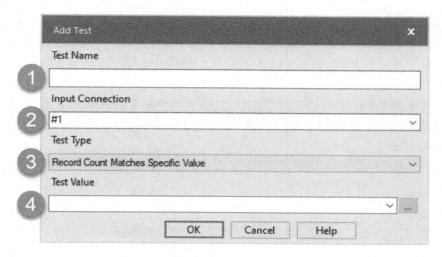

Figure 9.3 – Configuration of a new test in the Test tool

In the new test configuration, there are four fields to define:

1. **Test Name**: You define the test name, and this will be what is written into the logs if the test fails.

2. **Input Connection**: If you have multiple connections, you identify which input you want to run the test against.

3. **Test Type**: There are four test types for deciding how you are trying to evaluate the test. These options are as follows:

    *   **Record Count Matches Specific Value**
    *   **Record Count Matches Other Input's Record Count**
    *   **Expression Is True for All Records**
    *   **Expression Is True for First Record**

4. **Test Value**: This is the value you are testing or the expression you create for the test. If you select the **...** (ellipsis) button on the right-hand side of the **Test Value** window, it will open a formula editor window.

With this configuration set, you can design a test for the checks you need to apply. One example is when downloading from an API, as we did in *Chapter 4, Sourcing the Data*. In that example, we downloaded the place address for the London Eye using the **Google Maps Places API**. When a call was sent to that API, an **HTTP header response** was returned with the resulting dataset. We want a test that checks whether the response contains HTTP/1.1 200 OK, indicating a successful API query. The following screenshot shows the configuration we would use for this test:

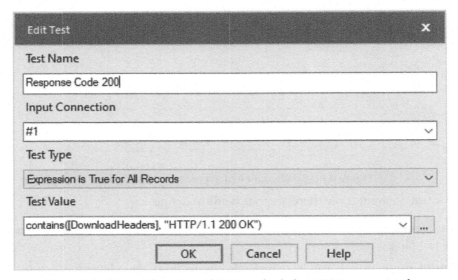

Figure 9.4 – The configuration of a test to check the HTTP response code

In this test, we check Input #1, which is the output from a **Download** tool from the *Leveraging external data sources from authenticated APIs* section of *Chapter 4, Sourcing the Data*. The test type will run the check for every call we make to the API endpoint and ensure that none of the calls failed. The actual check we are running is the formula contains([DownloadHeaders], "HTTP/1.1 200 OK"), which looks for the response we want in the DownloadHeaders field. For any record where HTTP/1.1 200 OK is not found, the check will return False and cause the test to produce an error. Using a Test tool allows you to define the tests you want, and there are a few common test types that have been created as part of the **CREW Macros** pack.

Using the Community CREW test macros

Many standard test processes appear when we create tests for your workflow. A community-developed macro pack called **CREW Macros** (http://www.chaosreignswithin.com/p/macros.html) took these common test types and packaged them together with a series of other helpful macros.

Once you install the macro pack, you will find a new tool pallet called **Crew/TestMacros**. The test macros contained in this tool pallet are as follows:

- **Expect Equal**: This is for checking that two data streams hold the same number of records. This is an extensive check designed to confirm that a **Join** tool has no unmatched fields from either input.

- **Expect Error**: This tool allows you to create a failing test inside a tool container. Then, if that negative test case does not fail as expected, the Expect Error tool will generate an error for you to fix.

- **Expect Zero Records**: If you are expecting an output or data stream to have no records, for example, in situations where you are joining data streams with a *spatial match* and you anticipate that every record should have a match, then this tool return an error about unmatched output if there are records in this output stream.

- **Test Runner**: This macro is for when you have multiple workflows running your tests. Using this macro, you create a subfolder for your workflow tests and then define a suite of tests in those subfolders to run. For example, this is useful for creating a data testing suite of workflows to validate the output of your pipeline.

With the CREW Test macros, you can extend the capability of the Test and Message tools to complete test suites for development and data validation.

In the next section, we will apply the testing tools to validate the results of our pipeline and automate the testing and validation process.

Validating data outputs

When we have created a data pipeline, we need to validate the records produced. This validation involves checking whether our dataset is what we are expecting, and, if there are any outliers, we can reprocess them after identification. This process needs to be as automated as possible, so actions are implemented quickly without general manual checks.

Automating the result monitoring actions

When you have built your data pipeline and added the testing steps in the *Workflow tests and messages* section, you want to minimize the number of interventions you need to make. However, any action you have to take manually is a possible point of failure, so we need to focus on automating a call to action in situations where our checks fail.

The most effective method is to use **Workflow Events** from the **Workflow Configuration** menu. We can see the **Configuration** menu in the following screenshot:

Figure 9.5 – Workflow Events menu

In the screenshot, the expanded **Add** button shows two options:

- **Run Command**: This option allows you to call the **Windows command line** and trigger a scripted process in response to the workflow running.

- **Send Email**: This option allows you to craft an email for your recipients based on the success or failure of the workflow.

These commands allow you to trigger processes and take action automatically when you run the workflow.

When configuring either the run command or the send email event, they both have the same **Run Event When** options:

- **Before Run**
- **After Run**
- **After Run With Errors**
- **After Run Without Errors**
- **Disabled**

These options define when the event will happen and allow you to control how you sequence a process when you run a workflow.

Configuring the Run Command event

The configuration of the Run Command event is a simplified version of the **Run Command** tool. The configuration is shown in the following screenshot:

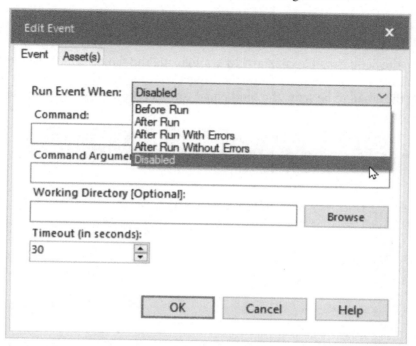

Figure 9.6 – Run Command event configuration with the Event trigger menu expanded

The configuration is triggered using the **Run Event When** menu. This menu is where you decide whether the command is run before or after the workflow, as shown previously.

You can then configure the workflow event after deciding when it runs. This event is anything that will run in a Windows **Command Prompt**. The event could be a **Batch**, **PowerShell**, or **Python** script.

Referring to *Figure 9.6*, we have the following fields under **Event** tab:

- **Command Arguments** are any additional parameters passed to the script or command you are running.

- **Working Directory [Optional]** is where you want to run the command. The default working directory is the directory location of the workflow.

- Finally, configuring the **Timeout (in seconds)** field defines the maximum time you expect the command to take to complete its execution.

We want to generate an exception for our workflow testing when an error has happened, triggering a post-run process to start. For example, this event could activate an example command to run an automated validation script or roll back any data uploaded by the workflow.

Configuring the Send Email event

Configuring the Send Email event starts by configuring the same event trigger as the Run Command event. Once you choose the trigger condition, you can move on with configuring the email to be sent. The send email configuration window can be seen in the following screenshot:

Figure 9.7 – Send Email event configuration

In the preceding screenshot, the **Edit Event** window shows the **Send Email** event and has two boxes highlighted with a configuration that performs different functions:

- **Email server configuration**: Box 1 defines how Alteryx will connect to your email server. This contains the standard configuration for locating the email server (SMTP and Port information) and the optional authentication information.

- **Email message configuration**: The second box details the email message configuration. This includes all the information that is required to send an email. For example, in the screenshot, any value enclosed with a percentage sign such as %AppName% constitutes a variable that will be populated at runtime.

These configuration options automate actions taken when running a workflow. This is the first way of creating an exception notification when a workflow fails, or you can automate the next step in the process (such as creating a support ticket for managing the issue).

Running tests on the output dataset

After a workflow has run, we need to validate the dataset created. Validating a workflow is about building a new workflow that will verify that the records in your dataset are the values that you expect.

One expectation is that we did not duplicate the data we uploaded with the workflow. We can check for this by running a validation process to confirm that our automated process is not resulting in duplicate values.

The automated process we want to validate is the Google Maps Places API data we extracted and saved to a Snowflake table in *Chapter 6, Destination Management*. We will apply the example test to identify any duplicate place searches in our dataset.

Identifying the duplicate places requires four steps, as shown in the following workflow snippet:

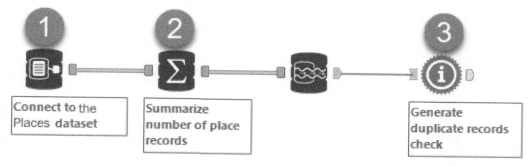

Figure 9.8 – Workflow to identify duplicate places in our dataset

The steps in the workflow leverage the **In Database (InDB)** capabilities of Alteryx to improve performance and minimize data movement over the network. The steps performed are as follows:

1. **Connect to the Places Data table**: This is the table that we created in *Chapter 6, Destination Management*, called `places_bulk_load`.

2. **Count the number of rows**: Using the **Summarize InDB** tool, we want to count the number of records for each name and formatted address.

3. **Stream records locally for duplicate checking**: After counting the number of records, we apply the logic check with the Message tool. We use the Message tool to have a message for every record that we have a duplicate for and remove the records when needed. The logic check we apply is as follows:

   ```
   [Count] > 1
   ```

   This check will identify any place name with more than one record and produce a warning message:

   ```
   "There is more than one record for " + [name]
   ```

With these steps, we can create a message, which we could define as either an error or a warning, and automatically trigger a remediation process with our workflow events.

Confirming the country of our place search

Part of a place search includes checking the country location of the returned result. Getting results from all over the world doesn't often provide useful information. We can confirm that the resulting place information is from a country in a reference list of countries. For example, we will be applying a check to ensure that our recorded place searches are found in either the United Kingdom, Ireland, or the United States of America.

A four-step process is required to validate our country, an overview of which can be seen in the following screenshot:

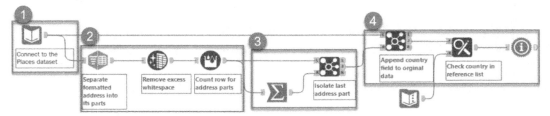

Figure 9.9 – Overview of the country validation process

Four steps are involved in verifying that the country appears in our reference list:

1. **Connect to the Places dataset**: Using the Input tool, select the database table that you saved the dataset to in *Chapter 6, Destination Management*.

2. **Separate the formatted address into its constituent parts**: The **formatted_address** field contains the address parts, including the street name and country, in a comma-separated list. We separate the process with the following workflow snippet:

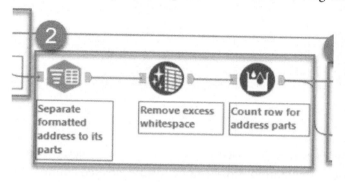

Figure 9.10 – Processing the formatted address field section

We can't be sure how many parts are in any individual place result, so we use the **Text to Columns** tool with the **Split to Rows** option to generate a new row for each address part. Any white space generated from the splitting operation is tackled using the **Data Cleansing** tool. Finally, a row count is created with a **Multi-Row** formula tool. In the **Multi-Row** tool, we create a new field called number of words. The formula expression is restarted with each new name (using the **Group By** checkbox list), creating a running count of rows: [Row-1:number of words]+1.

3. **Find the last address part**: In the formatted address field, the last address section is the country entry. We can identify the country entry by finding the maximum value for the number of words field created in the previous step. The maximum value is then joined back to the separated address list, which also filters that list to just the maximum value.

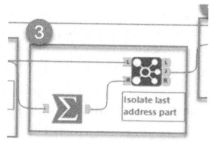

Figure 9.11 – Process for identifying the last address part

4. **Append the last address field to the dataset and check against the reference list**:
    The final step in the validation process is to append the country entry to the original
    dataset, as seen in the following workflow snippet:

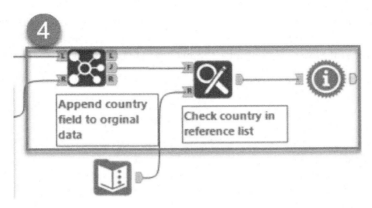

Figure 9.12 – Workflow snippet for validating the country entry against a reference list of countries

This part of the validation process appends the isolated country entry to the Places
dataset input. Then, using a **Find Replace** tool, we check that the country entry is
in our reference list. If the country appears in the reference list, then a value can be
appended to our original field. Using this behavior, if the appended field is null,
the following message is generated:

```
"The location " + [Country field] + " is not found in the
reference countries list"
```

This four-step process will allow us to ensure that we retain only places that exist in our
country reference list.

Centralizing the monitoring outputs with Insights

When we have a process that automates the checking and identification of problem
records, we need to build a system for monitoring the workflow. We can create a report
for this monitoring process, either a static report for records or a visual report for active
checking, that can be referenced when any checks identify an issue.

One method for carrying out this monitoring is a **Control Chart**. We can put this
control chart into an **Insights** dashboard, allowing us to view the results on our Alteryx
server easily.

Building a control chart monitoring system

We created a control chart in *Chapter 5, Data Processing and Transformations*, using the **Interactive Chart** tool. We can follow the same process to create the chart in the Insight tool, and publish it to your gallery reference on the server. This can be achieved by configuring the **Insight** tool in the top-right corner of the **Insight** configuration, where you select the gallery to publish the insight to.

For this control chart, we are going to use the smartphone Processors Ranking (`smartphone_cpu_stats.csv`). You can download this dataset from the Kaggle datasets page (`https://www.kaggle.com/datasets/alanjo/smartphone-processors-ranking`) or it can be found in the GitHub repository. To create our control chart insight, we will develop the following workflow seen in *Figure 9.13*:

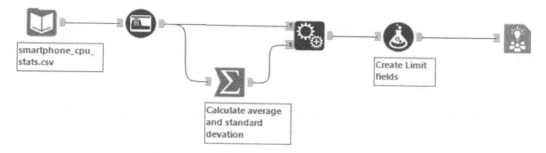

Figure 9.13 – An example workflow to create a control chart insights dashboard

The snippet extends the outlier detection workflow by creating the control limits before making a single chart insights dashboard.

The process for creating the control limits involves three steps:

1. **Summarize the dataset**: When summarizing the dataset, we need to calculate the standard deviation for all our smartphone performance records. The configuration for this is shown in the following screenshot:

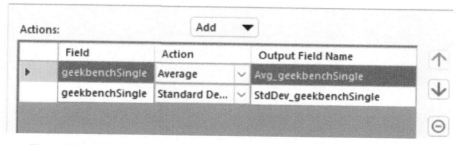

Figure 9.14 – Actions configured in the Summary tool to create a control chart

The preceding screenshot shows the configuration of the **Summarize** tool where we have aggregated the **geekbenchSingle** field to return **Average** and **Standard Deviation**.

2. **Append to the primary data stream**: Next, we use an **Append** tool to append each average and standard deviation to the primary data stream.

3. **Calculate the control limits**: Finally, we calculate the control limits for our dataset. The controls are the **Upper Control Limit** (**UCL**) and the **Lower Control Limit** (**LCL**), which are calculated using the following formula:

```
UCL = Round([Avg_geekbenchSingle] + 2 * [StdDev_
geekbenchSingle], 0.01)
LCL = Round([Avg_geekbenchSingle] - 2 * [StdDev_
geekbenchSingle], 0.01)
```

These two limits identify the expected range for our smartphone performance data.

Now that we have created the control limits, we build our dashboard using the Insights tool. With this tool, there are five sections to interact with, as shown in the following screenshot:

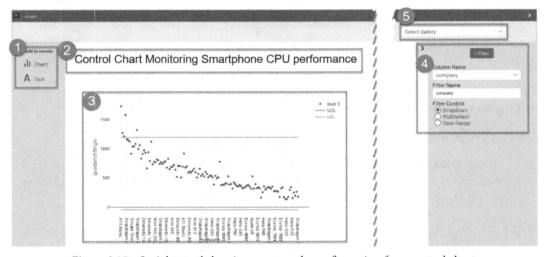

Figure 9.15 – Insights tool showing an example configuration for a control chart

In the preceding screenshot, the five areas are highlighted and have the following features:

1. **Canvas object addition options**: The first section provides two buttons for adding graphical objects. To add a new object, you drag the option onto the design canvas and then edit the window.

Figure 9.16 – The object addition panel in the Insights tool

2. **Text object for the title**: Across the top of the dashboard, we have added a text object. In this object, we can enter text and style it, as seen in the following screenshot:

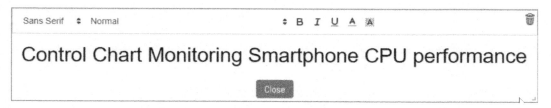

Figure 9.17 – Text object editing window

3. **Chart object with the control chart**: Next, we have a chart object. An **Edit** button will open the chart editing window when adding the object. This editing window is the same as we have seen for the Interactive Chart tool in the *Seeing the Null proportions visually* section of *Chapter 7, Extracting Value*.

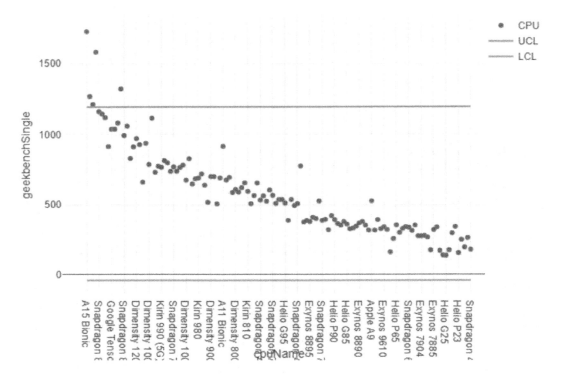

Figure 9.18 – Chart object in the Insights tool

4. **Global filter additions**: There is an expandable panel on the right-hand side of the Insights tool design window for adding global filters. For example, when more than one chart is added to the view, this filter will apply to all charts showing the same data context.

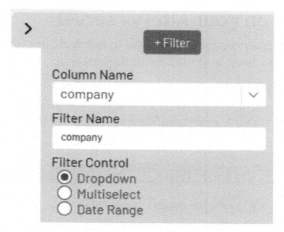

Figure 9.19 – Filter menu for the Insights tool

5. **Server Gallery publication menu**: When you have created your dashboard, you can publish the final dashboard to any Server Gallery you have signed in to (refer to the following callout) using the **Select Gallery** drop-down option.

Figure 9.20 – Server Gallery drop-down menu from the Insights tool

How to Sign in to an Alteryx Server Gallery from Designer

To save a workflow or insight to your Alteryx Server Gallery, you need to sign in to the server first. To sign into the Server Gallery, you navigate to the **Add New Gallery** menu. This menu is located under the **Open Workflow** submenu of the **File** option on the main toolbar menu or in the **Private Gallery** submenu, under **Save As**, of the main **File** menu.

Once we create a dashboard design, we can publish that dashboard to your Server Gallery for future use. The following section explains how you can use the dashboard once published to Alteryx Server and keep the data up to date.

Using insights on your Alteryx server

Using insights on your Alteryx server allows you to automate updating the data for your monitoring and scale the dashboard used to multiple people.

We saw the Server Gallery publication menu in the Insights tool in the previous section. This menu provides access to any server you have signed in to as a destination for your insights dashboard. An example of the dropdown is shown in the following screenshot:

Figure 9.21 – An example gallery in the insights dashboard published to the Server Gallery menu

When you select the Server Gallery for publication and save the insight, it will take a snapshot of the insight at that moment. Once you have saved the insight, you will get a success window with an advisory to save your workflow. This can be seen in the following screenshot:

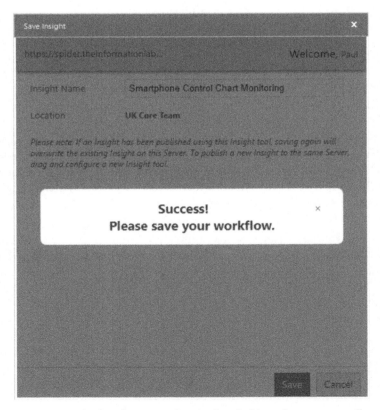

Figure 9.22 – Window for saving the insights dashboard to a server gallery

Our advice in terms of saving your workflow in the preceding screenshot is to save or publish the workflow to the same Alteryx Server Gallery. When you publish the workflow to your server gallery, you will be able to update the data either with a manual run of the workflow or according to an automated schedule, which we saw in *Chapter 2, Data Engineering with Alteryx*.

Summary

In this chapter, we investigated the different methods for testing a workflow and the data outputs. We learned how the Message and Test tools could be used to identify exceptions in your workflows. We also saw how those Test tools had been used in the CREW macros to extend the messaging capability for workflow analysis.

We then learned how to automate the validation of data outputs and generate a notification based on the results. We also used our skills to apply an outlier monitoring process to a dataset.

Finally, we learned how to centralize the monitoring of a workflow process and generate an insights dashboard. We learned how publishing that insight and the associated workflow could make the monitoring process available for other people to access.

In the next chapter, we will learn how to apply the DataOps principles to the workflow publication process. We will learn the methods for monitoring the Alteryx Server environment and create a monitoring insights dashboard for our server.

We will also learn how to create additional custom dashboards using MongoDB without having the dashboards impact the server when testing. We will then learn some of the skills required for implementing continuous integration using GitHub Actions.

10
Monitoring DataOps and Managing Changes

At this point in the book, you understand how to develop a workflow and add the workflow tests. In this chapter, you will learn how to monitor your Alteryx Server environment and the performance of the workflows you are running. Learning these skills allow us to build workflows leveraging the **Delivery** and **Confidence** DataOps pillars described in *Chapter 3, DataOps and Its Benefits*. Each step in this chapter builds on these pillars and allows us to create more robust data pipelines.

This chapter covers the following topics:

- Using the Alteryx Server monitoring workflow
- Creating an Insight dashboard for workflow monitoring
- Exporting the MongoDB database for custom analysis
- Using Git and GitHub Actions for continuous integration

Technical requirements

In this chapter, we will use Alteryx Server and MongoDB for persistence on the server host. To follow the examples in this chapter, you will need access to the server host (the Windows instance where you installed Alteryx Server) and the MongoDB password. Additionally, you will need Git installed and a GitHub account for version control and continuous integration.

The example workflows can be found in the book's GitHub repository here: `https://github.com/PacktPublishing/Data-Engineering-with-Alteryx/tree/main/Chapter%2010`.

The GitHub Actions example can be found here: `https://github.com/PacktPublishing/Data-Engineering-with-Alteryx/actions`.

Using the Alteryx Server monitoring workflow

Monitoring your server allows you to identify when workflows run, the workflow success rate, and user access. Alteryx has developed a workflow for extracting this information from MongoDB to start this process. This workflow is not part of the base install, but you can easily add it to your server, which we will learn in the following section.

Accessing and installing the server monitoring workflow

The Alteryx Server monitoring workflow can be found on `downloads.alteryx.com`. When you get to the Downloads page, navigate to the Alteryx Server page for your server version. For example, in the following screenshot, the current version download page has been selected:

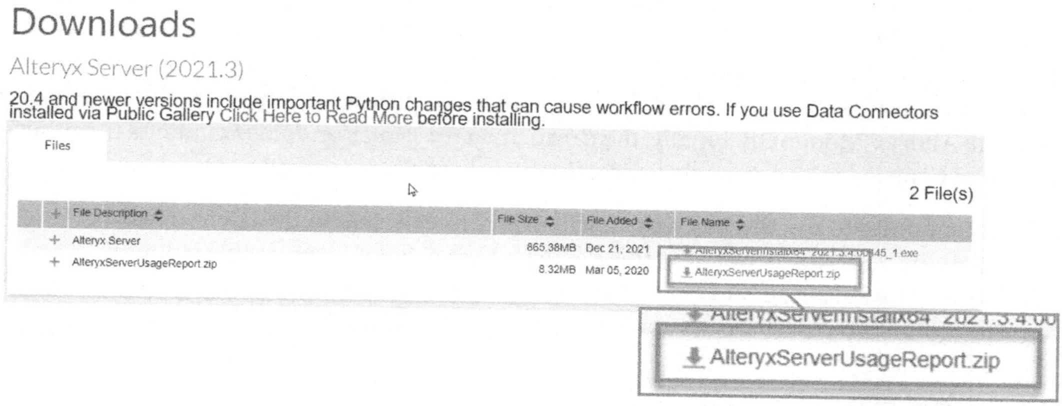

Downloads

Alteryx Server (2021.3)

20.4 and newer versions include important Python changes that can cause workflow errors. If you use Data Connectors installed via Public Gallery Click Here to Read More before installing.

Figure 10.1 – The Server usage report downloaded from the Alteryx Downloads website

As shown in the screenshot, there is a zip file called `AlterxyServerUsageReport.zip`. This file contains an example workflow and the macros required to extract the MongoDB data for the report.

Installing the workflow is a case of extracting the zip file containing the macros. The folder created is named `AlteryxServerUsageReport` by default, but you can customize that for your use. You will be able to insert the macro by right-clicking the canvas, selecting **Insert**, and then choosing the **Macro...** option from the **Insert** menu. Once you have inserted the macro, you will be able to interact with it in the same manner as any other tool in Alteryx. Alternatively, you can open the example workflow, as shown in the folder in the following screenshot:

Figure 10.2 – Contents of the extracted Alteryx_Server_Usage_Report folder

You can see an Alteryx workflow (the **.yxmd** file), an Alteryx macro (the **.yxmc** file), and a `Supporting_Macros` folder in the screenshot. The workflow is the example workflow we will investigate in the next section. The macro is the process that extracts the records from the Alteryx MongoDB. Finally, the `Supporting_Macros` folder contains the other functions required in order for the extraction macro to work correctly.

When attempting to use the macro, you will need direct access to the Alteryx Server MongoDB instance. Unfortunately, this database is usually only accessible from the Windows host where Alteryx is installed. Because you can only access MongoDB locally, you will need remote desktop access to troubleshoot the workflow.

Reading the PDF report

The fastest way to extract insights with the Server Usage Report is to use the PDF report included in the example workflow. The example workflow uses two macros, as seen in the following screenshot:

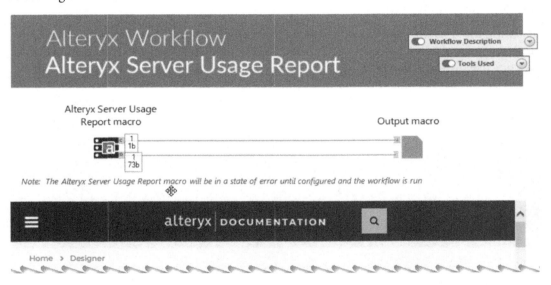

Figure 10.3 – The example workflow using the Alteryx Server Usage Report macro

The following screenshot shows the Alteryx Server Usage Report macro where the three highlighted areas provide the configuration that is required:

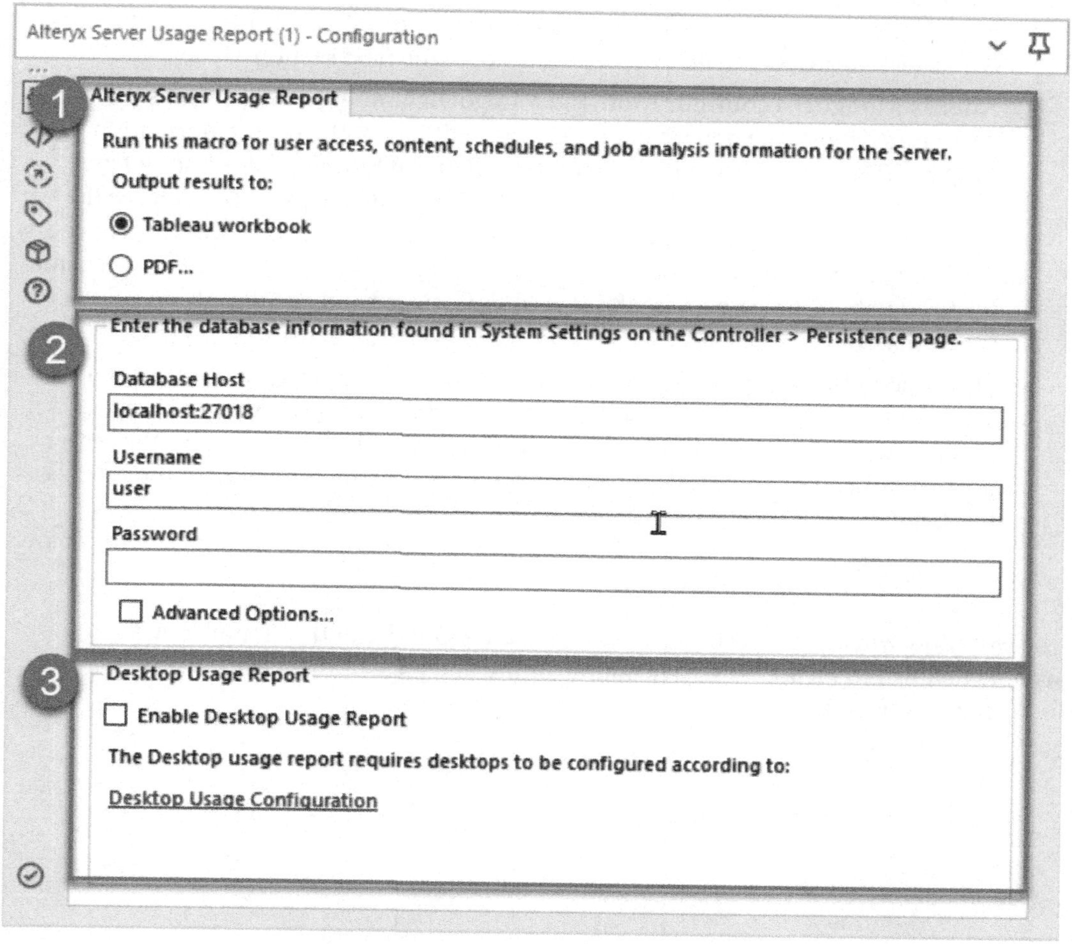

Figure 10.4 – The configuration of the Alteryx Server Usage Report

The **Usage** macro has three configuration areas:

- **The report type to create**: This section has two options for reports generated by the macro. The first option is an example **Tableau workbook**, while the second option is a generated **PDF...**, which we will examine in the next section.

- **Alteryx MongoDB configuration** The MongoDB configuration provides the database's details (the default is `localhost:27018`). The other information that we need is the username and password. You can find this information from the Alteryx Server settings on the **Controller | Persistence** page. You can see the Alteryx Server configuration details on the Alteryx help pages (`https://help.alteryx.com/20213/server/controller`). When you select the username for the database, be sure to use the standard password and not the admin password in the macro.

- **Optional desktop reporting**: The desktop reporting section is an optional report section that will extract the details about the users' activity on Alteryx Designer. An additional desktop configuration is required to save this information to the server. You can find an explanation on how to configure desktop reporting in the Alteryx Community post (`https://community.alteryx.com/t5/Alteryx-Server-Discussions/Re-Alteryx-Server-Usage-Monitoring-amp-Reporting/m-p/346796/highlight/true#M2984`).

The workflow will create a PDF report when you choose the **PDF...** report option in section **1** shown in *Figure 10.4*. An example of the first page of the report is shown in the following screenshot:

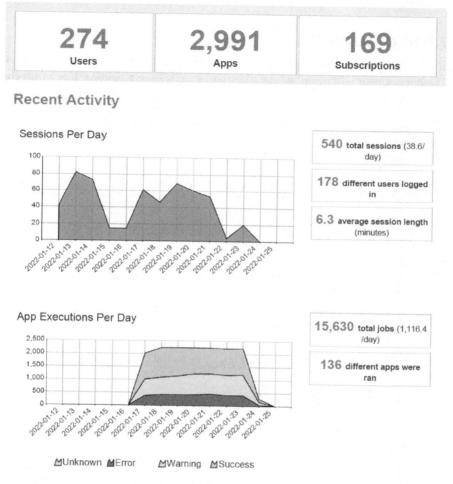

Figure 10.5 – An example of the first page from the PDF Server Usage report

The report highlights the server activity from the user sessions and the app executions perspective in the preceding screenshot. The report highlights server usage frequency as counted by users on the **Gallery** web interface, how many app workflows are run every day, and their success.

The following pages of the report detail the number of times each workflow has run and which users have run each workflow. These details allow you to identify the most common workflows on your server and who runs each workflow.

This report shows a brief summary of your server activity, but extracting deeper insights requires more in-depth interaction with the details from the macro. We will learn about this in the following section.

Using the data output

To identify further insights about your Alteryx Server, you must investigate the **data output** anchor. The data output will populate details about four topics; **Content**, **Job Analysis**, **Schedule**, and **Access**. You can isolate each of these topics by using the **Dataset** field.

The sample workflow provides a **Tableau workbook** as an example report. This workbook is populated using the MongoDB that was configured in the previous section. The following screenshot shows the content report from the example workbook:

Figure 10.6 – The Content dashboard from the example Tableau workbook

The left-side of this dashboard shows the content grouping in **Studio**, **Collection**, **Tag**, or **Author**. In comparison, the right-hand side provides more content attributes and content metrics for individual workflows.

An alternative to using the example workflow is to create your dashboard with the dataset. We will now create a dashboard to show the **Insights** tool's completion metrics.

Creating an insight dashboard for workflow monitoring

Creating a dashboard using the **Insights** tool gives you the ability to isolate any issues you need to be aware of and whether the performance of a workflow has changed. In this section, we will create an example dashboard that allows us to monitor the daily runtime performance of workflows. When trying to develop workflows following the DataOps principles, we need some method to *monitor quality and performance*, as described in the *Confidence* pillar from *Chapter 3*, *DataOps and Its Benefits*.

Creating a monitoring dashboard

The dashboard we will create has three charts:

- An area chart for the daily run count
- A line chart showing the average runtime of jobs
- A line chart showing the 90th percentile of the runtime for jobs

The completion success will split these three metrics to see whether the success of workflows causes any variation. We see the final dashboard in the following screenshot:

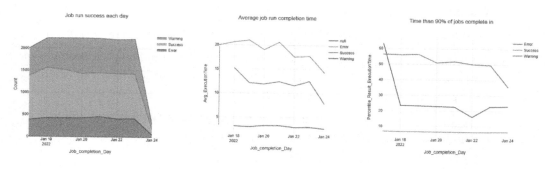

Figure 10.7 – Example dashboard that shows workflow performance metrics

The three charts above show the different areas that we want to monitor. We will build each chart in the following sections and publish it to a gallery to monitor. The charts we choose give us a view of some key metrics for Alteryx Server performance.

Preparing the data for all of our charts

As we saw in the *Using the data output* section, when you run the Server Usage macro and create a Tableau workbook, the data output provides the records to analyze the server performance. Therefore, we need to isolate the rows that provide the context to examine the job's performance. This process is shown in the following workflow snippet:

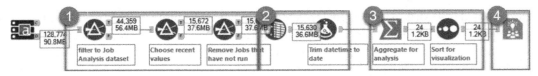

Figure 10.8 – Workflow that prepares data for the Insight dashboard

In the preceding workflow, there are four steps:

1. **Isolating to relevant records**: Isolating the records of interest involves selecting the Job analysis dataset, choosing only the recent values, and removing the jobs that haven't been run. We can remove the records with three filter tools and the following three formulas:

   ```
   [Dataset] = "Job Analysis"
   ToDate([Job_CreationDateTime]) >= "2022-01-01"
   !IsNull([Job_AlteryxResultCode])
   ```

   With the three previous formulas, we can focus on just the records of interest.

2. **Preparing columns for analysis**: Once we select the relevant records, we can prepare the columns for our analysis. We will prepare for this analysis in two steps:

   - First, remove all the null columns, as they are for different datasets.

   - Second, trim our date field to the day values rather than a complete timestamp.

   Removing the excess columns can be easily achieved with the **Data Cleansing** tool. One of the functions this tool can apply is to remove all null columns. For example, the null columns represent the columns for other datasets in our dataset.

   The second process is to trim the date field to the granularity of days of interest. You trim the date with a formula tool and the calculation:

   ```
   DateTimeTrim([Job_CompletionDateTime],"day")
   ```

This calculation will remove all the time information, meaning we can aggregate our dataset to the day level.

3. **Aggregating the dataset to appropriate granularity**: With our dataset prepared, we need to aggregate the records to the granularity of interest. In our example, that is the day level. The following screenshot shows the configuration window of the summary tool that we want to select:

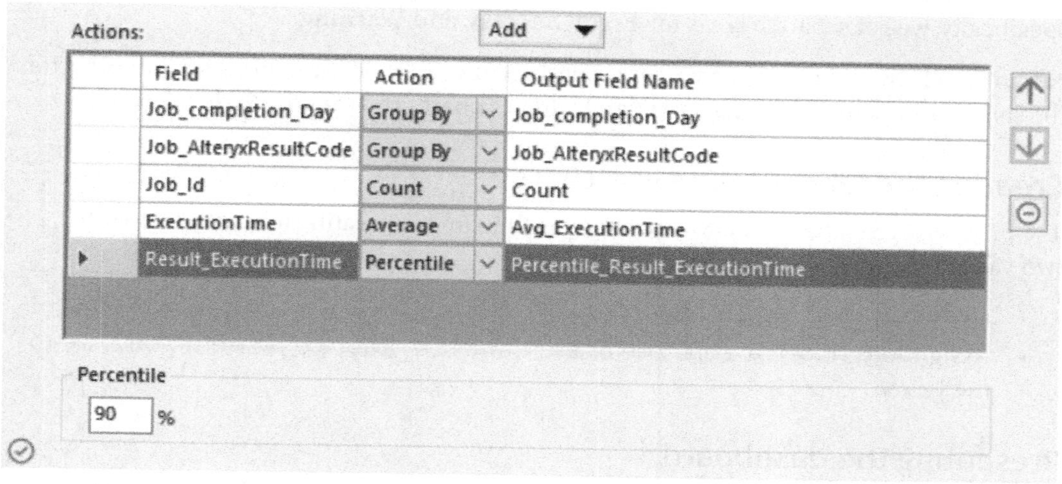

Figure 10.9 – Configuration of the Summarize tool

In the screenshot, we have grouped according to the fields `Job_completion_Day` and `Job_AlteryxResultCode` to provide the level of detail that we want in our charts, and we have also included the metric aggregations for the `Job_Id` count, `ExecutionTime` average, and `Result_ExecutionTime` percentile.

4. **Creating an Insight dashboard**: The final step in the process is to create the dashboard.

We will learn about the creation process in detail in the next section.

Creating the jobs run area chart

We want to create an area chart to show the overall number of runs each day and the proportion of those runs from each workflow result type.

The charts are created by adding a single layer and adding the following configuration options to the **Create | Layer** tab:

- Define the chart type as **Area**.

- Set the orientation to **Vertical**.

- Assign the `Job_completion_Day` field to the **x axis**.
- Assign the `Count` field to the **y axis**.

Once you define the layer, we can add a **Split** transformation to the **Create |
Transformations** tab. This transformation will apply to the layer we have created, and
we will split it according to the `Job_AlteryxResultCode` field. This split separates
our visualization into the separate results for each of the result types in our dataset;
specifically, we get separate areas for **Error**, **Success**, and **Warning**.

Next, we style the chart in any manner we wish. In the example, we confirmed the colors for
the split values in the **Style | Layer** tab and added a chart title from the **Style | Chart** tab.

Creating the jobs runtime line chart

The process for creating the two line charts is the same as creating an area chart with
two variations:

- Define the chart type as **Line**.
- Assign `Avg_ExecutionTime` or `Percentile_Result_ExecutionTime` to
  the y axis.

Presenting the dashboard

Once the three charts have been created, we can arrange them for our dashboard. For
example, in the earlier figure (*Figure 10.9*), we organized the charts side by side across
the page.

We can add some interaction with the charts arranged appealingly on the page. The
primary interaction we want is a date filter. On the right-hand side of the Insights tool,
there is a **+Filter** expansion button, where we can add the filters that we want to include.

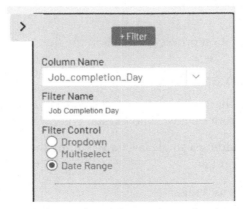

Figure 10.10 – The filter menu of the Insights tool with an added filter

When configuring a new filter, there are three options to configure:

- **The Column to filter**: This option is the field that you want to filter. To add a day filter, we would select the day field.

- **What name do you want to appear**: You can customize the name of the filter that would be displayed when published.

- **How you will interact with the filter**: The **Filter Control** option modifies how you will interact with the filter. The **Dropdown** option provides a single selection, and **Multiselect** provides the ability to choose multiple choices in the list. Finally, **Date Range** is for date field filters.

After creating the dashboard, we can publish this to our gallery and save the workflow to the server. Once we have created the dashboard, we can make the insight available and update the visualization.

Exporting the data output for external reports

There are times when you will want to extend beyond the reporting tools in Alteryx. In this situation, you will want to save the Server Usage report dataset to an external data storage location.

You can save the dataset by following the same process described in *Chapter 6, Destination Management*, to make the external reports possible. You will need to consider the excess columns for each dataset. When creating our dashboard in the *Preparing the data for our chart* section, we would need to manage the additional columns for each dataset.

You can manage the extra columns in two ways:

- **Split the entire dataset into four smaller datasets**: This method will create four separate datasets and then remove the extra null columns from each dataset.

- **Manage the columns in the external source**: This method will result in you publishing the dataset from Alteryx without any modifications and then managing the extra columns in your external analysis application.

Using the default **Alteryx Server Usage Report** macro for extracting the data will allow you to investigate many common questions regarding your Alteryx Server. However, when working with your server, you will often have more unique questions to answer. To examine these questions, you will want to extract more information directly from the MongoDB database.

Exporting the MongoDB database for custom analysis

MongoDB is a document store database that allows easy expansion and changes in the database schema. In addition, it gives the ability for different levels of data to be included in the database without needing to populate associated fields for every document.

These benefits mean that the database type is not ideal for completing the analysis, nor is the database very performant when running the types of queries that an analysis project needs. As with anything in technology, choosing the best tool or technology for the job is key. In the case of an analysis project, extracting the information we need from MongoDB and loading that into another database type, such as Snowflake for Analytics, will allow for the best performance.

The MongoDB schema

Alteryx Server frequently changes the MongoDB schema as the features and capabilities are updated, but some core collections appear in most analyses. The full details of the MongoDB schema can be found on the Alteryx help page (`https://help.alteryx.com/20213/server/mongodb-schema-reference`), but the collections that I focus on from the **AlteryxGallery** schema are as follows:

- **Users**: The Users collection holds all the information about every user on the server and the available permissions that this user has.

- **Sessions**: The Sessions collection identifies each gallery session and the user. This session information allows you to monitor the length of time that users are active on the gallery and when they last interacted during that session.

- **Collections**: Collections lists all the different collections on the server and their resources. Those resources include users and groups with permissions to view the collection and apps, workflows, insights, schedules, and results in the collection.

In the **AlteryxService** schema, the collections to focus on are the following:

- **AS_Applications**: The Applications collection holds all the workflows, macros, and apps on the server.

- **AS_Schedules**: The Schedules collection details all the schedules that run on the server. This information includes the schedule creator, its creation, and the next runtime.

- **AS_Queue**: The Queue collection lists the jobs run on the server and the success status of those runs.

With these collections, you can branch out into the supporting collections to answer any questions you might have. For example, if you want to know what department is using your server, you will start with the **Users** collection, join the **userGroups** collection for the department information, and supplement that with session information (from the Sessions collection) or application information (from the **AS_Applications** collection).

Modifying the Server Monitoring workflow

With knowledge of MongoDB, we can start modifying the **Server Monitoring** workflow. This option provides a starting point for building our results. A typical starting point to alter the workflow is to manage the amount of data queried and output with each workflow running.

When creating a continuous monitoring pipeline, we would be exporting the dataset to our holding database on a regular schedule. In this case, you would want to limit the records read each day to just the new records in the database. For example, when answering which departments are using the server, we would record each day's information and append any new records to the database.

We can isolate the user information into a separate workflow for modification. For example, we can see this starting point in the following screenshot:

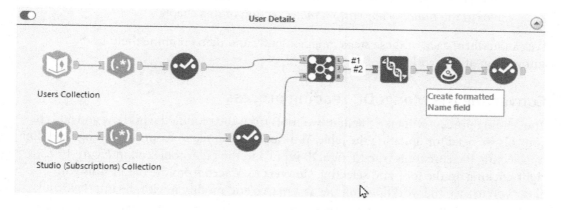

Figure 10.11 – The User Details section of the Server Usage report

We have the user information and their subscription membership from this workflow segment. Every time our workflow runs, we would complete a full extraction of the MongoDB to import all the records, rather than just the modified records for uploading.

We need to modify the workflow so that only updated records are passed to the next step to fix this. We can do this by adding a filter with a date condition as follows:

```
[DateUpdated] >= "2022-01-01 00:00:00"
```

This filter takes the `DateUpdated` field and applies a **greater than** condition with a date-time string in the format shown. For example, using this filter with the example timestamp, we would only return records updated after January 1, 2022, and not process any older or unmodified records.

This filter is still a static change and would not account for regular updates. Therefore, we need to make this process dynamic to make the MongoDB input dynamic to accept the maximum date from our database and the filter field. There are two steps to create this modification:

1. Convert the MongoDB input and filter to a dynamic macro.
2. Extend the workflow to pass the maximum date from the custom tables of our storage database as a parameter to the new dynamic macro. We will create the tables in the *Building our custom tables* section of this chapter.

We can perform each of these steps independently and then combine them in the automation of the workflow.

Converting the MongoDB reading process

The reading process will take the first two tools from the modified workflow and add the controls we need for updating the table. You can create a macro from an existing workflow by selecting the core tools (the MongoDB input and the Filter tool seen in *Figure 10.12*), right-clicking on the tool, and selecting **Convert to Macro** from the menu. This will allow you to save the workflow snippet as a macro and modify it with the interface tools in the new workflow window that opens. For example, we can see the macro filter in the following screenshot with the interface tools added:

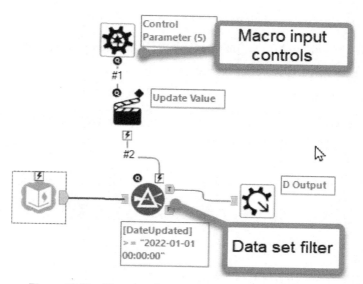

Figure 10.12 – User details input macro with a date filter

In the preceding figure, we can see the standard MongoDB input. In the future, we can add additional controls for choosing the collection or other parameters for increased flexibility. In this tool, we have the filter as we previously configured and a *control parameter* for updating the target date. The configuration for the **Action** tool that makes the change can be seen in the following screenshot:

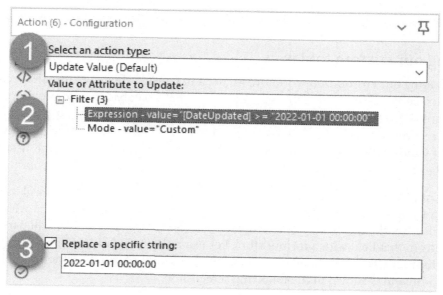

Figure 10.13 – Configuration of the action tool to update the date filter

In the preceding screenshot, we have applied the following steps:

1.   We have chosen **Update Value (Default)** for the **Select an action type** field.

2.   We have chosen **Expression - value** as the update target.

3.   Finally, we have selected the specified date string that we want to update.

After saving the workflow as a macro (.yxmc file), we can use the filtered input in our main workflow, replacing the initial connection as seen in the following figure:

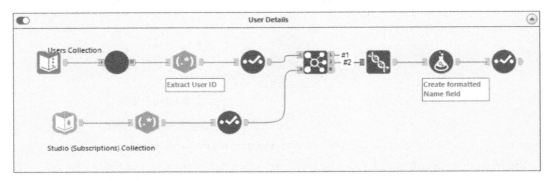

Figure 10.14 – Updated user details workflow with the added input date filter

We can feed the filter's date record with the added macro. We provide the date record from a static text field. We can replace the text input with a query from the output database tables we will create in the next section. By changing the text input, the maximum date will update on each run of the workflow, creating a dynamically updating workflow.

Building our custom tables

When creating our customized workflow, we need to consider how we store the records we are extracting. A simple flat table saved to a Snowflake database would provide a performant query target for our advanced analytics. However, if we want to update the **User** records based on the changes, we need to consider how we add **Primary Key** required by the database. As we add additional details, such as the groups each user is a part of, the simple table would duplicate records and break the primary key conditions.

In our example, we will be building the users table. To identify each user, we will use the content of the _id field, which is the document identifier in MongoDB. When we extract the records from the database, _id is returned as a JSON string so that we will parse the ID value from that field with a formula tool. For example, in *Figure 10.15*, the RegEx tool with the **Extract User ID** annotation extracts the identifier information for our table. The RegEx command is shown in the following screenshot:

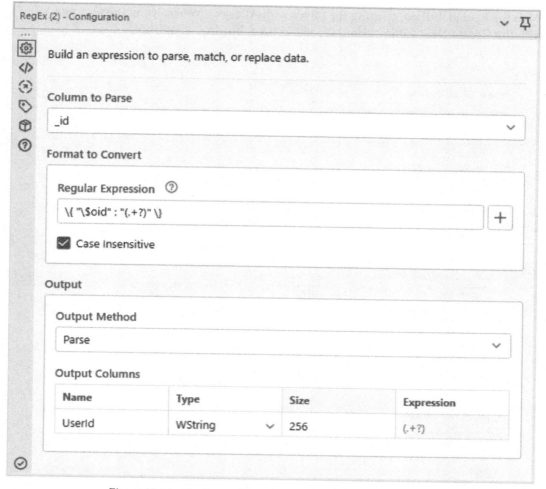

Figure 10.15 – RegEx configuration to extract the identifier field

The regex command ensures that the JSON string matches the identifier we are expecting and then parses **_id** field to create **UserID** for use, as seen in the preceding screenshot. The regex formula we use is as follows:

```
\{"\$oip":" (.+?)" \}
```

In the expression, the section we are extracting is the part that contains the parentheses (.+?) and is the user identifier.

With the field identified, creating the tables with Alteryx involves using the Output tool with the **Create New Table** option, as seen in the following screenshot:

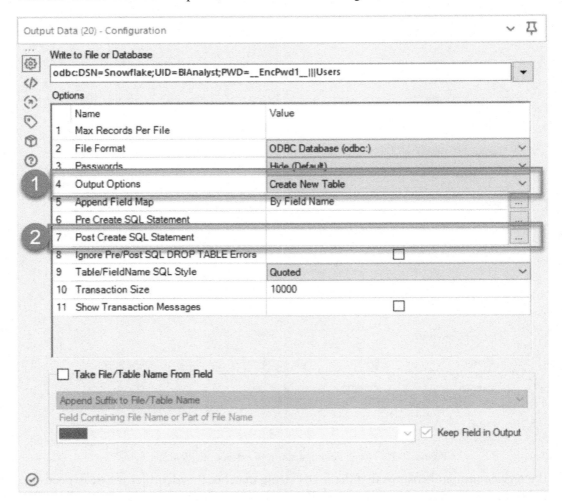

Figure 10.16 – Output tool configured to create a user table

Output Options is set to create a new table and highlighted as point one in this figure. The second highlighted area is to execute **Post Create SQL Statement**. This statement will add the primary key to update records and the user information changes. The syntax of the statement required depends on the database you are using. For Snowflake, the command is as follows:

```
ALTER TABLE "Users" ADD PRIMARY KEY ("UserId");
```

In this command, the `Users` and `UserId` entries are specific fields you create, but the rest of the command will add the primary key to the `Users` table and use the `UserId` field as the key.

With the primary key added, we can finalize our workflow, so we update our tables (rather than rebuild them) and change the input macro to use the most recent date from the `Users` table. We can see this in the following updated workflow screenshot:

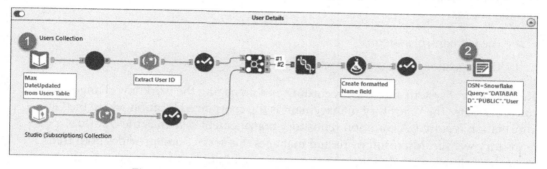

Figure 10.17 – Final workflow to update the Users table

In the final workflow, we can use the Output tool's **Update: Insert if New** option, which will keep all our records updated. Also, if we add a new user, it will add the new user to our records.

We now have a process for monitoring our Alteryx Server performance using built-in tools and creating external monitoring dashboards by exporting the MongoDB tables. As we are applying our DataOps principles, we want to treat the *workflows as code*. This principle encourages us to deploy a method to save workflow changes' history and apply additional workflow standards we might want to implement. We can use a version control system to maintain the workflow changes and apply the workflow standards as part of this process.

Using Git and GitHub Actions for continuous integration

Applying standards and maintaining the change history is a process that can be achieved using a **Software Version Control** (**SVC**) system such as **Git**. The version control allows you to monitor each change in a workflow XML, the text code that defines the workflow. By using SVC, in addition to the published version control that exists in an Alteryx workflow, you can have rich monitoring and collaboration on a project.

Implementing SVC also enables us to treat *analytics as code*, part of the Delivery pillar of DataOps. This allows us to manage the datasets, and the Alteryx workflows that create them, easily switching between versions should a recovery be needed.

Saving workflow changes with Git

When you want to work with Git for version control, there are two parts that you will need to understand:

- The Git control system
- The repository management process

The Git control system allows for recording and managing the workflow changes that you will create. The repository management is the centralized location where the Git information is stored. A common repository management system is the GitHub.com repository website. Microsoft owns and manages this service and provides both free and paid accounts for individuals and companies and public and private repositories for security.

When working at an organization, you will likely already have a version control host that you use. If you don't have an SVC system in place, you can follow along using a free GitHub account. The instructions for getting started can be found at https://docs. github.com/en/get-started. In addition, your company will often have a defined set of processes to use for version control. Therefore, you can include those processes and applications when using version control for an Alteryx project.

Getting started with Git

Using Git will require you to install the **Git for Windows** application (https:// git-scm.com/book/en/v2/Getting-Started-Installing-Git). This application installs the command-line processes to run a Git repository. This application does require you to learn the command-line references, thereby creating a barrier to starting an Alteryx Git project. Suppose you are using GitHub as your repository manager. In that case, you can use the GitHub Desktop application to connect your local Git repository to the repository stored on the GitHub.com website and provide a simple user interface for managing the project. You can download and install the GitHub Desktop client from https://desktop.github.com.

Once you have installed GitHub Desktop, you can create a new repository. For example, the following screenshot shows the **Add | Create a new repository** menu in GitHub Desktop:

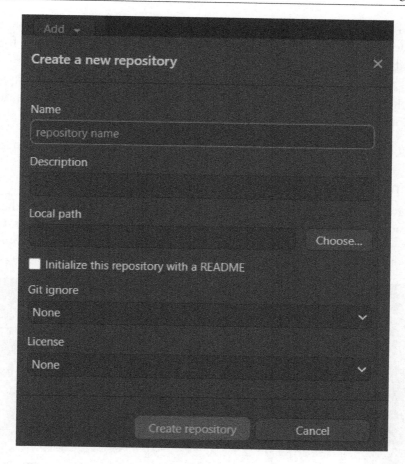

Figure 10.18 – The Create a new repository menu in GitHub Desktop

This window defines the repository name, usually the project name, and where the local repository will be saved. These two values are all that is required to create a new project. The other options add additional detail files to the repository:

- **Description**: This description will be seen on GitHub and let people know what the repository project is.

- **Initialize this repository with a README**: The README option will add a Markdown file for recording the purpose of the workflow and project.

- **Git ignore**: This file will exclude some files from the repository. The Git ignore file is a management method to ensure that you do not publish secure files (such as your database keys and configuration files) and that they do not get uploaded to the repository.

To add a file to Git ignore in GitHub Desktop, right-click on the file you want to exclude from your repository and select **Ignore File (add to .gitignore)** from the context menu.

- **License**: If your workflow requires a shared license for use or interaction, you should include it here. You will likely have created a private repository, so this probably won't be needed.

With our Git repository initialized, we can populate it with the workflows for our project.

Committing the workflow changes

Once you have created the local repository, you can commit those changes to the repository each time you have any changes in the workflow. Using GitHub Desktop, you add the files you want to save to the repository, and then add a name for the commit and a description of the changes. The commit window can be seen in the following screenshot:

Figure 10.19 – File changes window in GitHub Desktop for adding files to the repository

In the preceding screenshot, there are three boxes:

1. **List of changed files**: This lists the files that have been added, removed, or modified in the folder where the repository is saved.

2. **The commit message**: This is the message that will be associated with the commit so users can understand the purpose of the change.

3. **File changes from the previous commit**: This window shows the differences between the changed file and the prior version of the workflow.

Once we have added files to our local repository, we want to publish the repository so we can collaborate with other team members and have a central location to reference the information.

Publishing workflows to GitHub

Once we have committed the changes in the workflow, we need to save those changes to our remote repository. By saving it to an external location, we remove the dependency on each person. This makes the process more resilient to contributor changes. You publish the changes by pushing the local Git repository to GitHub (or your chosen repository management software). For example, in *Figure 10.19*, annotation number 4 will publish the repository to GitHub. In the following figure, we can see the publishing location options, **GitHub.com** or **GitHub Enterprise**, where you can remotely save the workflow:

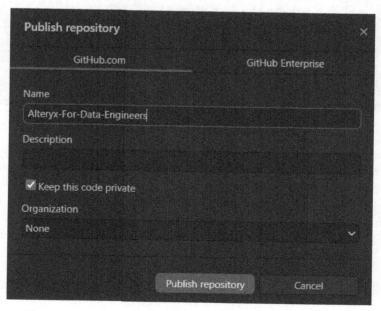

Figure 10.20 – Git Publish repository window to save our project

Now that we have a method for sharing and centralizing our repositories, we can leverage how changes are recorded for CI automation.

Knowing how Git records workflow changes

When using Git to manage changes in your workflow, you will need to know how Alteryx interacts with the file and how the interactions are represented in the workflow. For example, when you open a workflow in a text editor, such as Windows Notepad, you will see the file presented as an XML text document, as seen in the following screenshot:

```
1   <?xml version="1.0"?>
2   <AlteryxDocument yxmdVer="2021.3">
3     <Nodes>
4       <Node ToolID="19">
5         <GuiSettings Plugin="AlteryxBasePluginsGui.TextInput.TextInput">
6           <Position x="294" y="18" />
7         </GuiSettings>
8         <Properties>
9           <Configuration>
10            <NumRows value="1" />
11            <Fields>
12              <Field name="date" />
13            </Fields>
14            <Data>
15              <r>
16                <c>2012-01-01 00:00:00</c>
17              </r>
18            </Data>
19          </Configuration>
20          <Annotation DisplayMode="0">
```

Figure 10.21 – An example of an Alteryx XML file

In the preceding screenshot, we can see the XML attributes, which define the workflow. One of the **attribute** types is the Node attribute, with its **sub-elements**. Each node represents a tool in the Alteryx workflow. When changes are made to the workflow, such as when tools are added or removed or settings are changed, the tool's nodes are updated to record that change. So, when Git records the changes for version control, it will be looking at each of these nodes and attributes to identify changes in the workflow to record.

One challenge when using Git with an Alteryx project is the fact that each movement of a tool in the workflow will result in Git identifying changes in the workflow. This can result in noise in the file differences and, if multiple people are working on the workflow, can cause conflicts when trying to merge changes from multiple people with the main workflow. Because of this, it is advised that only one person makes changes to a file in a project to reduce the commit conflicts.

Verifying the XML workflow

In *Chapter 8*, *Beginning Advanced Analytics*, we applied testing processes to monitor the workflow's quality and the records in the workflow. When using version management, we can add additional procedures for **Continuous Integration** and **Continuous Deployment (CI/CD)**. For example, one method we can undertake is to deploy XML validation to confirm that our workflow contains meta-information that we want to include.

One of the tree nodes in the workflow XML is the **MetaInfo** node, which is part of the **AlteryxDocument | Properties** XML tree. This node contains all the details about the workflow and its uses. The fields that we can record include the following:

- Description
- Tool Version
- Category Name
- Search Tags
- Author
- Company
- Copyright
- Example information

These meta-information pieces provide details about the workflow that adds context for new users who need to work with workflows. We can use this node to create additional validation for the XML as part of our testing process. We can include these tests with an Alteryx Test workflow or a script for use in a CI/CD test pipeline.

Validating XML with Alteryx

We can create a new testing workflow to validate the workflow XML with Alteryx. To import the workflow as an XML, we use the input tool and set the **File Format** type to **Extensible Markup Language (*.xml)**. We can tell Alteryx to read **XML Child Element Name** of **MetaInfo** in our validation workflow. This configuration is seen in the following screenshot and allows us to focus the dataset on just the MetaInfo fields we are interested in:

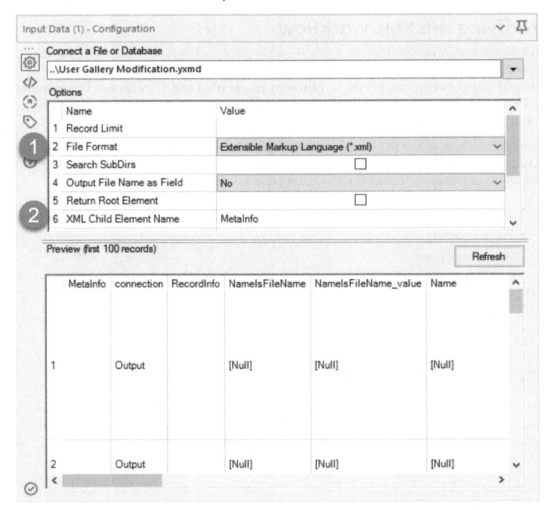

Figure 10.22 – Configuration of the Input tool to read an Alteryx workflow as XML

Once we have read the MetaInfo node, we can apply our test to ensure that the workflow meets the required standards.

The check we will run is to remove the records with information in the `Connection` field. The MetaInfo for these records is related to any connection tool rather than the overall workflow.

With the overall workflow MetaInfo isolated, we can create our validation check using a messaging tool. The Message configuration we want to apply is to create an error for any record where the `Description` field is `Null`. For example, this configuration is shown in the following screenshot:

Figure 10.23 – The configuration of the message tool for the XML validation

With the configuration seen in the screenshot, we have also created the error message to notify if the workflow has no description, so we know why the test has failed.

Validating XML with Python code

We can create a validation process with a code language to check the same conditions that we discussed in the *Validating XML with Alteryx* section. One benefit of using code for the XML validation is that you can add the test to your CI/CD pipeline and automatically check whether the workflow has the requisite information anytime a commit is published to your system.

Using Python, you can check the XML in four steps:

1. Identify any workflows in the repository folder.
2. Read the workflow as an XML document.
3. Find the correct **MetaInfo** element.
4. Identify whether there is content in the description element.

To find the files in our working folder, we can use **list comprehension** with the `listdir` function and locate any files that end in an Alteryx file type of yxmd, yxmc, or yxwz:

```python
from os import listdir
import os

ayx_file = ('.yxmd', '.yxmc', '.yxwz')
files = [f for f in listdir(os.getcwd()) if f.endswith(ayx_
file)]
```

To read the workflow as XML, we need to use the `ElementTree` package. By using this package, we can parse functions to import the file and convert the XML tree in the records into an iterable object:

```python
Import xml.etree.ElementTree as ET

for file in files:
    tree = ET.parse(file)
    root = tree.getroot()
```

Next, we will find the correct `MetaInfo` node by running an XPath search:

```python
desc = Root.findall('./Properties/MetaInfo/Description')
```

> **About XPath**
>
> If you want to learn more about XPath, you can follow the tutorial on W3Schools at `https://www.w3schools.com/xml/xpath_intro.asp`.

Finally, we can assert or validate that `Description` contains information. If you assert an empty string in Python, it will return as `false`. So, if we assert the text of the description from the previous step, if there is any content, the assertion will pass. On the other hand, if the text is empty, the assert will raise an error:

```
assert desc.text
```

To make this work as a full process, the final script would appear as follows:

```
from os import listdir
import os
import xml.etree.ElementTree as ET

ayx_file = ('.yxmd', '.yxmc', '.yxwz')
files = [f for f in listdir(os.getcwd()) if f.endswith(ayx_
file)]

for file in files:
    print("checking workflow: " + str(file))
    tree = ET.parse(file)
    root = tree.getroot()
    for desc in root.findall('./Properties/MetaInfo/
Description'):
        print(desc.tag, desc.text)
        assert desc.text
```

We have now seen two methods of verifying the workflow by treating it as XML. With this capability, we can use our version control repository in GitHub and Python code verification to automate the validation checks with GitHub Actions.

Applying standards with GitHub Actions

GitHub Actions is an automated continuous integration process that allows you to run automated checks on your code base. With this automatic process, we can validate our workflows anytime they are pushed to our GitHub repository and enforce or warn users if the workflow does not meet the required standards.

To allow GitHub Actions to use the testing script we created, we need to change the checking loop into a function. That function needs to have the word `test` in the name somewhere. We also need to save the Python script we created to have the word `test` in the name. This means we can create a `testing_workflow_validation.py` file with the `test_description` function inside it. We can add as many additional tests as additional functions or additional test files in the workflow.

Once we have made that change, we can go to the **Actions** tab of your GitHub.com repository and add a new action:

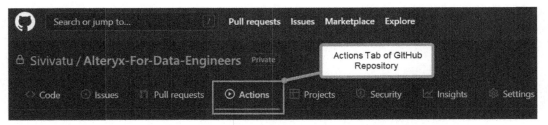

Figure 10.24 – Where to find the Actions tab on a GitHub.com repository

We can add a Python package action to this tab and apply that action without any additional configuration. This action will run the `pytest` module and check for any Python scripts with `test` in the name (in the same way we changed our test file to be) and run the tests contained in that file.

When a test fails (the description files are not populated), the actions will produce a red-colored *fail cross,* and you can read the failure report to identify the workflow at issue. In addition, when all *tests pass*, you will find a green tick for the pass. You can see both of these results in the following screenshot:

Figure 10.25 – GitHub Actions page with passing and failing test jobs

The commit called `Create python-app.yml` identified a workflow where the description was not added when the actions were first added in the preceding screenshot, *Figure 10.25*. In a later commit called **Merge branch 'main'**, the missing description was added, and all tests passed.

By extending the XML validation process, we can apply automated standards to our workflows and ensure the meta-information that we want appears in our workflows. We could further enhance this by leveraging the Alteryx Server APIs and extending the CI/CD process to publish the completed workflow to our server with the validation accepted.

Extending the CI/CD process can be kept as simple as a description appearance check or as complex as multiple validation steps with publication to an Alteryx test server to validate the workflow deployment further.

Summary

In this chapter, we have investigated methods for managing the DataOps process. First, we learned how to monitor the performance of an Alteryx Server with the Server Usage reports and how we can use the Usage Report macro to extract the data records. We then created an Insight monitoring dashboard using the Usage Report macro. We were able to deploy the insight to our server and keep it updated to monitor performance over time. Finally, we learned how to export the Usage Report records and extract the MongoDB database to create an analytical database that we can query to establish insights into the performance of our Alteryx server.

After gaining knowledge and insights from the Alteryx Server reporting, we learned about methods for additional workflow validation and how to use software version control to maintain our workflow code base. First, we learned how to use Git and GitHub to record workflow changes and how those changes are found in the XML and Alteryx workflow. We then learned how to check the workflow XML to ensure that workflow standards, such as a workflow description, are added to our workflows. Then we leveraged that capability to use GitHub Actions to automate the validation of our workflow standards using a CI/CD pipeline and version control.

In the next chapter, we will discover how we can share content and manage access to the workflows and content we have created.

11
Securing and Managing Access

At this point in our data engineering pipeline, we have created our workflows to process the data. We can also monitor the quality of the dataset we have created and the performance of our workflows. The next consideration we have is how to manage the content assets on our Alteryx Server and how users will access the content.

In this chapter, we will examine the requirements for managing an Alteryx Server and the considerations for securing the content.

In this chapter, we will cover the following topics:

- Organizing content on Alteryx Server
- Managing collections
- Securing the data environment

Technical requirements

This chapter will focus on using Alteryx Server and how to control the environment. To implement the concepts discussed in this chapter, you will need to be an administrator on your server. Additionally, we will discuss how to secure the data environment. In this discussion, we will use **Amazon Web Services** (**AWS**) as an example cloud provider, but the concepts will apply to other cloud providers and on-premises situations as well.

Organizing content on Alteryx Server

With a centralized location for your Alteryx data pipelines, you need methods to manage your published content. Alteryx has built three ways of organizing the content you have published on your server; **My Workspace**, **Districts**, and **Collections**. Navigation links to **My Workspace** and **District** can be immediately seen in the left-hand navigation menu from the **Server Gallery** home page. The navigation link for **Collections** appears in the same navigation menu after you have authenticated to the server. These three features provide different capabilities for managing your data and allow varying access requirements.

The primary deciding factor is what security controls you apply when deciding on what organizational method you want to use. User access defines each organization's method and then provides different capabilities once that access is restricted. The high-level controls are as follows:

- **My Workspace**: My Workspace is where you save your content on the server. As the publisher, you should be the only person who has access to My Workspace, and it provides the personal space for development and any server-level testing you need to apply.

- **Collections**: Collections are a group space that requires authenticated access to use. To access a collection, end users must sign in to the server before the **Collections** navigation link appears in the left navigation pane.

- **Districts**: Districts are the organization for the public space of your Alteryx Server. To access a district, users do not need to authenticate, but it provides a method for organizing the content that any user is allowed access to.

With these three areas, the capabilities and control mechanisms change, allowing you to manage how users access your server's content. The access separation can be seen in the following diagram:

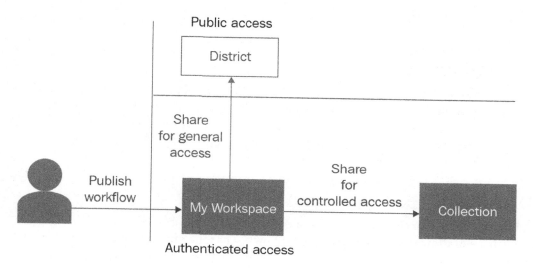

Figure 11.1 – How Alteryx Server content access is managed

In the preceding diagram, there is a dividing line between the **Public access** area, the space that anyone who can reach your server URL can access, and the **Authenticated access** area, where a user must log in to view any content.

The public area contains any freely accessible workflows, and these workflows can be organized into **Districts**, making the content easier to find.

The authenticated area contains the content that requires access control. Users, both you as the data engineer and your end users, must log in to the server before viewing anything in the authenticated area.

My Workspace

The **My Workspace** area is the first place where the content resides when published to the server. Every new **artisan** (a person using Alteryx Designer who publishes to Alteryx Server) has a My Workspace instance automatically created for them when they first join the server. This space is a personal development area for each data engineer.

Collections

A **Collection** in Alteryx is a method for collaboration and sharing content between your server users. To access a collection, you need to log in, which allows for security over the content. Then, any user who has the correct permission can create new collections. The collection owner and designated collection administrators then manage the new collection.

Districts

A **District** allows for the management of content made available to the public. When you publish a workflow to the server, the content owner has the option to make that content public. When the workflow is public, anyone who can access the server can find and interact with the content. The user does not need to authenticate to view the content in this situation. The limitation is that there is no default organization of the public space. A district is a sub-section of the public space where you can find all workflows with a specific **tag**. The server **Curators** (**Administrators**) create the tag, and then associate it with a district and add it to workflows.

There are three steps to organizing your public workflows into districts:

1. **Creating a tag**: In the **Administrator** section of your Gallery, navigate to the **Workflows** tab. The top half of the **Workflows** tab previews all workflows published to the server. Because this is an administrator area (and only users with the **Curator/Administrator** role can access this area), administrators can see all the workflows for publication management. The bottom half of the tab has access to the tags created on your server currently. The following screenshot shows the **Workflows** tab:

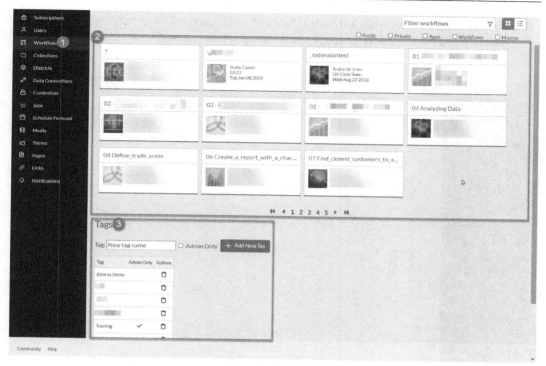

Figure 11.2 – Screenshot of the Workflows admin pages on Alteryx Gallery

In the preceding screenshot, the three annotated areas represent the **Workflows** tab, the workflow area, and the **Tags** area. To create a new tag, you enter the name of the tag, identify whether the tag is only to be used by administrators, and then click to create the tag as per the following screenshot:

Figure 11.3 – Steps to create a new tag on the Workflows admin page

Now that you have made the tag, it can be associated with a district.

2. **Associating the tag with a district**: You can enable and disable existing districts on-demand on the **Districts** page. Additionally, you can add new districts and tags associated using the **Add New District** button (section **2**):

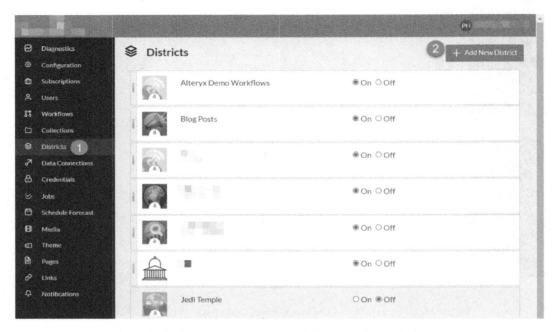

Figure 11.4 – The Districts tab of the Gallery Administration pages

When we select the **Add New District** button in the preceding screenshot, we navigate to the **Create District** page. On this page, we define the following in relation to the district: **Title**, the navigation link, **Nav Link** (which we can customize), and **Tag**, to associate with the district. Finally, we add the explanatory **Excerpt** and **Description** options for the district, so users understand the district's purpose. You are required to populate all the district options except **Excerpt**, which is an optional field. The new district page is shown in the following screenshot:

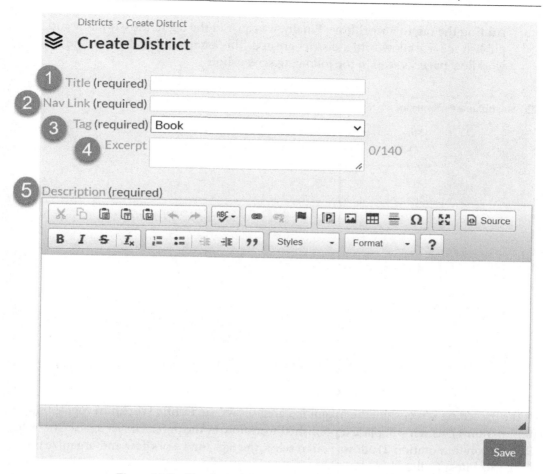

Figure 11.5 – The Create District page with fields highlighted

3. **Adding the tag to a workflow**: Finally, we can add the tag to the workflow and publish the workflow with a district created. This association is done on the workflow page, as seen in the following screenshot:

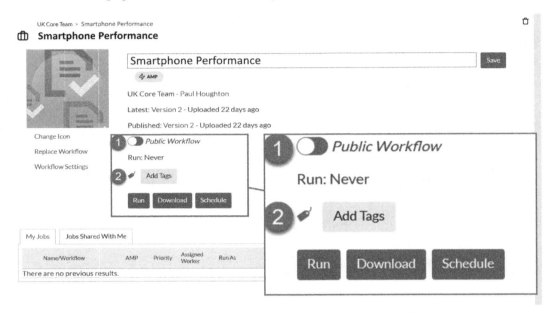

Figure 11.6 – Process for adding a tag to a published workflow on Alteryx Gallery

In the preceding screenshot, the magnified area shows the **Public Workflow** toggle button (annotation **1**), which will place a published workflow in the public server space. The **Add Tags** button (annotation **2**) allows you to select the tags for a workflow and organize the workflow into a Gallery based on that tag.

The public spaces of Alteryx and Districts have few permission management options. The workflows are either fully public or privately secured. Therefore, when you start using the private sharing controls of collections, you have more flexibility in managing the content and the users who can access the collection.

Managing collections

As a content creator or a server administrator, you will often need processes for sharing content in a controlled manner. For example, managing access to published workflows, insights, and schedules for the groups of users who require that content allows you to keep the content secure and discoverable for all your end users.

When managing the content in a collection, two aspects need managing—the content in the collection and the access required for the collection.

Creating collections

In the Alteryx Gallery, curators can assign the collection creation permission to any user. To confirm whether you have the **Collections Creation** permission, navigate to your **profile page** and check whether the **Create New Collections** permission is checked, as in the following screenshot:

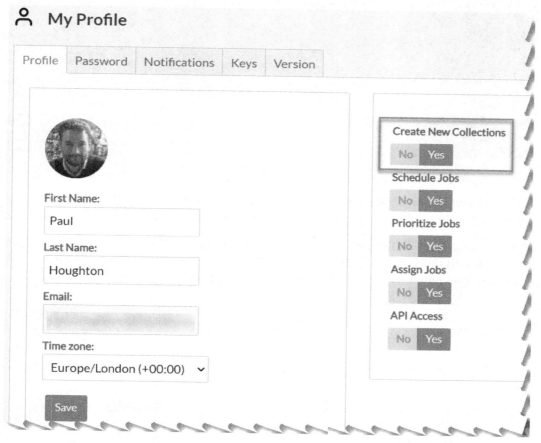

Figure 11.7 – Gallery Profile page with the Create New Collections permission

When you have the **Create New Collections** permission, you will see an **Add New Collection** button when you navigate to the **Collections** page of the Gallery. After selecting this button, you can define the collection name to create a new collection, as shown in the following screenshot:

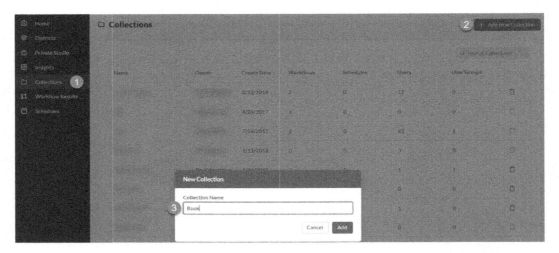

Figure 11.8 – The New Collection dialog with the annotated steps to open the window

With a new collection created, we can start managing the content as well as access to it. Once you have the collection created as the owner, you gain complete control.

After opening the collection, you will see the details of the collection and all the tabs associated with the asset contents and users. For example, the following screenshot shows the asset tabs annotated in section **1**, with user management in section **2**:

Figure 11.9 – A new Collections page with the asset and user management tabs highlighted

The three highlighted sections in the preceding screenshot give control to the collection owner. The following sections will describe each of these collection editing options.

Managing content in Collections

The first section of the Collections page manages the assets in the collection. An asset is anything that a data engineer has created and published to the server. It also includes the automation that is applied to the published workflows.

Three asset types can be placed in a collection:

- **Workflows**: Workflows are any of the pipelines a data engineer creates in Alteryx Designer. This asset can be a standard workflow, a macro, or an analytic app.
- **Insights**: You can add any Insight dashboards that you create to a collection for sharing with users.
- **Schedules**: When you automate the running of a workflow, you can add the schedule to the collection to see the success logs and workflow results. The collection then allows multiple people to monitor the schedule results.

The asset type is added from each of the asset type tabs and then the **+ Add Workflow** button (magnified in the screenshot) is selected for the **Workflows** tab in the following screenshot:

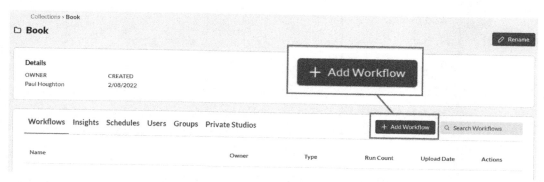

Figure 11.10 – Add Workflow button for adding workflows to a collection

Once you select the **+ Add Workflow** button, as seen in the preceding figure, you can choose the asset to add to the collection.

Managing access to Collections

With the content you want in the collection, you add users for collaboration. You can add users in two ways, either individually or in groups. When adding users, the preferred method is to use groups for management. Using the group management features allows you to define the permissions for a group of users rather than specifying them for each individual user.

Adding individual users

The process for adding individual users is very similar to adding content. First, click the **Add User** button from the **User** tab and select the user you want to add. Once you have specified the user, you can apply custom permissions for that user, as seen in the following screenshot:

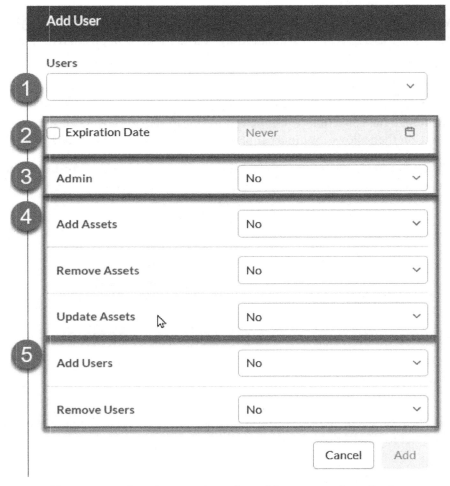

Figure 11.11 – Permission options when adding users to the collection

In the preceding screenshot, there are five annotated sections:

1. **User selection box**: This box is where you select the user you are adding.
2. **Expiration Date**: This box gives you the option to end a user's access to the collection automatically upon the stipulated day.
3. **Admin permissions**: This option will automatically allow all the asset and user permissions.
4. **Asset permissions**: An asset permission allows for the discrete control of how a user can interact with the assets in the collection. For example, these are the permissions you would use for any other data engineers, data analysts, or data scientists collaborating on the collection and workflows.
5. **User permissions**: These two permissions define whether the user can add or remove additional users to or from a project. You can assign user permissions to team leaders who might want to manage the users in a project, but do not need to collaborate on the workflows or assets in the project.

The permissions you defined for a user have the same options to apply to groups. However, there is a new set of steps for configuring groups. We will look at these next.

Adding groups of users

Creating a group for use with Collections requires administration permissions. However, you do not need administrator permissions to add the group to the collection.

The **Groups** option can be found under the **Users** tab on the left-hand navigation panel of the **Admin** pages. You can see this page in the following screenshot:

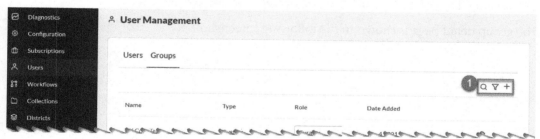

Figure 11.12 – Group management admin window

In the screenshot, the highlighted area on the page shows a *search* button, a *filter* button, and an *add group* button. When creating a new group with this button, you first need to define the group name and the default role for the group as follows:

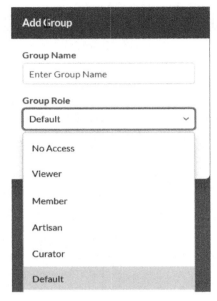

Figure 11.13 – The Add Group pop-up window

The next process is to add those users you want to group with the group created. Each user in the group will get the same permissions. If you wish to assign different permissions to different groups, such as one group of people collaborating on a collection and another group using the collection, you will need multiple groups for those teams.

The group detail page is shown in the following screenshot:

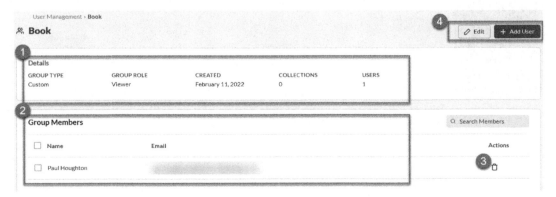

Figure 11.14 – Group page with group details and members highlighted

In the preceding screenshot, there are four highlighted areas:

1. **The group details**: This section lists the summary details of the collection. The group type can be either **Custom** for an Alteryx group or **Active Directory** if you use Active Directory for authentication.

2. **Group members**: This section lists all members of the group. You can check this list for the group membership and confirm users' permissions.

3. **Remove group member button**: To remove a user from the group, the trash can icon on the right side of the page deletes that user.

4. **Edit and Add User buttons**: There are two buttons in the group page's top-right corner: the **Edit** button and the **Add User** button. The Edit button allows you to modify the configuration options set when you created the group, specifically **GROUP TYPE** and **GROUP ROLE**.

The **Add User** button is used to add individual users to the group. To add a user, you search for the user's username or email. The **Add User** pop-up window is seen in the following screenshot:

Figure 11.15 – Add User pop-up window for a group

Once a group has been created, you can assign it to a collection with the same permission controls as adding individual users, namely, adding *Admin* permissions, *Asset* permissions, or *User* permissions.

Using Collections, we have created a system to effectively share assets with our users. It allows us to manage who can access the workflows and data assets and control the interactions with them as well. We also have to consider how the server hardware interacts with the underlying data sources. We need to put in place the mechanisms to securely communicate with the data sources while not exposing those data sources to people outside our organization.

Securing the data environment

When looking to secure Alteryx inside your data environment, you need to consider where your data is and how it will move around your environment. Of course, the ideal situation is that most of your Alteryx environment is inside a private network, with only the gallery accessible to your users and not external parties.

This section will focus on deploying your environment in an **Amazon Web Services (AWS)** environment. I use this as an example as it will show the processes we are trying to achieve when deploying an Alteryx Server, but the plans will apply to any other cloud provider. If you want a more in-depth look at working with AWS, you could read Packt's *AWS Certified Solutions Architect – Associate Guide*, by Gabriel Ramirez and Stuart Scott (`https://www.packtpub.com/product/aws-certified-solutions-architect-associate-guide/9781789130669`).

When looking to secure the environment, we will look at two scenarios: a single node server and a multi-node environment. But first, we will take a look at Alteryx Server's architecture in the following section.

Alteryx Server architecture

Building Alteryx Server architecture involves defining how **public** and **private network subnets** will minimize data exposure and keep the environment secure.

A single-node system will have all the processes running on a single node. The only way to isolate the components from user network access is to use a load balancer. An example AWS environment for a single node is shown in the following diagram:

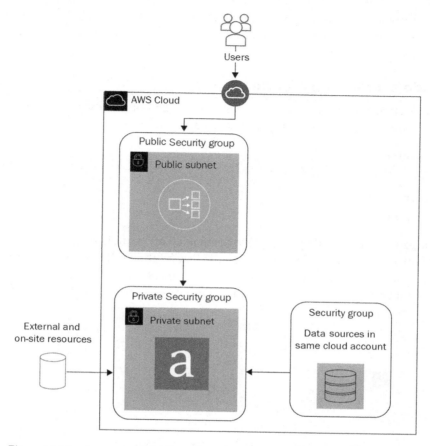

Figure 11.16 – An example single-node architecture in an AWS cloud environment

The preceding diagram shows an example environment where a load balancer is presented to our users in a public subnet while the Alteryx application stays secure in a private subnet.

The other area to consider is what you will do with the log files. In *Chapter 10, Monitoring DataOps and Managing Changes*, we investigated methods for monitoring Alteryx performance with the MongoDB records. Another resource for monitoring your server is the log files that Alteryx generates. To find the log files, first you define where the log file will be saved in the **Alteryx Server System Settings**. You can find details about configuring this in the Alteryx Help pages (https://help.alteryx.com/20214/server/configure-and-use-server-logs). The simplest method of saving those files when working in a cloud environment is to use the native log management system for AWS, either **CloudWatch** Logs or **S3 object storage**.

Minimal additional configuration is required. The single server contains all the processes. A multi-node system provides additional server processing capacity, redundancy, and configures high availability.

Multi-node server architecture

A multi-node environment allows you to secure the different processes from external access. There are four processes that you have control over in Alteryx:

- **Controller**
- **Gallery**
- **Worker**
- **MongoDB**

Of the four processes, the only process that users need access to is the gallery. This is because all other processes are only accessed directly by the underlying application and have no end user input requirements. Using this information, we can assemble an architecture that best secures the environment. You can see this in the following diagram:

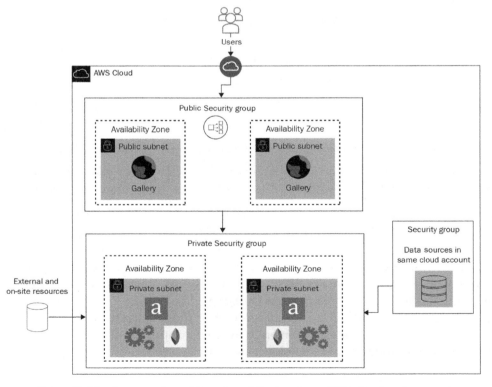

Figure 11.17 – An example multi-node architecture in an AWS cloud environment

The Gallery processes are accessed via a load balancer placed in a public subnet in this architecture. The other processes, **Controller**, **Worker**, and **MongoDB**, would all be put in the private subnet. When scaling Gallery, Worker, or MongoDB nodes, the new processes are added to new **Availability Zones** (**AZ**) to allow data center redundancy. If any single zone goes offline, then the other AZ would still be available, and the server would still operate.

Controlling URL access with firewalls

In both the environments described previously, the Alteryx Gallery access controls are defined in two permission sets:

- User access to Alteryx Gallery

- Server access to company data sources

To define access to Alteryx Gallery, you control who can access the URL. In an AWS environment, you achieve this by managing the public subnet's IP access with **Security Group** rules. You can find details on creating security group rules in the AWS documentation (`https://docs.aws.amazon.com/AWSEC2/latest/WindowsGuide/security-group-rules.html`). The same options are available with Microsoft Azure **network security groups** (`https://docs.microsoft.com/en-us/azure/virtual-network/network-security-groups-overview`) and Google Cloud **security groups** (`https://cloud.google.com/identity/docs/how-to/update-group-to-security-group`) or any other cloud provider.

Data source access

When securing your data environment, the final consideration is how Alteryx Server can access data sources. This situation requires that you determine how Alteryx can communicate with cloud-based data sources, such as **Snowflake** or **AWS Relational Database Service** (**RDS**) instances, and how you can access on-premises resources such as network files and databases.

For data services on your chosen AWS, the cloud provider used in our example, we would create a security group rule for the private subnet to allow communication between the worker nodes and the data resource subnets. This access would be contained inside the AWS environment and not require any resources in the public subnet.

To access an external cloud environment or one that is based on-premises, you need to define a secure connection between them. This is because the cloud-based data sources will often provide resources on the same cloud infrastructure as you are using. In the case of Snowflake, when creating your account, you define the cloud provider to be AWS. With Snowflake on AWS, you can use the **AWS PrivateLink** service. This service allows a secure connection between your Snowflake instance managed by Snowflake and your Alteryx Server in your organization's AWS environment. You can learn about connecting Snowflake and your cloud provider from the Snowflake documentation (`https://docs.snowflake.com/en/user-guide/private-snowflake-service.html`).

When you want to connect with on-premises resources, you need to join the environments differently. To establish a secure connection between the environments, you can create a dedicated network connection to AWS with **AWS Direct Connect**. You have secure communication between your on-premises location and an AWS Direct Connect service. Then you can route the communication to your AWS resources and your Alteryx Server. You can find details about AWS Direct Connect from the documentation (`https://docs.aws.amazon.com/directconnect/latest/UserGuide/Welcome.html`), while other cloud providers have similar offerings.

These two communication methods allow you to create isolated, secure communication pathways between your Alteryx Server and your data source. This means that any communication does not traverse general internet traffic and provides the security you need for data manipulation.

Summary

In this chapter, we learned the methods for organizing your Alteryx server so that workflows can be discovered and users can collaborate on Alteryx projects.

Next, we learned how to manage assets and users in Collections. We also learned how users can collaborate on projects and workflows on the Alteryx server with these skills.

Finally, we learned how to secure the Alteryx environment with the example of a server in AWS. We learned the basic server architecture and how to use security groups to control access to those resources. We also learned how to connect our Alteryx server environment with company data sources and enable a connection between a cloud environment and an on-premises environment.

In the next chapter, we will learn how to take the content on our Alteryx server and data sources from our environment and make them discoverable with **Connect**.

12
Making Data Easy to Use and Discoverable with Alteryx

Building a data pipeline and a dataset provides the foundation for data operations. Getting to the dataset solves the initial request that a data engineer will receive, but it will always leave end users with questions about the dataset you have created. Questions such as *What does the field xyz represent?* Or, *How was this metric calculated?* You can also have a situation where, because the dataset is unknown to most users in your organization, you get duplicate requests for the same data, or the dataset gets recreated, often with slight differences. This divergence in datasets leads to different teams reporting different results for the same question. **Alteryx Connect** was created to solve the data duplication and discovery challenge.

In this chapter, we will cover the following topics:

- What is Alteryx Connect, and how does it help DataOps?
- Publishing the data lineage to Alteryx Connect
- Syncing the Connect data dictionary with other data catalogs

Technical requirements

This chapter will focus on using Alteryx Connect. To follow the descriptions and examples, you will need access to a Connect instance. Additionally, the section on syncing a data dictionary using APIs will use the Tableau REST API for synchronizing the environments for different user groups. You can look at the example workflows in the book's GitHub repository here: `https://github.com/PacktPublishing/Data-Engineering-with-Alteryx/tree/main/Chapter%2012`.

What is Alteryx Connect, and how does it help DataOps?

Alteryx Connect is the data catalog and collaboration hub for your data assets. Connect provides a central point for describing datasets and understanding data relationships. It also provides a location for cross-department knowledge-sharing regarding the departments' datasets.

One example of a data catalog is **Kaggle Datasets** (`https://www.kaggle.com/datasets`). This site is a central repository for the discovery of Kaggle datasets and provides the context information for any datasets that have been produced. The catalog ensures that all Kaggle users understand what the datasets are and what the fields mean, meaning their analysis can be comparable.

According to the Alteryx Connect Product page (`https://www.alteryx.com/products/alteryx-connect`), Connect is described as:

> *A powerful data catalog combined with advanced analytics empowers everyone to quickly find, manage, understand, and collaborate across departments and the organization.*

This definition describes how Connect enables people to work together and share common resources throughout the organization. In addition, the **Delivery pillar** and the **Confidence pillar** of the DataOps principles are supported by Connect.

The Delivery pillar is supported by allowing datasets to be reused by different departments and teams. Connect reduces the duplication of effort and improves the cycle time of requests by providing a well-understood starting point for any dataset variations, rather than needing to start from the raw datasets with every request.

Connect supports the Confidence pillar by allowing reflection on the created data pipelines. This reflection starts by understanding how the multiple steps in a data pipeline interact and how much the organization uses a dataset you have made. Connect also facilitates the sharing of pipeline-specific knowledge in a central repository for the entire organization to leverage.

What is Connect?

The core function of Connect is to provide a robust data catalog for an organization. By providing a central location for teams to find datasets and learn the definitions of the data assets, teams can share the data assets for consistent analysis results. It also provides a location to highlight any reports created that might answer a user's question, saving them the time required to develop the report themselves.

There are three main areas where Connect allows end users to gain more significant insights into their datasets:

- **Find data assets and track lineage**: Using the search functions in Alteryx connect, end users can find any data asset in the organization. Users can find the data asset they need by populating the data catalog with data files, databases, reports, and Alteryx assets. You will also have an automatically populated data lineage, meaning the relationships between different data assets and the transformations a dataset has undergone can be identified.

- **Search and access trusted content**: Data stewards and experts can identify high-quality, reliable data sources (the kind of datasets you create following the DataOps principles) in the **data dictionary**. A data dictionary is a single location where all the data assets can be described and the contents defined for users to look up and understand. By highlighting the organization's curated dataset, everyone can save time finding the best dataset for their analysis.

- **Maintain context across your teams**: Having all teams across your organization understand the same data language allows for more coherent collaboration across teams. The Connect data dictionary and glossary allow the definitions of data assets and standard business terms to be consistent across the organization.

These three areas support our DataOps in two primary ways:

- By increasing the confidence users have in the data assets
- By improving the discoverability of the data assets that we create

This allows data engineers to get the best returns on the time and energy that they invest due to increasing the data confidence and discoverability in our data assets and data pipelines.

Now that we know how Connect is supporting our DataOps principles, we can look at the specifics of how to use Connect and how to derive the benefits for our operations.

Areas of the Connect interface

The **CONNECT** home page is the central location where users search for the data assets they need. The following screenshot shows the main areas of the Connect interface:

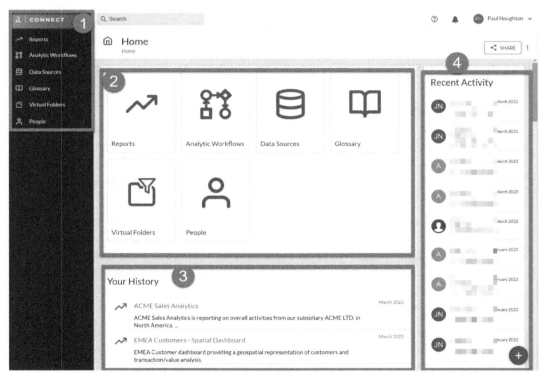

Figure 12.1 – The Connect home page with the main sections highlighted

On the Connect home page, there are three sections:

- **Navigation areas**: On the home page, there are two main navigation areas; the menus on the left side of the page (annotated as **1**), and the navigation buttons in the center (annotated as **2**).

- **Your activity history**: At the bottom of the page is a history of your page navigation on Connect. It lists all the places you have visited and gives a quick method for returning (annotated as **3**).

- **All users' recent activity**: This final section (annotated as **4**) highlights the updates by other users. It shows where people are adding content to your Connect environment and what changes your data community makes.

These areas in the interface allow users to navigate to the content they are interested in and have an overview of what activities are happening on the server.

Also on the home page is a search bar for finding the content of interest by keyword. This feature will search for the given keyword in any populated field for the data assets in Connect.

Using Connect for DataOps

When trying to find data assets on the server, there are two methods:

- Navigating to the content type
- Searching the data assets

These two methods allow you to find the content depending on what you already know about the data asset you are trying to find. We will look at these different methods in the following sections.

Navigating to the assets directly

If you know what asset type you are trying to find, for example, a database table, you can navigate to the asset directly. To find a database, search in the Data Sources area of Connect, after following the order as shown in the following screenshot:

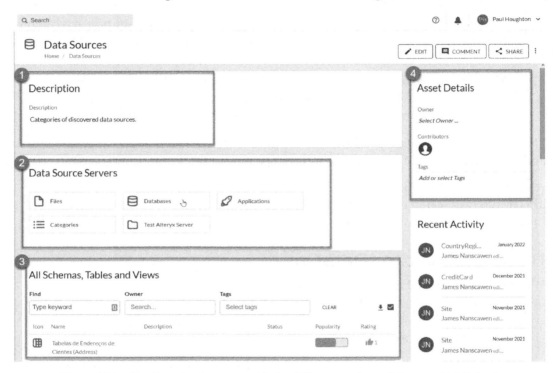

Figure 12.2 – The Data Sources page with the different sections of the page highlighted

Four areas are highlighted in the **Data Sources** page screenshot that provides information about the data sources. All the data assets on the server are laid out in a similar way. You can follow the annotations:

1. **Description**: A description of the data source you are viewing

2. **Data Source Servers**: Grouping the top-level content for the data source type

3. **All Schemas, Tables and Views**: Specific entries in the overall data source

4. **Asset Details**: Details about the data source, including the owner, contributors, and search tags

The four sections described provide multiple avenues to find your desired data asset. When you know you are looking for a specific database, you can navigate to the **Databases** button link in section two. Then, you can find all the database servers listed on the next page. The **Database servers** section is shown in the following screenshot:

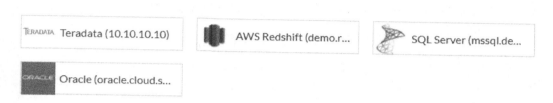

Figure 12.3 – The Database servers section of the Databases page in Connect

Once you have located the database (the **SQL Server** option from the preceding screenshot, which is then displayed in *Figure 12.4*), the final step in finding your data asset is to identify the table or schema of interest. On the **Databases** page, seen in the following screenshot, there are a series of description fields to help locate the data asset of interest:

Figure 12.4 – An example database entry with section four highlighted

The preceding screenshot shows the main Database page, which contains general information, such as the server, common alternative names for the database, and the hostname. Additionally, the **ACTION** button (highlighted in red) allows you to request access to the data source from the owner. If you already have access to the data source, you can create a new workflow with the data source included.

At the bottom of the page, the same page as *Figure 12.4*, are the details of every table in the database. In addition, the following screenshot provides a more detailed view of this section:

All Tables

Find		Owner	Tags		
Type keyword		Search...	Select tags	CLEAR	⬇ ☑

Icon	Name	Description	Status	Popularity	Rating
⊞	Tabelas de Endereços de Cientes (Address)				👍 1
⊞	AddressType				
⊞	AWBuildVersion				
⊞	BillOfMaterials				

Figure 12.5 – A detailed view of the All Tables listing

The preceding screenshot contains information about the table names, a description of the table, the status of the data source, the popularity, and the rating of the data source. Each of these individual entries gives additional context about the data source, allowing you to isolate the most relevant and best quality data source for your application.

Searching the data assets

The second method for finding your dataset involves the search capability of Alteryx Connect to identify the data source you need. The search box is located across the top of every page, next to the Alteryx Connect logo. For example, we can find a dataset called account and perform a search from the search box, shown in the following screenshot:

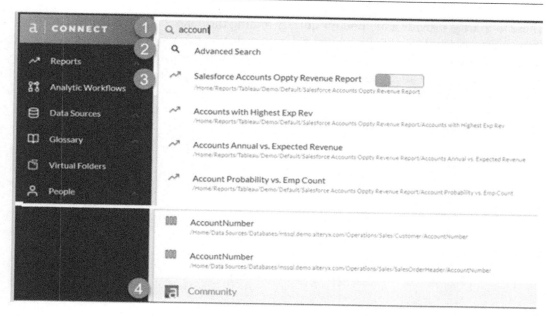

Figure 12.6 – An example search looking for an account asset

Four areas are noted:

1. **The initial search box**: This box is for entering your initial search query; in this case, *account*.

2. **The advanced search link**: The second entry provides a link to the advanced search page, providing the capability to narrow your search parameters further.

3. **Quick matches with popularity and certification indicators**: The next section lists your initial search results. The list is organized according to asset type (as indicated by the icon next to the entry), with certified data assets appearing first, followed by the most popular data assets. The popularity of an asset is used as a proxy for the quality of the data source.

4. **Community results list**: At the bottom of the results list, several results are returned from the **Alteryx Community** (`community.alteryx.com`). Additionally, there are direct links to the community results and for creating a community question.

These four areas provide a method for quickly finding the dataset you are interested in. If the quick search does not give a good dataset result, you can refine your search further with the **Advanced Search** option. The following screenshot shows the advanced search for the *account* query after you select the **Advanced Search** option from the previous screen that we discussed:

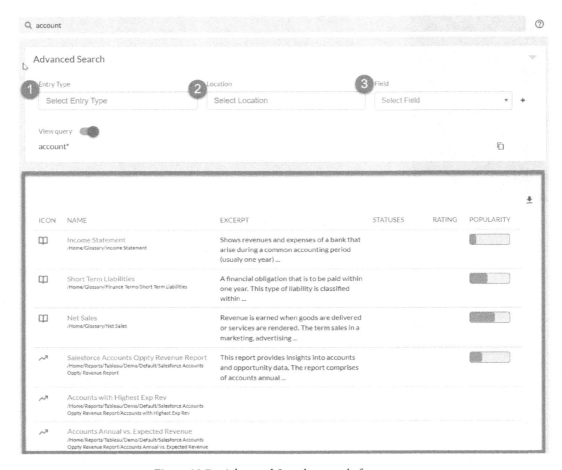

Figure 12.7 – Advanced Search example for account

The **Advanced Search** box shows additional filtering options for **Entry Type**, the **Location** data source is in Connect, and finally, the field you wish to search in. The entry type and location allow you to isolate your search. For example, if you are looking for a database table, you can set **Entry Type** to an *application table* and **Location** to *data sources*.

This advanced searching allows you to find a known data asset type, even if they aren't sure of the data source's naming.

Publishing the data lineage to Alteryx Connect

We have been looking at a data catalog where all the individual assets, such as the tables or fields, have the information already populated. For this information to be available, you need to populate the data asset information into Connect. There are three methods for populating the Connect data assets:

- Loading metadata directly from Connect
- Using the prebuilt workflow apps
- Creating a custom-built data source with the Connect APIs

These methods allow you to populate your Connect data dictionary with the information that exists in your data asset. For databases, Alteryx will extract any comment information in addition to tables, field names, and field types. Let's take a look at them one by one.

Loading metadata directly from Connect

The first method for loading metadata is directly from Alteryx Connect. To initialize the metadata collection from Connect, there are two prerequisites:

- You must be an Alteryx Connect administrator.
- You have the Alteryx Gallery Admin API enabled.

Using these two Alteryx permissions, you can populate records in the Connect database and create the workflow on your Alteryx Server (via the Alteryx Gallery interface) to extract the metadata from the target data sources.

Configuring Alteryx Connect to extract the metadata requires two configuration steps:

1. Creating the Alteryx Gallery connection
2. Defining the Data Source connections

The first step enables the API execution of workflows on your Alteryx Gallery, while the second step defines what data sources you want to populate.

Creating the Gallery connection

The core requirement for creating a Data Source connection is to define the **Alteryx Gallery** authentication details. You define the Gallery connection information in the **Administration Console** connection. First, you will navigate to the **Alteryx Gallery** tab, as shown in the following screenshot:

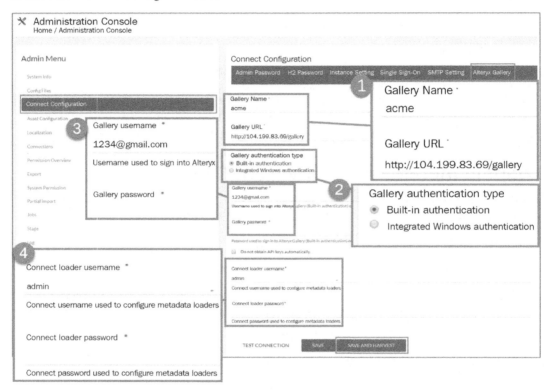

Figure 12.8 – Alteryx Gallery configuration in the Connect Admin console

In the screenshot, four sections are shown that need to be populated:

1. **Gallery location**: The **Gallery Name** and **Gallery URL** fields of the server that will run the connect loader workflow.

2. **Gallery authentication type**: The authentication type defines how users authenticate to your Alteryx Gallery. If you are using Windows Authentication, you will need to include the **Windows domain** information as part of the authentication.

3. **Authentication name**: The Alteryx Gallery login details for running the metadata loader workflow. This user needs to have Admin API credentials to create the workflow run.

4. **Connect authentication**: The **Connect** authentication information is used to populate the Connect database.

Once you have populated the four areas, you can use the **TEST CONNECTION** button to confirm whether the configuration is correct. Once this is working correctly, you can start defining the data sources you want to populate.

Defining the data source connection

You create a **data source connection** in the **Connection** tab of the Connect **Administration Console** window. The following screenshot shows the connections page with the **ADD CONNECTION** button highlighted:

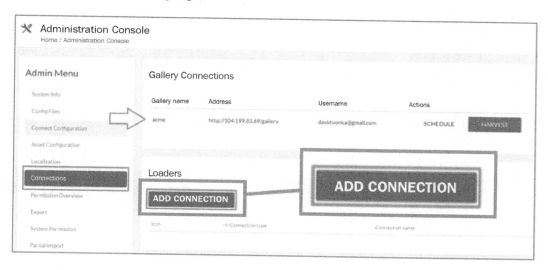

Figure 12.9 – The Connections administration page with the ADD CONNECTION button highlighted

After clicking the **ADD CONNECTION** button shown in the preceding screenshot, you can populate your data source's authentication information. First, you will select the technology you're creating a data source for. This technology could be a database, filesystem, or business intelligence server.

In the Connection details, the following screenshot shows an example of a filesystem. You will populate the information for both the target data source and the Connect server you want to populate.

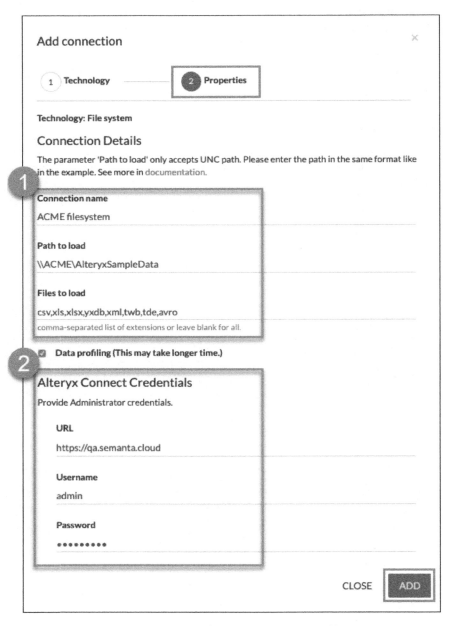

Figure 12.10 – Example of a new connection to a filesystem

In the screenshot, the first section highlighted shows the connection information for the target data source. A filesystem data source will take a name, a UNC path that you want to load, and the file type extensions you wish to load.

The second section is the Alteryx Connect catalog you want to populate. This information needs to be populated as Alteryx Gallery performs the processing and extraction process you configured in the *Creating the Gallery connection* section. This Gallery connection also needs to have access to the data source location you will populate. This requires network access through company networks and firewalls and authentication permissions to access the data source target that you are trying to load.

Scheduling the metadata extraction

Once you have a Gallery connection and a data source defined, you can extract the metadata in a one-off process or create a schedule to update the metadata regularly. Both methods for extracting the data require **Alteryx Gallery Admin API** authentication to run. That is why permissions are required when creating the Gallery connection.

You execute a one-off manual run with the **Harvest** button on the **Connections** admin page that we saw in *Figure 12.9*. This will send the connection directly to your Alteryx Server (defined in the *Creating the Gallery connection* section) and run as soon as possible.

Manually updating the metadata is helpful for static or one-time data sources. However, regularly updating the metadata is preferable for changing or evolving data sources. Creating a schedule for updating uses the **Schedule** button to define a **Cron** expression. Cron expressions are a Linux OS task process (a full explanation of Cron expressions is available on the Linux manual pages: `https://man7.org/linux/man-pages/man5/crontab.5.html`). A cron expression takes seven individual numbers separated by a space, and each number represents a different section of time (the time fields) when the schedule will run.

The fields are as follows:

```
#Seconds #Minutes #Hours #Day-of-Month #Day-of-Week
#Year(optional)
```

Each section of time combines to define when a workflow runs during the day. Additionally, there are special characters that provide flexibility to the expression. An example of a special character is *, which represents any value.

Using Connect to load the metadata leverages the Gallery Admin APIs and automatically populates the Connect loader workflow apps. While creating the workflows directly in Connect is a simple method for extracting the metadata, you can get the same functionality using the prebuilt **Loader apps**.

Using the prebuilt workflow apps

The prebuilt workflows are provided as an installer file from the Alteryx downloads page (http://downloads.alteryx.com). On this page, navigate to the Connect installer files page and choose the **Alteryx Connect Loaders** installer. For example, this is seen in the following screenshot:

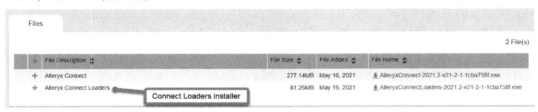

Figure 12.11 – Download page for Alteryx Connect Loaders

The connect loaders are installed on a local computer with an Alteryx Designer license. You use the Designer application to configure and prepare the connection configuration for the Connect loaders app. When scheduling the metadata loader to run, the workflow will also need to be published to the Alteryx Server or the Connect metadata loaders installed on the server.

Once you have downloaded the connect loaders, a new menu will appear in your Alteryx Designer Help menu, specifically, **Help | Sample Workflows | Alteryx Connect Metadata Loaders**. This menu is shown in the following screenshot:

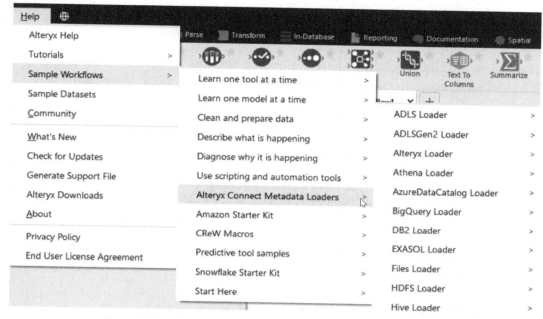

Figure 12.12 – Help menu location of the Connect metadata loaders

From the Help menu shown in the preceding screenshot, you can select the data source from which you want to extract metadata. You can find the complete list of existing metadata loaders on the Connect help page (`https://help.alteryx.com/20211/connect/load-metadata`). After selecting the metadata loader, you can run the loader as an analytic app using the Run as an analytic app button beside the **Run** button, as shown in the following screenshot:

Figure 12.13 – The Run as an analytic app button

By selecting the run as an analytic app button, you can populate the data source and connect the instance configuration. You apply the configuration in two steps: first, the connection information for the target data source, and second, the connection details for your Connect instance.

Creating a custom-built data source with the Connect APIs

The final method for populating Alteryx Connect is to create a custom connect loader. When building a custom loader workflow, there are three main steps involved:

1. Creating an **XML file** containing the data source structure
2. Creating an XML file to define the Connect Load Job configuration
3. Uploading the metadata using the Connect helper macros

We have already investigated creating a workflow in *Chapter 4, Sourcing the Data,* and *Chapter 5, Data Processing and Transformations.* The same skills learned in those chapters are applied here to build the workflow, so we will discuss the process and logic needed to create a custom loader. You can read the full details for using the Connect Loader SDK on the Alteryx help pages (`https://help.alteryx.com/developer-help/build-connect-loaders-connect-sdk`).

Creating the data source XML structure

The first step in creating a custom loader is to define your data source's structure. Next, the structure is recorded in an XML file and then loaded into the Connect database.

The structure required to create a data asset is defined in the example `county.xml` file. You can download this file from the Alteryx support pages (`https://help.alteryx.com/developer-help/configuration-files-creation-example`). Using this structure, you build a form to upload for Connect to interpret. The form starts with the data source identification information:

- `xid`: The unique identifier for the application.
- `icon`: A base64-encoded icon for displaying in the Connect interface.
- `entry-name`: This is the label for users to interact with.

You use these tags to identify the data source so that users can interact with the created asset in Alteryx Connect.

The next section defines the data source structure in a grid formation. This tag contains the metadata that is contained in the data source, including the following:

- `id`
- `name`
- `fields` (a tag that includes the individual fields for the data source identified)

These individual components are repeated for each table or object imported into Alteryx Connect.

After the table objects are defined, you can define the relationships in your custom data source to populate the **data nexus**. These relationships are defined by adding a `group` tag with the `id` tag of `Nexus` and a `name` tag of `Relationships`. In this relationship group, you define the additional tags for the relationships you want to appear in the nexus.

Finally, you populate the `list` tag to define which fields will appear in the listed entries. For example, these fields would be the individual columns of a database or table, along with the additional details you want to share, including the field description.

Creating the Connect Job definition

Once the data source structure definition has been created, we need to tell Connect how any updated records will be imported from the staging table. This staging table is defined in the **Connect helper macros** that you will use in the next section. The Connect API uploads new records to the primary data dictionary.

Much like the data source definition XML, the job definition takes the instructions in XML form. In addition, it defines how the staging table records we uploaded get translated into the main Connect application.

The job definition starts by creating a new XML file with the `loading-instructions` outer XML and `loading-instruction` as the first level down the XML tree. Once inside the loading instructions, we can define how the staging table is imported:

- `job-id`: This is the unique identifier that you will call in the API when triggering each job run.

- `for-each-row`: This opens the sub-job processes executed for each row in the Data Source definition. In this level of the XML tree, we then define the next set of parameters for the individual rows:

  - `sub-job-id`: This allows you to create a hierarchical structure to import the data source with multiple levels (such as a schema containing tables that hold fields).

  - `of-query`: This is the SQL query that you use to select the importing records.

  - `define-entry`: This section will define how your staging asset maps into the Connect UI. The tree nodes that appear in this section will identify the data source you are importing and will change based on what you want to appear. Because of this variability, it is best to find which specific fields you want based on your dataset.

Once you define the method to import each table, you can repeat the process for each level of the data source schema, table, and column hierarchy. You can use subsequent for-each-row tree nodes to traverse the levels of your data source.

Uploading the metadata with the Connect helper macros

The final step for your custom loader is to upload the data to a staging table and import it into the **Connect User Interface (UI)**. To upload the metadata, the Connect helpers will automatically extract the metadata from your data source.

An example workflow method is shown in the following screenshot:

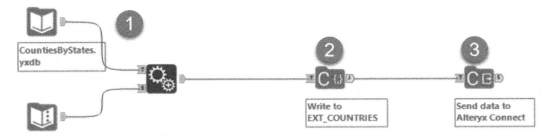

Figure 12.14 – An example data loader using the Alteryx Connect helper macros

In the preceding screenshot, the three basic steps involved in building the table to upload to Connect are as follows:

1. Extract the initial records from the data source, including any information about the fields. You append a LOAD_CODE field to each record as part of this initial information. This LOAD_CODE identifies the staging table records that will need to be removed by this loader.

2. After collecting the field information from your data source, the **Connect Json Builder** helper macro will take the input field and convert the metadata into the correct JSON format. The Connect JSON builder only requires you to define the staging table name. This table should have a prefix of EXT_ to help manage the cleanup of the table after it has been imported.

3. Finally, upload the correctly formatted JSON file using the **Connect Output** helper macro in the **Connect Output - Configuration** macro. A screenshot of the configuration window is shown here:

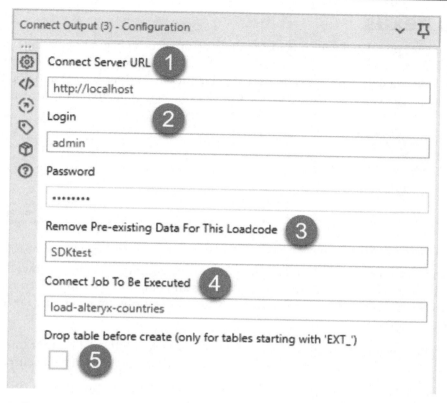

Figure 12.15 – The configuration window of the Connect Output helper macro

In the preceding screenshot, five areas need to be configured:

1. The URL of your Alteryx Connect instance.
2. The login information for the server. These login details need to have permissions to update the Connect database.
3. The load code that you defined in the first step of your custom loader and appended to the sample records.
4. Identify the Connect Job that will need to be executed. This job was created in the *Creating the Connect Job definition* section.
5. Finally, If you have applied the prefix EXT_ to your staging tables, you can clear those records as part of the configuration. It is best practice to use this option to keep the database clean and performant.

These three steps are the core requirements for building a custom loader. Each of these steps will be augmented by preparing the data source you are interested in. This should include the different hierarchies you want in your final Connect data asset.

Data nexus

Once you have populated your metadata, Alteryx Connect can begin populating relationships between data assets. For example, Alteryx Connect can find the different locations where a data asset has been used and identify that asset's lineage and popularity. This lineage is displayed to the user in the Data Nexus seen in the following screenshot:

Figure 12.16 – An example data relationship shown in the Data Nexus lineage view

At the center of the nexus is the data source you are examining. The nexus shows the relationship between the data source and its inputs and outputs. The simple relationship example shown can also be expanded with any transformations applied to the raw data to generate the final data source.

When examining an intermediate data source, you can explore the data source lineage back to its source and follow the additional transformations and output data sources.

In addition to the **Lineage** view, you can change the mode type to **Joins** or **All**. The Joins mode type provides information on how multiple data sources are combined to create an output or report.

The **All** mode type provides details about the data asset content. It shows the individual fields and any manually added metadata, including tags, descriptions, and the frequency associated with the data source.

Now that we have the methods for populating our Connect instance and our data dictionary, we need to consider how our users will access the information we have populated. Not all of our end users will want to access the data dictionary outside their usual work applications, so we can provide the information in the best way for them.

Syncing the Connect data dictionary with other data catalogs

While populating your data dictionary gives you a single location to reference your organization's knowledge, not all the users in your company will use Connect, and, as we mentioned in *Chapter 3, DataOps and Its Benefits*, we know that the specific tool you use is of secondary importance. Making sure the data assets you have created can be used again will allow you to extract the most value from your data assets. We can synchronize our Connect data dictionary into other data management platforms using the Connect APIs to achieve this.

Using the Connect API methods

The Connect API uses a cycle of logging in to the server, performing your actions, and then logging out. An example process for this activity is shown in the following screenshot:

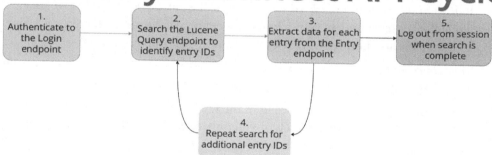

Figure 12.17 – An example cycle for using the Alteryx Connect API

In the diagram, we can see a cycle where you do the following:

1. **Log in to the Connect API**: You authenticate to the Connect API with the Login endpoint. The response from this endpoint includes `session_cookie` in the body as follows:

   ```
   {"session_cookie":"JSESSIONID\u003d435"}
   ```

   This `session_cookie` proves your permissions for any subsequent API interactions.

2. Once you have a `session_cookie`, you can begin the cycle of querying the API endpoints for the information you need. To extract the primary information, such as the entry type, primary data, and data source fields, you can use the **Lucene** endpoint to search for the matching entries.

    You query the Lucene endpoint by providing a Lucene query (as defined in the **Apache Lucene query parser syntax** standard at `https://lucene.apache. org/core/2_9_4/queryparsersyntax.html`) to the `/rest/1/lucene` URL endpoint.

    The Lucene query endpoint response includes an `xid` that can extract more details about the data source relationships.

    An example query from the Alteryx help pages searches for `ancestorsandme`:

    ```
    curl -X GET "http://localhost:8080/rest/1/lucene?query=
    ancestorsandme%3AMzRlM2RhZTAtMzc1YS00YTBjLTk5ODMtYzQz
    YTBiMDFiNWFh&offset=0&limit=4" -H "accept: application/
    json;charset=UTF-8"
    ```

    In this query, the endpoint is defined by the `/rest/1/lucene` path. Then, following the question mark, `query=` begins the entry you are trying to query, while the `offset` and `limit` parameters define what page of the response you want to view and how many entries you want to see with each page.

    This query will return all the information about this specific entry, but to populate any relationship information, you need to drill into the **entry** endpoint.

3. Next, you can take the `xid` returned in the Lucene search and search for that entry's parents and children. Additionally, if you only need the information for a specific entry (and you know what that entry's `xid` is), you can use the entry endpoint to ascertain that information.

    The entry endpoint takes the host address and searches for the `/rest/1/entry/ {xid}` path. If you append `/parent` or `/children`, you will extract the upstream and downstream relationships.

4. After searching for the initial information, you can repeat this process to extract additional details for your entries. For example, you can repeat an entry query loop to find the grandparents or great-grandparents of the original entry. Alternatively, you could start a new **Lucene** search to find additional information on the following database or report set you are interested in.

5. Once your query process is complete, you call the `/logout` endpoint to finish your session.

Each query needs the `session_cookie` you received in *step 1* through *steps 2 to 5*. This `session_cookie` is passed into the `--cookies` flag of your `curl` command, defining the cookie name of `JSESSIONID`.

Tableau Data Dictionary API example

The final step to synchronizing your data dictionaries is to format your extracted Connect assets and upload any additional data dictionaries. This step is unique to each data dictionary and requires matching what each Alteryx Connect field represents to the equivalent in your target dictionary.

As an example, if you are trying to populate a **Tableau Data Catalog** (an example catalog page is shown in *Figure 12.18*), you would use a combination of the **Tableau Metadata API**, which leverages the **GraphQL** language for interaction, and the metadata methods in the **Tableau REST API**.

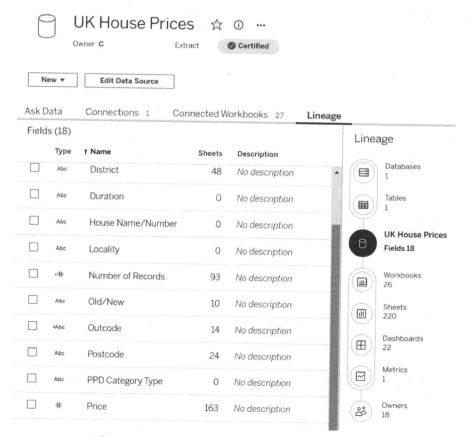

Figure 12.18 – An example Tableau data catalog page

Even though you are trying to synchronize the Alteryx Connect data catalog and the Tableau data catalog, the information you need in both applications is different. For example, because the Tableau data catalog focuses on the data assets inside the Tableau environment, it does not require the entire lineage of transformations that occur in relation to a data source. Instead, the information that is needed is that the Tableau data source is a transformed asset and a link back to the Connect asset for the transformation details.

To update the description of a table asset in the Tableau catalog, you would PUT data in the **update tables** endpoint. The query you would send is as follows:

```
PUT api/<api-version>/sites/<site-id>/tables/<table-id>
```

In the preceding URI, `<site-id>` and `<table-id>` are both parameters to update, which are the unique identifiers for the table you want to edit. The `<api-version>` parameter depends on the version of Tableau Server you are using to update.

With the URI configured, you would then add the **request body** to that to update the table entry. The request body is provided as an XML formatted field as follows:

```
<tsRequest>
  <table isCertified="certification-status"
    certificationNote="certification-note"
    description="new-description-value">
    <contact id="new-contact-id">
    </contact>
  </table>
</tsRequest>
```

There are four optional attributes in the table element in the request body. These attributes are as follows:

- `isCertified`
- `certificationNote`
- `description`
- `contact id`

In our example, where we want to update the description with a URL back to the Alteryx Connect asset, we would populate the `description` field with the Connect information and description details we extracted from our Connect query in the previous section.

We have discussed a single example of synchronizing our data catalogs. Using the skills we learned when interacting with APIs in *Chapter 4*, *Sourcing the Data*, we can authenticate with our target data dictionary (the Tableau data catalog was the example we provided) and update that information with the Download tool. We achieve this by setting the **HTTP action** verbs according to the API requirements.

Summary

In this chapter, we learned why Alteryx Connect is a good tool for managing our data asset discovery and how that helps our DataOps deployment. We learned how to use the Connect navigation and search functionality to find and understand our data assets. We discovered the community knowledge-sharing functions available in Connect to build a rich understanding of what data resources exist and how we can access them.

We then learned the methods for populating our data dictionary. Next, we explored the different ways of populating the Alteryx Connect data catalog. The first was to populate the analytic apps directly in Connect, using the Alteryx Server API to run the workflow in the background. Second, we learned how to deploy the Connect loader apps in Alteryx Designer and scheduled those apps with the methods we learned in *Chapter 2*, *Data Engineering with Alteryx*. Finally, we learned the final technique to directly update the Connect data catalog with the APIs. This provided the mechanism for creating custom loaders for any data asset we required.

The final action we learned was how to synchronize our Connect data catalog with other data management systems. We remembered that following DataOps means we use whatever tool makes the most sense for an application and that not all users would interact with the Alteryx Connect environment. With this knowledge, we saw an example of populating the information extracted from Connect into a Tableau data catalog where many business users might be operating.

With the Alteryx Connect catalog created, we have completed the process of developing an Alteryx data pipeline and applied the DataOps principles. The final chapter will bring all the steps we have created from the first chapter to this one, into a single narrative to clarify the end-to-end process we have followed.

13
Conclusion

Throughout this book, we have been learning the methods and reasons to create data pipelines in **Alteryx**. In addition, we have been learning the skills required to take a raw dataset from internal resources or public **Application Programming Interface (APIs)** and transform them into valuable resources for your organization.

This final chapter will consolidate our learning into an end-to-end process. It will remind us of the DataOps approach we implemented, the skills and methods we used to process our datasets, and the governance methods we will apply to manage our data pipelines for our organization's use.

In this chapter, we will summarize the following topics:

- The Alteryx data engineer
- The functional steps in DataOps
- Governance of DataOps with Alteryx
- Our Alteryx data pipeline

The Alteryx data engineer

The **Alteryx Software** stack, comprising **Alteryx Designer**, **Alteryx Server**, and **Alteryx Connect**, is the core tool an Alteryx data engineer uses to build, deploy, and publicize the datasets and data pipelines created. Following an iterative development process, a data engineer quickly finds a dataset, transforms the dataset, and then provides the dataset to end users.

In *Chapter 1, Getting Started*, we introduced the components of the Alteryx platform and demonstrated their use in a simple example. We also introduced the working definition of data engineering as follows:

Data engineering is the process of taking data from any number of disparate sources and transforming it into a usable format for an end user.

This definition provided a starting point for building a process for accessing data sources and making them a valuable resource for our end users. Using Alteryx provided three key benefits for you as a data engineer:

- Speed of development
- Iterative workflow development
- Self-documentation

These three benefits are found throughout the platform to make your data pipelines more accessible and faster to deploy.

We introduced Alteryx Designer as a tool for high-speed development, allowing the rapid iteration of a workflow to find a solution for any challenge your end users present to you. This chapter was also where we introduced the Designer interface, which we see in *Figure 13.1* as follows:

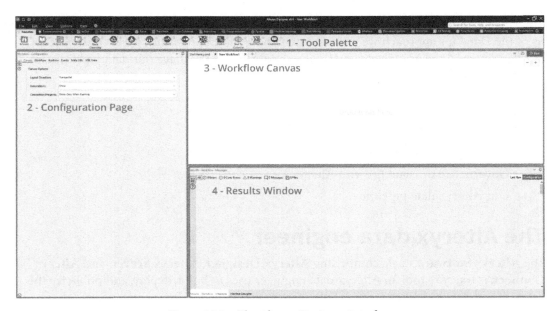

Figure 13.1 – The Alteryx Designer interface

This interface provides the data engineer with easy access to all the resources and tool configuration settings close to hand.

We also looked at the server resources with Alteryx Server and Alteryx Connect. These two components allow **data engineers**, **data scientists**, and **analysts** to automate their data pipelines and connect with end users.

Alteryx Server provides a platform to automate data pipelines on time-based schedules and provides APIs for web automation. Alteryx Server also helps data engineers scale their data pipelines and analytics to end users. End users can manually trigger workflows, access the reports created, and monitor data quality using browser-based interactions. The capabilities of Alteryx Server allow data engineers to reach beyond their immediate users and have their work used productively by a wider audience.

Alteryx Connect is the communication layer for Alteryx, providing a data dictionary for all the assets in an organization so end users can find what assets are available, what the contents of an asset are, and what the lineage of the asset is.

The three Alteryx software tools provide components of an Alteryx data engineer's tech stack. With these tools, a data engineer can build a data pipeline to solve the questions from our end users. These tools provide a way to develop your data pipelines, but it doesn't describe how we implement the data engineering process with Alteryx.

In *Chapter 2, Data Engineering with Alteryx*, we learned how to develop an Alteryx data pipeline. We also introduced what a data engineer was to separate the person from the task. We defined a data engineer as follows:

The person that takes any available tools to collect data together then cleanses and transforms the raw data to create an enriched dataset. The raw data can be from any company, commercial, or public source. The final enriched dataset is a cohesive, interpretable, and usable data source that end users trust.

With this definition of a data engineer, we have an adaptable person who creates value for end users. It also shows that, while not tied to any particular tool, a data engineer needs a flexible tool that can quickly iterate over multiple datasets and pipelines.

Chapter 2, Data Engineering with Alteryx, also introduced the main areas where we leverage DataOps with Alteryx. Those areas are as follows:

- Data sourcing and processing

- Storage and value extraction

- Governance and monitoring

- Improving access

These four areas appear throughout the DataOps life cycle, where we create a data pipeline in an Alteryx Designer workflow. We then automate the storage and analysis of datasets with Alteryx Designer and Server.

We then move on to leveraging automated workflows and **Alteryx Insight Dashboards** to monitor the quality of a dataset and the performance of workflows running on your Alteryx Server.

We also use Alteryx Server to manage the visibility of and access to workflows, analytic apps, and created insights.

Finally, we use Alteryx Connect to improve the visibility and understanding of the datasets that we have created. Using the data dictionary and community-sourced knowledge relating to the records, alongside the lineage information, highlights the workflow's source and what resources might be accessing the assets.

The final chapter in *Part 1, Introduction* was *Chapter 3, DataOps and Its Benefits*. This chapter details the three DataOps pillars shown in *Figure 13.2*:

The DataOps Pillars

People	Delivery	Confidence
• Continually satisfy your customer	• Improve cycle times	• Quality is paramount
	• Simplicity	• Monitor quality and performance
• Embrace change	• Reuse	• Reflect
• Daily interactions	• Value working analytics	
	• Orchestrate	• Reduce heroism
• It's a team sport	• Analytics is code	• Make it reproducible
• Self-organize	• Analytics is manufacturing	• Disposable environments

Figure 13.2 – The DataOps pillars from Chapter 3, DataOps and Its Benefits

As we see in the preceding diagram, the three pillars are **People**, **Delivery**, and **Confidence**—each of the pillars groups the principles that need to be adopted to build a functioning DataOps process.

- The **People** pillar contains the principles that unite the individual DataOps practitioners. It focuses on the interactions between the practitioners and between the practitioners and end users. Each principle highlights a practice we embed in the organization's data culture.

- The **Delivery** pillar encompasses the principles that get a data asset from concept to the end user—finding methods for integrating faster development, reducing work duplication, and building a constant improvement mindset toward any data asset and pipeline created.

- The final **Confidence** pillar helps both data engineers and end users understand what the datasets are and where they are sourced. In addition, it gives the freedom to test new methodologies for data extraction without fear of irreparably breaking critical data assets.

Within the DataOps framework, Alteryx products support all aspects of the framework and allow users to test and deploy any solution and communicate the contents of the data asset.

Armed with our understanding of Alteryx and the DataOps framework, we transitioned our learning into the functional steps of creating a data pipeline with Alteryx, using the DataOps principles as a foundation of how we will structure our pipeline project.

The functional steps in DataOps

In *Part 2, The Functional Steps in DataOps*, we saw how within a DataOps project, we take five overarching steps:

1. Sourcing the data
2. Data processing and transformations
3. Destination management
4. Value extraction
5. Beginning advanced analytics

We detailed each step in a separate chapter. We also split the value extraction step into two chapters, allowing for the getting primary value extraction details and extending our analytic capabilities with the advanced spatial and machine learning features in Alteryx.

Sourcing the data

Chapter 4, Sourcing the Data, began our data pipeline construction by connecting to three different data source location types:

- Internal organization data sources
- Downloading public files
- Using public APIs for data extraction

These three data locations provide the basis for most of the data sources you find as a data engineer. The internal data sources are any files or databases your organization owns and are accessible using the **Input Data** tool. This tool is the primary method for connecting to files on your local computer or stored on network drives. It is also the primary way to connect to databases, such as Snowflake, Microsoft SQL Server, or Postgres. Using the Input Data tool gives a common starting point for those data sources, which are seen in the following screenshot:

Figure 13.3 – The Data connections options as seen in Chapter 4, Sourcing the Data

In instances where your data is provided by external sources, such as government agencies or commercial APIs, accessing the data from them requires the use of the **Download** tool. You can access public files from a consistent URL or authenticate with a secured API to acquire the data records with the Download tool. We learned the most straightforward method for downloading from public resources and a standard procedure for authenticating with URL parameters.

Data processing and transformations

Understanding how to connect to a data source, we moved on to the common data transformation skills required in a data pipeline. *Chapter 5, Data Processing and Transformations* introduced the series of transformations and cleansing steps common to all data pipelines. These processes can be completed in any order and include the following:

- Selecting the fields of interest

- Selecting the records that are required

- Transforming the shape of your dataset to meet your requirements

These three steps are the core of any data pipeline for two reasons; they provide the records required for analytic processes and the skill set required for most other transformations in Alteryx. In addition, these steps demonstrated the skills needed to modify the records in your dataset.

Once we had transformed our dataset, we undertook an initial profiling and summarization process to understand our dataset to be confident that what we had created would meet our requirements.

Destination management

We have created an initial dataset at this point of our data pipeline. It might require future processing and enrichment, but we have fulfilled the core requirements for the data. Now, we need to save our data for future use. In *Chapter 6, Destination Management*, we looked at the different methods for persisting our data to files and databases. In addition, we examined the ways to make file locations robust and repeatable and how to use other database connection mechanisms to ensure our data pipelines will work in all of our data environments.

When connecting to files, we looked at using both relative file paths and leveraging **Universal Naming Convention** (UNC) paths for referencing our files. With these different file controls, we can deploy our data pipeline to Alteryx Server or share the workflow with our data team, confident that the workflow will run without errors. We can see the use of UNC paths in *Figure 13.4*:

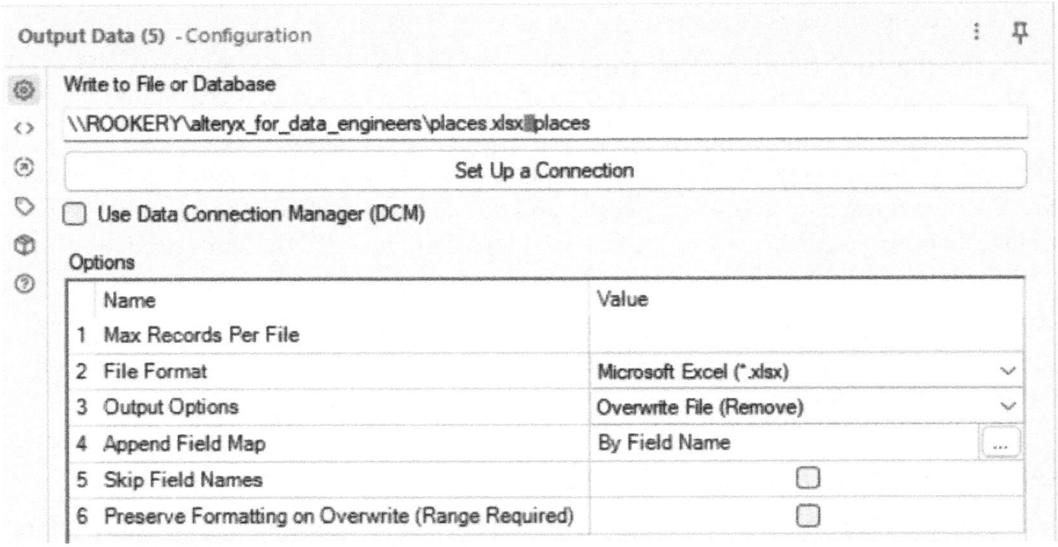

Output Data (5) - Configuration		
Write to File or Database		
\\ROOKERY\alteryx_for_data_engineers\places.xlsx‖places		
Set Up a Connection		
☐ Use Data Connection Manager (DCM)		
Options		
Name	Value	
1 Max Records Per File		
2 File Format	Microsoft Excel (*.xlsx)	⌄
3 Output Options	Overwrite File (Remove)	⌄
4 Append Field Map	By Field Name	...
5 Skip Field Names	☐	
6 Preserve Formatting on Overwrite (Range Required)	☐	

Figure 13.4 – An example of an Excel file saved to a network location using an UNC path

When connecting to databases, we had a similar set of considerations for ensuring the workflow would work in different environments. Using a **DSN-less** connection, we can remove an **ODBC manager** dependency and make the data connection portable. We also considered how we would upload the records to the database. When using a standard ODBC connection, records are written one row at a time, resulting in slow uploads for large datasets. This method does allow the flexibility of updating existing records (provided the database table has a primary key defined) but at the cost of slow writing.

The alternative is to use the bulk upload connection. With these methods, the upload process is faster as a single SQL command writes the data, but you lose the flexibility of modifying existing records. Additionally, if there are any primary key conflicts, you need a method to identify and reprocess those records.

The final customization we applied is to use the database's custom **command-line interface** (CLI) tools. With these CLI options, you have full access to the database functionality, but it requires you to create the SQL code needed for the process you want to deploy.

Extracting value from data

After we have persisted, the dataset can begin using the data for analysis. *Chapter 7, Extracting Value*, and *Chapter 8, Beginning Advanced Analytics*, look at the options for how we can extract value from our data.

The analytics process starts in *Chapter 7, Extracting Value*, with exploratory data analysis. We begin by identifying the overall profile of our dataset. This profile gives us an understanding of the type of records present in each field. We can quickly get an overview of our data using the **Basic Data Profile** tool and then reshape the profile for future analysis.

We can identify possible data quality issues by taking the basic data profile output. For example, `Null` values can cause model development issues for data science projects, so having a method to remove or process those `Null` values is an important feature that we will need to implement.

Once we had an initial understanding of our data profile, we investigated the distribution of our dataset. This exploration allows us to identify whether the data shows a common distribution pattern, like a normal distribution. In addition, investigating the distribution can also provide the first clues that any unexpected values appear in our dataset.

Following the single value explorations in *Chapter 7, Extracting Value*, we investigated the interactions between fields. Finding relationships requires leveraging the **Association Analysis** tool to create a **Correlation Matrix** (as shown in the following *Figure 13.5*):

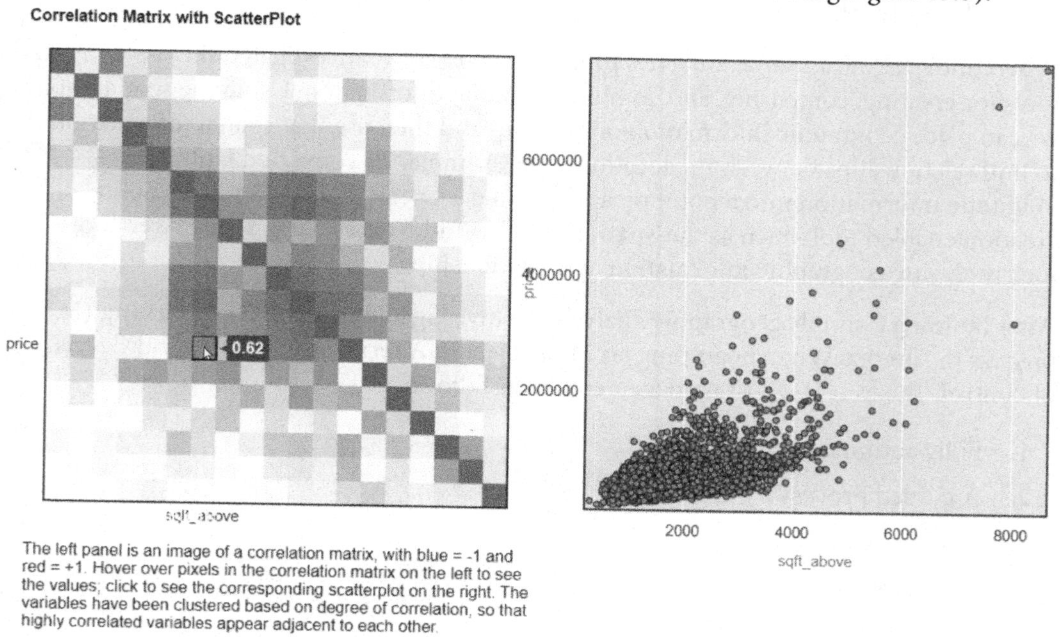
Correlation Matrix with ScatterPlot
price
0.62
sqft_above
6000000
4000000
2000000
2000
4000
6000
8000
sqft_above
The left panel is an image of a correlation matrix, with blue = -1 and red = +1. Hover over pixels in the correlation matrix on the left to see the values; click to see the corresponding scatterplot on the right. The variables have been clustered based on degree of correlation, so that highly correlated variables appear adjacent to each other.

Figure 13.5 – An example correlation matrix from Chapter 7, Extracting Value

The correlation matrix provides a visual representation of how variables interact and correlate with each other. It gives an insight into showing whether multiple values might be representing the same information or interacting predictably. We can use this insight to reduce the complexity of our dataset without losing any context through dimensionality reduction techniques.

The final step in the initial value extraction is to create a standard report. To create a standard report in Alteryx requires the creation of layout objects with the reporting tools. Using these reporting tools, such as the **Table** and **Report Text** tools. After creating the collection of layout objects that hold the different components of your desired report, we then combine them with the **Layout** tool.

Beginning advanced analytics

After completing the primary value extraction process and producing standard reports, we can consider extending our analysis complexity with advanced analytics. Advanced analytics extends the general value extraction processes to include spatial analytics and machine learning. We began our journey into advanced analytics in *Chapter 8*, *Beginning Advanced Analytics*. This chapter was only a beginning as these topics have a depth and breadth on which you could build an entire career. Because of this depth, we used this chapter to introduce how you could get started with these advanced topics and begin using Alteryx for the analysis.

When undertaking a spatial analytics project in Alteryx, we investigated the use of **Spatial** tools for creating, comparing, and combining spatial information. Using the spatial tools, we can place geographic information onto a map and then use that spatial information to find relationships between the locations. For example, we converted latitude and longitude information into a point on a map using a **Create Points** tool. This point creation enabled tools such as the **Spatial Match**, **Find Nearest**, and **Trade Area** tools for processing geographic information and relationships.

After building a simple geographic analysis, we investigated the **machine learning (ML)** process in Alteryx. When beginning an ML project in Alteryx, you can take four levels of control. The four levels of management are as follows:

1. Fully automated
2. A guided process
3. Deploying pre-build model macros
4. Fully custom ML code

This control depends on whether you have a license for the Alteryx Intelligence Suite or if you are using R-based predictive tools. Having multiple levels of model-making control allows you flexibility over the speed at which you can develop a new model or the accuracy required for a specific application.

When using the intelligence suite, you can build a fully automated model with the AutoML tool or a guided process with the **Assisted Modeling** tool. There is no configuration required when using the AutoML tool, and the model is built using the input data and the target field. The assisted modeling process allows for some customization of the ML pipeline along a guided path. Following is a snippet of the workflow created by the **Assisted Modeling** tool:

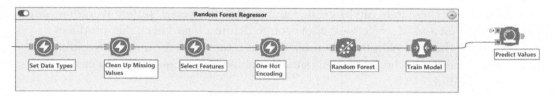

Figure 13.6 – A snippet of the workflow created by the Assisted Modeling tool

These options follow a predetermined process for building the application and interpreting the results during the model creation. By contrast, using the pre-built model macros with the R-based tools or the intelligence suite gives you greater flexibility in the transformation methods you want to apply. In addition, when using these tools, you are responsible for all the decisions regarding feature engineering and preparation, model type, and model hyperparameters. By allowing control over each of the decisions in this process, you can create more accurate models for your predictions.

The final ML option is to create a fully custom model with the **Python** or **R** tools from the **Developer** tab of the **Tool Palette**. These tools allow you to create custom code for the model you are trying to build and lets you leverage all the capabilities of the underlying language you choose.

Throughout the functional steps section, we interacted with Alteryx Designer to create workflows and data pipelines to transform our raw data into a valuable resource. The final section focused on taking those pipelines and applying the robustness needed for production applications and implementing the controls required for monitoring the quality of the data pipeline and the dataset.

Governance of DataOps with Alteryx

After developing a data pipeline, automating and scaling the workflow is the next task for a DataOps deployment. This automation and scaling utilize the server-hosted components of Alteryx with Alteryx Server and Alteryx Connect. Before you save a workflow to Alteryx Server, you want to make sure your workflow includes tests as part of your workflow. Including these tests ensures that our data pipelines are robust and we will take action if something falls outside our expectations.

Testing workflows and outputs

Implementing the testing mechanisms uses the **Message** tool and the **Test** tool. We investigated how these tests can be created and used in *Chapter 9, Testing Workflows and Outputs*. The Test and Message tools allow you to define a logic check that produces a response from the tool. With the Test tool, you can return an error into the workflow when your conditional check fails. This situation allows for simple output to ensure we meet the condition.

By contrast, the Message tool allows for more flexibility in returning the test result to the workflow. The Message tool enables you to produce the message types:

- **Message**
- **Warning**
- **Field Conversion Error**
- **Error**
- **File Type Message**

You can create other event logging actions within your workflow with these different messages. The configuration of a Message tool is shown in *Figure 13.7*:

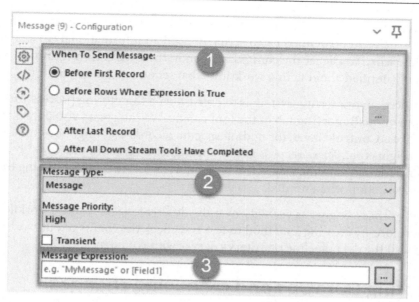

Figure 13.7 – The Message tool configuration from Chapter 9, Testing Workflows and Outputs

The next test system we wanted to create was a method for validating our dataset and having a plan to trigger an action if the workflow produces an error automatically. We are still using the Message and Test tools in this situation, but we use them in conjunction with the **Workflow Events** configuration tab. We can trigger an automatic Send Email or Run Command event with this combination. This menu is shown in *Figure 13.8*:

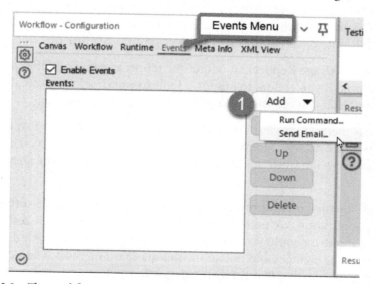

Figure 13.8 – The workflow events menu from Chapter 9, Testing Workflows and Outputs

We can configure an event with the **Events** menu to automatically run some command-line process, such as a predefined batch script, or send an informational email. In addition, we can define when to trigger the communication in the **Events Configuration** window, so we are only notified about failing workflows that require our intervention.

The final process in our testing system is to create a data monitoring process with the **Insights** tool in the **Reporting** tab of the tool palette. We can create visual tracking processes, like a **Control Chart**, for finding specific records that might be out of place using the Insights tool. These records might not trigger an error in our workflow as the dataset could contain extreme values, but we would need a method for finding those records to take action when needed.

These testing processes give us visibility over the different places where a workflow can fail. Furthermore, by creating a method to test and check the results of our workflow, we can publish the data pipeline on Alteryx Server with confidence.

Monitoring DataOps and managing changes

Getting the workflow from a local development environment onto Alteryx Server starts the next system that needs to be maintained. We learned some methods for managing the Alteryx Server environment in *Chapter 10, Monitoring DataOps and Managing Changes*. Every workflow published to your Alteryx server produces job success information and completion time details. By monitoring these two metrics, you can understand the stability of your Alteryx server.

The simplest method for extracting the performance information is to run the **Alteryx Server Usage Report** workflow. This workflow extracts not only these two performance metrics, but a full suite of standard Alteryx Server monitoring processes.

The **Alteryx Server Usage Report** can output the report as either a PDF report or as a **Tableau workbook**. If you choose to output a Tableau workbook, you can also access the report dataset that you can then customize to answer your questions.

Another analysis method is to customize the usage report workflow to extract different information from the Alteryx MongoDB installation. In this situation, you can pull any of the record information from the Alteryx Persistence layer to find the answer to any question you have.

We investigated the final process of deploying workflow changes with a **software version control** (**SVC**) application. We used the **GitHub** platform with **GitHub desktop** as an example SVC system you could use. The benefit of using SVC is that your development team can monitor the changes and updates with a standard method. Additionally, you can use that system to implement **Continuous Integration** (**CI**) processes.

An example of CI processes is to use **GitHub Actions** to automatically enforce company standards policies for the metadata contained within a workflow. We can do this by validating the Alteryx workflow **XML** and ensuring that specific XML tree nodes are populated. In addition, if we use a testing suite, such as the `pytest` module found in the **Python Package** action, it is compatible with GitHub Actions.

Implementing the DataOps methodologies and change management can ensure that workflows perform well when automated on Alteryx Server. In addition, the metadata they contain holds the information that we require.

At this stage of the DataOps process, we have created a robust and performant workflow. We have applied standards to the documentation and delivery of a workflow for production, and we have systems in place for continuous monitoring. We now need to consider how we share the datasets and workflows with other users in a secure manner.

Securing and managing access

Next, we need to manage access to the content published on Alteryx Server. Therefore, we investigated the controls for securing an Alteryx server in *Chapter 11, Securing and Managing Access*. In this chapter, we learned about the two security control areas: content and user security, and server infrastructure security.

We first considered how to organize the content we publish to the Alteryx server and the best methods for making that content available. When publishing content to the server, we access the workflows from the following three areas:

- **Private Studio**
- **Collection**
- **District**

Each of these sharing locations allows more people to view and interact with a workflow. The sharing locations also have different methods for organizing the content and all the locations can be used together.

Private Studio is where a workflow owner saves the content. Only the workflow's owner, the data engineer who created the workflow, has access to this location. **Private Studio** is a secure location for ensuring your data pipeline works as expected on the server.

The next level of content management is the **Collection**. In a collection, we assign permissions to individual users or groups of users so they can access assets such as workflows, schedules, results, and insights. Depending on each user's role in a collection, you can assign different levels of permissions. We can see an example collection in the following screenshot:

Figure 13.9 – An example Collection page from Chapter 11, Securing and Managing Access

The final location for sharing content is to use the **Districts** feature in Alteryx Server. Districts use tags to organize the content into different searchable areas of the Server for users to interact with content. The primary difference between Collections and Districts is that collections require a user to log on to the server and the collection permissions to be assigned for each user. By contrast, a district does not require any authentication. A district is just a method for organizing the public space of your server.

After considering your content's organization, you should also consider the server environment installed on the Alteryx server. Using the example of an **Amazon Web Services** (**AWS**) deployment, we learned the different access requirements that Alteryx Server components require. In addition, we saw how the **Gallery**, **Controller**, **MongoDB**, and **Worker** components interact to inform us of the access needed in a deployment.

In the AWS environment, we saw how we could use multiple **Security Groups** to control access between the components to limit external access as much as possible. By separating the different communication requirements into separate security groups, we can isolate the resources and data source access to the component requiring access.

With an organized and secure Alteryx server, we are finally ready to make the data sources and content we have created widely accessible and discoverable. Using Alteryx Connect, we can share the data sources and educate our users about the data.

Making data easy to use and discoverable with Alteryx

The final step of our DataOps deployment is to improve the discoverability and clarity of our data assets. In *Chapter 12, Making Data Easy to Use and Discoverable with Alteryx*, we investigated the use of Alteryx Connect in creating a central data dictionary for data assets. Alteryx Connect provides a centralized location for building confidence in our data assets and reducing the duplication of processes in our data estate.

Alteryx Connect provides final visibility of the datasets we have created for our users and includes all the context information needed to use effectively the datasets that we make. Using the connect loaders, we can populate the connect catalog with all the content information from our data persistence locations and view all the transformation touchpoints throughout the data pipeline.

We also investigated using the Connect APIs for synchronizing the Connect data catalog with other data tools. These tools are an essential consideration as not all data consumers will have access to our Alteryx data pipelines. For example, a business user might only have access to their Business Intelligence tool, such as Tableau, and only find the data context information they need from that platform. Using the Connect APIs, we can cross-populate the data dictionaries in both applications and decide which application is the primary resource that holds the definitive information about a data asset.

Throughout the DataOps application process, we followed an example pipeline to demonstrate how to achieve the various steps in the process.

Our Alteryx data pipeline

The Alteryx data pipeline we created was an example of downloading place information from an authenticated API and using this as a dataset to enrich internal data records.

The data sourcing step from *Chapter 4, Sourcing the Data*, used the **Google Maps Places** API. We wanted a place location dataset to identify places that could impact our business. Following a DataOps process, we needed to quickly create a dataset for this future analysis and make the dataset robust enough to be used for other applications later.

Once we had a raw dataset, we needed to transform the download into a format from which our users could extract value. The data we downloaded from the API was in **JavaScript Object Notation (JSON)** format. This format works for many applications, but performing analytic processes in Alteryx required transformation into a more common tabular form. We followed a five-step process using many tools common to various analytical techniques. The five steps we followed were as follows:

1. Converting the JSON data
2. Isolating the header information
3. Splitting key fields into identifying parts
4. Cross-tabbing records into a text table
5. Setting our data types

These five steps provide a typical process for transforming a dataset from one format into another for a different application. In addition, the tools used in each stage are used in many Alteryx applications.

We also performed initial profiling of our dataset to ensure an accurate download of data and confirm that our application's key fields are in the expected ranges.

With a dataset created, we persisted the records into the database, **Snowflake**, for future analysis. This process made use of the bulk loading option for the Snowflake output. We prefer the bulk load option for this application as running the workflow would result in new locations being added to our records. In addition, by having a complete history of the locations we searched for, we could provide additional depth to any future analysis.

We then moved on to the value extraction steps of a DataOps project. Because extracting a large sample for analysis would take time using the Google Maps Places API, we transitioned to analyzing the sample datasets provided with the Alteryx Designer installation.

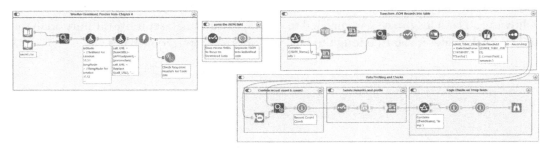

Figure 13.10 – The structure of the complete Alteryx data pipeline

We discussed the value extraction steps in *Chapter 7, Extracting Value*, and *Chapter 8, Beginning Advanced Analytics*, in the *Functional Steps in DataOps* part. The examples we used were also examples for our Alteryx data pipeline. Next, we followed an exploratory data analysis process and then transitioned into the spatial and machine learning topics.

We applied the skills used in many analytical methods during this entire process. As a result, the tools used comprised the most common and practical tools you can use in your data pipelines.

We were also able to implement the Governance steps for testing our workflow using messages, test tools, Test Runner macros from the CREW macro pack, and XML validation of our workflow with Alteryx test workflows and GitHub Actions using Python.

The entire DataOps process can be deployed to our Alteryx server and published in Alteryx Connect for discovery.

Final summary

DataOps is a framework that transforms how data engineers and Alteryx practitioners develop robust workflows for their users. The framework provides a set of principles that fit with Alteryx's iterative way of working.

But, as with any technology, it evolves. Even during the writing of this book, sections have been updated and changed as functionality has changed. Evolution will occur. It is the nature of software, and better methods are developed constantly. DataOps is the latest example of this evolution.

Keeping up with the changes in technology is continuous and rewarding. Finding a new method to improve your data pipelines gives a sense of personal achievement and is encouraged in the DataOps framework.

One day, the best tool for your application might not be Alteryx because of your specific project's requirements. Or Alteryx might be a templating tool for a particular data science project. No matter the situation, the principles discussed in this book will provide value and give a basis for future projects.

I will continue to evolve my use of Alteryx and leverage the new features available. Sharing what I have learned is always a critical method for solidifying my understanding. Whether teaching in front of an eager class, in a small workshop consultancy, in texts such as this book, or on my blog at `https://databard.co.uk/`, sharing knowledge is always rewarding, and I thank you for taking the time to learn from me.

Index

`Packt.com`

Subscribe to our online digital library for full access to over 7,000 books and videos, as well as industry leading tools to help you plan your personal development and advance your career. For more information, please visit our website.

Why subscribe?

- Spend less time learning and more time coding with practical eBooks and Videos from over 4,000 industry professionals

- Improve your learning with Skill Plans built especially for you

- Get a free eBook or video every month

- Fully searchable for easy access to vital information

- Copy and paste, print, and bookmark content

Did you know that Packt offers eBook versions of every book published, with PDF and ePub files available? You can upgrade to the eBook version at `packt.com` and as a print book customer, you are entitled to a discount on the eBook copy. Get in touch with us at `customercare@packtpub.com` for more details.

At `www.packt.com`, you can also read a collection of free technical articles, sign up for a range of free newsletters, and receive exclusive discounts and offers on Packt books and eBooks.

Other Books You May Enjoy

If you enjoyed this book, you may be interested in these other books by Packt:

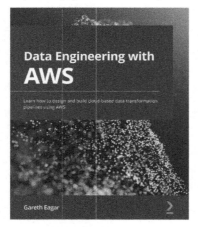

Data Engineering with AWS

Gareth Eagar

ISBN: 978-1-80056-041-3

- Understand data engineering concepts and emerging technologies
- Ingest streaming data with Amazon Kinesis Data Firehose
- Optimize, denormalize, and join datasets with AWS Glue Studio
- Use Amazon S3 events to trigger a Lambda process to transform a file
- Run complex SQL queries on data lake data using Amazon Athena
- Load data into a Redshift data warehouse and run queries
- Create a visualization of your data using Amazon QuickSight
- Extract sentiment data from a dataset using Amazon Comprehend

Learning Alteryx

Renato Baruti

ISBN: 978-1-78839-265-5

- Create efficient workflows with Alteryx to answer complex business questions
- Learn how to speed up the cleansing, data preparing, and shaping process
- Blend and join data into a single dataset for self-service analysis
- Write advanced expressions in Alteryx leading to an optimal workflow for efficient processing of huge data
- Develop high-quality, data-driven reports to improve consistency in reporting and analysis
- Explore the flexibility of macros by automating analytic processes
- Apply predictive analytics from spatial, demographic, and behavioral analysis and quickly publish, schedule
- Share your workflows and insights with relevant stakeholders

Packt is searching for authors like you

If you're interested in becoming an author for Packt, please visit authors. packtpub.com and apply today. We have worked with thousands of developers and tech professionals, just like you, to help them share their insight with the global tech community. You can make a general application, apply for a specific hot topic that we are recruiting an author for, or submit your own idea.

Share Your Thoughts

Now you've finished *Data Engineering with Alteryx*, we'd love to hear your thoughts! Scan the QR code below to go straight to the Amazon review page for this book and share your feedback or leave a review on the site that you purchased it from.

https://packt.link/r/1-803-23648-5

Your review is important to us and the tech community and will help us make sure we're delivering excellent quality content.

Made in United States
Orlando, FL
11 December 2022

26142460R00200